TRADITIONS AND INSTITUTIONS OF THE SANTALS

TRADITIONS AND INSTITUTIONS OF THE SANTALS

P.O. BODDING

GYAN PUBLISHING HOUSE
New Delhi-110002

TRADITIONS AND INSTITUTIONS OF THE SANTALS
(Tribal Studies, Anthropology)

ISBN: **9788121206723**

Published in 2016 in India by
Gyan Publishing House
5, Ansari Road
Daryaganj,
New Delhi-110002

Phones: **011-47034999, 9811692060**

E-Mail: gyanbook@del2.vsnl.net.in
Web Site: www.gyanbooks.com

CONTENTS

EDITOR'S PREFACE

It having proved impossible to get this translation published before the author's death the manuscript was left in the care of Professor O. Solberg, who had repeatedly rendered invaluable assistance in bringing out other important works of his and who has since then published his SANTAL RIDDLES and his WITCHCRAFT AMONG THE SANTALS, Oslo 1940. At his request I have undertaken to act as editor of the translation, and I am happy to be able to do this last service to a deceased friend.

I have considered it to be my duty to check the translation with the original Santal text wherever I was in doubt, but I have only occasionally found it necessary to make some slight and insignificant verbal changes. On the whole I have faithfully reproduced the readings of the manuscript.

I have felt more free with regard to the numerous and sometimes rather long notes which had been added and which were sometimes apt to divert the reader's attention from the text itself. Since the translation was drafted some important works of our author have been published, and his SANTAL DICTIONARY, Oslo 1932—1936, is in reality a comprehensive encyclopaedia of Santal lore. A reference to its statements usually gives full information about such details which would else have to be explained in lengthy notes. I have therefore to a considerable extent substituted such references for the notes of the manuscript.

The text here laid before the ethnologist is a genuine account of Santal traditions and institutions, taken down from the mouth of Kolean, an old Santal, who had learnt it from his own teacher. We cannot say how far back these traditional tales can be carried, from generation to generation. But as we have them before us, they are evidently the result of a comparatively long development.

We know nothing about the different phases of this development. It is evident that there are borrowings from Aryan sources, but it is also clear that a considerable portion is genuine Santal lore, and it is often difficult to distinguish between both elements. Thus the name Ṭhạkur of the vague supreme god seems to be Aryan; and such is certainly the case with his additional designation Jiu 'soul, spirit'. But that need not imply that the whole conception is Aryan. Several customs and institutions described in the text have admittedly been taken over from the Hindus, but also here there are numerous doubtful points, which only future research can clear up.

The account of the wanderings of the Santals does not make it possible for us to trace their way to their present home with anything like certainty, because it is usually impossible to identify the names of locality. It is true that the wanderings of the tribe in modern times seem to have been directed towards the east, and we seem to know that kindred tribes were formerly settled much farther to the west than at the present day. But we cannot say whether there may be traces of old migrations in the opposite direction below the traditional tales.

Kolean's narrative was noted down in the year 1871, and several changes have taken place since that time. Nobody would have been better qualified to draw attention to such innovations than our translator, and some remarks will be found in the Dictionary articles quoted in the notes. To try to bring the whole account up to date would, however, mean to interfere with its genuineness, and it would represent an enlargement in one direction only, towards our own days, while the antecedent stages of the development would remain in the dark. We do more justice to the traditional account, if we leave it as it was originally noted down.

The additions to Kolean's narrative have been taken from other, younger sources, and have not the same interest. They have been left as the translator had drafted them.

Sten Konow.

FOREWORD

Fifty years ago, in 1887, the late Rev. L. O. Skrefsrud published The Traditions and Institutions of the Santhals, Hoṛkoren Mare Hapṛamko reak̓ Katha, as a guide for the Santals, especially in the customary matters dealt with in the book, and also on account of its ethnological value. It was re-edited by me, in 1916 and 1929, only with a short preface and a few pages of fresh matter, added at the end, at the request of certain Santals. What here follows is a translation with a number of explanatory footnotes and some additional matter. As only a very few would be able to use the work in the original Santali, and as it is of considerable ethnological interest, I have repeatedly been asked to translate it. My translation is absolutely literal, in order to enable the reader, as far as possible, to understand the Santal mentality and way of expression.

With the exception of a short story of the Santal insurrection of 1855 the original work was taken down by Skrefsrud from the mouth of an old guru, named Kolean. According to a statement towards the end of the book the dictation was finished on the 15th of February, 1871.

Skrefsrud once told me, that he had hunted everywhere among the Santals to find a man who knew his people and their traditions and customs, and that Kolean without comparison was the best authority he had been able to find. Skrefsrud further told me, that the book contains absolutely nothing of his own, the whole being a faithful record of Kolean's words and language.

I cannot, however, help thinking that Skrefsrud had something to do with the arrangement. The language is easy and fine, and Kolean's narrative was based on oral tradition handed down verbatim by teacher to disciple, from generation to generation, a practice which, as Skrefsrud states in the Annual Report of the Mission for the year 1887—88, "has now fallen into disuse".

This does not exclude the possibility of our learning something from other sources, and some Santals have actually narrated things which Kolean did not mention. Sometimes we can see that such tales are adaptations of Hindu lore, as when some gurus maintain that their ancestors followed Rama to fight Ravona in Ceylon. In other cases, especially with regard to Santal customs and institutions, we may have to do with independent lines of tradition.

Kolean hailed, as he tells at the end, from a village called Pabea in a "country" (rural district) called Paṇḍra in the district of Manbhum to the southwest of the Santal Parganas.

He stated that he was a disciple of a guru named Buku. Together with other Santals he had emigrated eastwards. His old home being in Manbhum explains that some very few of his statements are different from what is the present custom in the Santal Parganas.

Kolean was a guru, a designation borrowed from the Hindus but adapted to suit Santal society. A Santal guru is a man who is supposed to know certain things, e. g., what should be recited at some ceremonial functions, and who is able to act as a reciter when called upon to do so. Any Santal can become a guru, by attaching himself to an older guru and gradually learning from him. In this way we cannot expect absolute uniformity throughout.

The use of such recitations may partly be due to imitation of Hindu customs, and there are definite statements in the traditional tales here translated to the effect that the ancestors on a certain occasion, after long deliberations, decided to abandon some customs of their own and to adopt Hindu usages instead. In this connexion it is of interest to note that the Santals often use songs in a foreign language, notably Bihari, during their festivals and at cremations. And it is a curious fact that many Santals do not understand these songs. It is evident that we have, to some extent, to do with borrowings, but it would be an exaggeration to maintain that the whole has been borrowed.

The traditional history of the world as contained in the first part of Kolean's narrative is recited twice in connexion with the life of every Santal, first at the caco chaṭiar, when a child is ceremoniously given full social right, and finally at the bhaṇḍan, the funeral ceremony, when the deceased is handed over to the next world and to the care of the departed ancestors.

P. O. Bodding.

I. THE ANCESTORS' STORY

As the old Kolean has told it.

Towards the rising of the sun (the East) was the birth of man. At first there was only water, and under the water there was earth. Then Ṭhạkur[1]-Jiu created the beings that live in water, the crab, the crocodile, the alligator, the raghọṗ boaṛ fish, the sọlẹ prawn, the earthworm, the tortoise and others.

Thereupon Ṭhạkur said: "Whom shall I now make? I will make man". Then he decided to make two of earth. He had just finished making the two; then when he was going to give them souls (life) the Day-horse[2] came down from above, trampled them to pieces and left. Thakur became awfully grieved by this.

Then Ṭhạkur said: "I will not make them of earth; I shall make birds". Then he made the two Hãs Hạ̃sil birds[3] pulling (the material) off from his breast. He placed them on his hand; they were looking very beautiful. Thereupon he breathed on them, and they at once became alive and flew upwards. They moved about flying, but as they could not find a place to alight anywhere, they therefore always alighted on Ṭhạkur's hand. Then the Day-horse came down along the gossamer thread to drink water. When he was drinking water he spilt some froth of his mouth and left. It floated on the water; thereby foam was formed on the water.

Ṭhạkur then said to the two birds: "Do alight on the froth". They did so. When they had alighted they moved about over the whole sea, the froth carrying them along like a boat. Then they implored Ṭhạkur: "We are moving about, that is so, but we do not find any food".

Then Ṭhạkur-Jiu called the alligator: he came; and the alligator said to Ṭhạkur: "Why did you call me, Ṭhạkur?" Ṭhạkur said to him: "Would you be willing to bring up earth?" The alligator answered him: "If you tell me to do so, I might bring it up". Then having gone down in the water he was working bringing up earth; all was dissolved.

Thereupon Ṭhạkur called the prawn. He came. Having come he said to Ṭhạkur: "Why did you call me, Ṭhạkur?" Ṭhạkur said to him: "Would you be willing to bring up earth?" The prawn answered him: "If you tell me to do so, I might bring it up". Then

---

[1] lit. 'the Lord'. [2] The Siń sadọm is mentioned only here and once below. Santals will connect the name with the sun. [3] Hãs is the Hindi name for goose or swan; hạ̃sil is the female. Other Muṇḍā peoples have a similar story; the Muṇḍās have only one egg, out of which both the first human beings were hatched.

he went down in the water; having gone down he worked bringing it up in his claws; all the earth was dissolved.

Thereupon Ṭhạkur called the raghọṕ boaṛ fish[4]. He came. Having come he said to Ṭhạkur: "Why did you call me, Ṭhạkur?" Ṭhạkur said to him: "Would you be willing to bring up earth?" The raghọṕ boaṛ fish answered him: "If you tell me to do so, I might bring it up". Then having gone down in the water he bit (the earth); he was bringing some of it in his mouth and some on his back; all the earth was dissolved. Since that time the boaṛ fishes have no scales on their body.

Thereupon Ṭhạkur called the stone-crab. He came. Having come he said to Ṭhạkur: "Why have you called me, Ṭhạkur?" Ṭhạkur said to him: "Would you be willing to bring up earth?" The crab answered Ṭhạkur: "If you tell me to do so, I might bring it up". Then having gone down in the water he worked bringing it up in his claws; all the earth was dissolved.

Thereupon Ṭhạkur called the earthworm. He came. Having come he said to Ṭhạkur: "Why did you call me, Ṭhạkur?" Ṭhạkur said to him: "Would you be willing to bring up earth?" The earthworm answered Ṭhạkur: "If you tell me to do so, I might bring it up, provided the tortoise stands on the water".

Thereupon Ṭhạkur called the tortoise. He came. Having come he said to Ṭhạkur: "Why have you called me, Ṭhạkur?" Ṭhạkur said to him: "No one is able to bring the earth up. The earthworm has promised to bring it up, provided you will stand on the water". The tortoise answered Ṭhạkur: "If you tell me to do so, I might stand. Then he stood on the water. When he had taken his stand there Ṭhạkur chained his four legs in the four directions. The tortoise became immovably quiet on the water. Then the earthworm went down to bring up the earth; he reached the earth. Now he had put his tail on the back of the tortoise, and with his mouth down below he is eating earth, and this he brings out on the back of the tortoise. Then it was spread out and fixed like a hard film. He continued to bring up earth; he brought up enough for the whole earth.[5] Then he stopped.

Thereupon Ṭhạkur caused the earth to be harrowed level. By continual harrowing some was heaped up on the implements; this became mountains. Then when the earth had been brought up and levelled, the foam that was floating on the surface of the water stuck to the earth, and as Ṭhạkur sowed sirom seed[6] on this foam the sirom plant sprang up first (before all other plants). After this he let the dhubi grass[7] be sown and come up; after this the karam tree[8], thereupon the tope sarjọm, the labaṛ atnaḱ, the laḍea matkọm[9], and after this all kinds of vegetation. The earth became firm. In all places

---

[4] The Santals know a fish called so; this is the Silurus glavis. I know no English name. [5] The foreign influence in the story seems here evident. [6] Sirom is Andropogon muricatus, Retz. [7] The dhubi grass, Cynodon dactylon, Pers. [8] Adina cordifolia, Hook. f. & B. [9] Sarjọm is Shorea robusta, Gaertn.; the prefixed tope is used in the meaning of "cut off", or, "short"; atnaḱ is Terminalia tomentosa, W. & A.; labaṛ means "highly coloured". Matkọm is Bassia latifolia, Roxb.; laḍea means "crooked", or, "bent".

where there was water, there he let sods be put, and in all places where water was bubbling up, there he let it be closed up by pressing pieces of rock down on it.

Thereupon, having made a nest in a clump of the sirom plants, the two birds laid two eggs. The female bird would sit on the eggs, and the male bird would find and bring food. Keeping on in this way they hatched the eggs: O mother! two human beings were born, one boy and one girl. Then both of them sang:

O dear dear, on the sea,
O dear dear, these two human beings,
O dear dear, have been brought into the world,
O dear dear, these two human beings,
O dear dear, where are they to be put?

O dear dear, you two please tell him,
O dear dear, the great Ṭhạkur Jiu,
O dear dear, the two have been brought into the world,
O dear dear, these two human beings,
O dear dear, where are they to be put?

So they implored Ṭhạkur saying: "How shall we two support these two human beings?" Ṭhạkur gave them some cotton and said to them: "Whatever you two eat, press the juice out of these things and make a place on the cotton wet therewith, and put this into their mouths to suck." By sucking and getting food in this way they grew and commenced to walk. But as they were growing the anxiety of the two birds increased, viz., where they should put the two when they grew up.

So they besought Ṭhạkur, and he said to them: "Do fly round and find for us a place for them to stay. Then they flew towards the setting of the sun; they discovered Hihiṛi Pipiṛi. Having returned they told Ṭhạkur of this. He said to them: "Do take them there". Then they took them along carrying them on their backs. They put them down and left them there. What became of Ḫās Ḫạsil, this the ancestors of old have not told us; therefore we do not know.

The names of these two human beings were Haṛam and Ayo[10]. Some people call them Pilcu Haṛam and Pilcu Buḍhi[11]. There in Hihiṛi Pipiṛi they grew up eating the grain of the sumtu bukuć grass and the ears of the sama grass[12]. They had no clothes, they were both naked; still they felt no shame, and they lived in great peace.

---

[10] Haṛam is the common word for an old or elderly man; Ayo means in Santali "mother", a word borrowed from an Aryan language. [11] Pilcu haṛam and Pilcu buḍhi are the common designations of the first parents. Haṛam is explained above; buḍhi is the common word for an elder, especially married woman; pilcu means "small, tiny". Buḍhi is an Aryan word. [12] The sumtu bukuć grass is Eleusine aegyptiaca, Pers., and sama grass Panicum colonum, L.

One day Liṭạ[13] came to them and said to them: "Where are you, grandchildren? How are you? I am your grandfather; I have come to pay you a visit. I see you are well; but there is one great joy that you have not tasted. Do brew beer, it has a very sweet taste". Then he taught them to prepare the fermenting stuff. All three went to the forest. Liṭạ showed them the roots. The two dug up and brought these. When they had brought them Liṭạ said to Pilcu Buḍhi: "Now you make the rice wet for us". She did so. Having made it wet she pounded it into flour; they jabbed the "medicine" (fermenting stuff), they squeezed it and kneaded the flour with the "medicine"-juice; having kneaded it into a dough they made balls of it; having made the balls they put these into a basket together with straw and put this aside. When next day came, at the time they had made the balls, at the same time they uncovered them; having done this they threw the straw away and spread (the balls) out on a winnowing-fan; spread out there the balls became dry, and they put them aside. When this was done they gathered the sumtu bukuć and sama ears and pounded them. They boiled the grain and thereupon let it cool; when cooled they kneaded the fermenting stuff into it; thereupon having assembled all they covered it up in leaves and kept it there. In five days the fermentation was complete. In the afternoon they poured water on it. Then Liṭạ said to them: "Now both of you drink this after first having poured on the ground some to Maraṅ buru. To-morrow I shall come again and visit you".

Thereupon they made three leaf-cups and filled these; having done this they poured on the ground the contents of one in the name of Maraṅ buru; then they drank themselves. When they were drinking, they commenced to toy amorously; continuing this they both drank all and also became very drunk. It became night, they lay down together.

When it became dawn Liṭạ suddenly came. He called out to them: "How is it, grandchildren, have you got up or not? Do come out". When they had regained consciousness they recognized that they were both naked and felt very ashamed; therefore they answered him: "O grandfather, how can we possibly go out; we are awfully ashamed; we are both of us naked; last night when we had become drunk from beer, we have done something bad".

Liṭạ then said to them: "It does not matter". And smiling to himself he went away. To cover their shame Pilcu Haṛam and Pilcu Buḍhi made a skirt and a loin-cloth for themselves of ficus-leaves. Now they got children, seven boys and seven girls. The name of the eldest boy was Saṇḍra, the one following him was Saṇḍhọm, the one after him was Care, the one following him was Mane, and the youngest one was Acaredelhu. The eldest girl was Chitạ, the following Kạpu, the one after her was Hisi, and one was Ḍumni. We have forgotten the names of the others.

---

[13] Liṭạ is said to be the real name of the principal boṅga of the Santals, always referred to as Maraṅ buru, lit., the great mountain. Liṭạ ak̕, the name for a rainbow.

So they lived on; living on they grew up and became big. Haṛam on his side was in the habit of going with the boys to hunt in one direction, and in another direction Buḍhi on her side was going with the girls to pluck and bring vegetables and leaves, and when it became evening they used to come together at home. One day the young men went to Khaṇḍerae forest to hunt by themselves alone, and the girls also had gone alone to Sũṛũkuć[14] forest to pluck vegetables. When they had finished doing this, they came out at the foot of the Capakiạ Fig tree[15] and were playing swinging on the pendulous roots of the Fig tree. Thereupon they shifted and commenced to dance ḍahar[16] and sang:

The ants, the ants swarm, O mother,
On the lower branches of the Capakiạ Fig tree they swarm.

Having become tired from hunting the young men were coming out of the forest bringing a boi bindi deer[17] with them. Hearing the singing of the girls they said: "Listen you, who are singing?" Then they left the deer there and went to the girls and commenced to dance with them. Dancing along they became delighted. The eldest young man chose for himself the eldest girl and the youngest boy the youngest girl, and in this way all of them did. Thereupon the eldest young man and the eldest girl went to have a look at the deer. At that time the other ones sang:

Along under the Fig tree to the young deer,
O mother, quick to see the young boi bindi deer.

Then all of them became pairs of their own accord. Having observed this Haṛam and Buḍhi said: "They have found each other, we shall marry them". Then they (two) built a house; in this they made seven rooms; when this was ready, they brewed beer; having done this all of them drank; when they had drunk, Haṛam and Buḍhi put them, one pair in each of the seven rooms, the eldest young man with the eldest girl, the youngest boy with the youngest girl, in this way all of them. In this way their marriages were performed.

After this all of them got children. They were growing up. Then Haṛam and Buḍhi said: "When there were no others, we two joined and became a pair and brought forth and multiplied them, seven boys and seven girls, and these children we have also married, brothers and sisters; but these we two shall make into septs; let no brothers and sisters be married". Then they divided them into septs. The eldest boy became Hãsdaḱ, the one following him Murmu, the next Kisku, the one after him Hembrom, the one following him Mạrṇḍi, the one after him Soren, and the one following him Ṭuḍu. Then they said to them: "Join them together in marriage in this way: don't marry them with one of their

---

[14] The forest names probably refer to the names of the trees there. Khaṇḍerae is the name of a bush known in Muṇḍari, but not any more in Santali; sũṛũkuć is Salix tetrasperma, Roxb., common in the Santal country. [15] Ficus tomentosa, L. [16] Ḍahar, a cart-track, a road, also the name of a certain Santal dance.
[17] A mythical unknown deer.

own sept. The bride may be of any sept, provided the young man is of a different one". Then they lived on; living in this way a very long time passed, and they multiplied exceedingly.

Thereupon they went to Khọj kaman[18]. Living there mankind became very bad, they became like buffaloes and buffalo-cows, they did not respect each other. Seeing all this Ṭhạkur became very angry, and he firmly made up his mind to destroy mankind, if they did not return to him. So he called them to come: "Come, mankind, come back to me". But they did not heed his word. Therefore Ṭhạkur called to him whether it was Pilcu Haṛam and Pilcu Buḍhi or another holy pair (some people say that Pilcu Haṛam and Pilcu Buḍhi died in Hihiṛi Pipiṛi) and said to them: "Mankind does not listen to my word; therefore I will make an end of them. But you two go into the cave in the Harata mountain; there you two will be saved".

These two listened to (obeyed) Ṭhạkur's word. They went into the mountain cave. When they had gone in there, for seven days and seven nights Ṭhạkur let fire-rain (some gurus say, sky-rain) stream down from the sky and destroyed mankind and animals, every one of them, only the two who were in the Harata mountain cave were saved and left alive. About this they sing:

Seven days seven nights fire-rain,
Seven days seven nights uninterruptedly,
Where were you, you two human beings?
Where did you two find shelter?

It is there, it is there the Harata,
It is there, it is there the mountain-cave;
There we were we two,
There we two found shelter.

Then it cleared up; when it had cleared up the two human beings were coming out from the cave; then they saw a buffalo-cow that had fallen down there. Thereupon they found a cow; this one was pressed down under a halfburnt big log; one side of the cow was burnt and stripped off, and one side was whole. They sing:

Glowing cinders, the cow fell under the log,
Pulverized ashes, the fallen down buffalo cow.

---

18 Some gurus mention a number of different countries where the ancestors stayed for "who knows for how many years" (as they express themselves). From Hihiṛi Pipiṛi they went to Hohoro Bomboro (also called Haharo Bambaro, by some); from there to Ayaro Payaro, then to Jhạl dak̕ (lit., long water); from there to Dudumul, and then to Aere Kaeṇḍe; from there to Haradata and then to Khọj kaman. Some gurus do not mention Jhạl dak̕ and enumerate from Dudumul to Ajodana, thereupon to Haradata, to Khọjkanọl, thereupon to Sasaṅ beḍa and then to Aere Kaeṇḍe; from there to Jạrpi and from this country to Cae Campa. Again others mention the countries in the following order: Ayarọ Payaro, Dudumul, Ajodana, Jhạl dak̕, Aere Kaeṇḍe, Haradata, Khọj kamọl and through Toṛe Pokhori Baha Bandela to Cae Campa.

And they found, who knows which other animals. When they had come out from the cave, Ṭhạkur gave them clothes. They made themselves a home near the foot of the Harata mountain. They lived and got children. They multiplied very much.

Thereupon they went from Harata to a very large plain called Sasaṅ beda[19]. There they stayed for a long time. There they became tribes. Haṛam and Buḍhi divided them into septs like the septs of old, viz., Hãsdak̕, Murmu, Kisku, Hẹmbrọm, Mạrṇḍi, Sọrẹn and Ṭuḍu. Besides these original septs they made five more, viz., Baske, Besra, Pãuria, Cõṛẽ and one sept that has been lost, they were called Bedea[20]. They sing:

In Hihiṛi Pipiṛi we were born,
In Khọj kaman we were called for,
In Harata we grew up,
In Sasaṅ Beḍa we became septs.

After they had been divided into septs in Sasaṅ beḍa the ancient ancestors came to the Jarpi country. While living there, for some cause or other they became unable to stay, and they were coming along through forest after forest. Then they reached a high mountain. Wandering along they became exhausted by again and again trying to find a way to cross. As they were unable to find this they said: "The spirit of this mountain has doubtlessly blocked the way; come, let us make a vow, that he may let us pass through". Thereupon they made a vow to him, viz., "O Maraṅ buru (O Big mountain), if thou lettest us pass through, we shall worship thee when we shall have found a country (to stay in)". O mother, a short while afterwards they suddenly at morning time found a way to pass across, and they saw it, the sun rising as soon as it became morning[21]; otherwise when they had again and again been trying to find a way to cross, the sun had been rising only late. This pass they called Siń duar (the Day, or Sun, and door, or pass; may also mean the shut door). There is a song about this:

From the Jạrpi country I,
Through Siń duạr, Bãih duạr
The people of the country have come out.

Then they were passing through, who knows how long a time it took. Having come out from the Bãih duạr[22] they found the Aere country. Having stayed there they moved to the Kaeṇḍe country. Having lived in the Kaeṇḍe country, for some cause or other they came to the Cae country. There the people stayed for a very long time and greatly multiplied. But there also they were unable to remain; therefore they came running

---

[19] Sasaṅ turmeric, Curcuma longa, Roxb., and beḍa a level stretch of land along a river. [20] Cf. Santal Dictionary s. v. pạris. [21] The description presupposes that they were on the western side of a long range of high mountains. No mountain range in India would seem to justify a description like that here given. [22] Siń duạr is the entrance and Bãih duạr the eastern end of the pass.

(migrated) to the seven-river land Campa[23]. There were two passes, one Cae pass and the other the Campa pass.

In Campa they built a great many forts in order to ensure that enemies should not be able to overcome them. One was the Khạiri fort; this was the fort of the Hẹmbrọm people; one was the Kọeṇḍa fort; this belonged to the Kisku people. One was the Campa fort; this belonged to the Murmus. One was the Badoli fort; this belonged to the Mạrṇḍis; and one was the Sim fort; this belonged to the Ṭuḍu people. There were still other forts; but we have forgotten the names.

In Campa we stayed for ages, and there we were a great people. At that time we were not subordinate to anybody. The "kings" (rulers) were persons of the Kisku sept. The Murmus were from olden times our priests; we call them Murmu Ṭhạkur. The Sọrẹns were peons; they were fighters. The Hẹmbrọms were the nobility, the Mạrṇḍis were the wealthy class, and the Ṭuḍus were drumming the dancing- and the kettle-drums, and they were making all kinds of things of iron. The Baske people were buying and selling (merchants). What special work those belonging to the remaining septs had, we do not remember.

Having settled in Campa they placed Marań buru, the Five-Six and the Jahẹr era[24] in a sacred grove at the end of the village-street and were worshipping them. The Day-spirit they worshipped at sun-rise every fifth year.

Our ancestors of old have, people say, told, that in olden times, when Ram raja was living, at that time all Kharwar people went with him to Lońka (Ceylon) and helped him to vanquish Rabona raja; for this reason from then on for a very long time we had no fighting or anything of this kind with the Dekos[25]. They were living in the plains and we in the forests and on the hills. But afterwards we got very much fighting with the Dekos; until this day we have no happy relations with them. As soon as we have cleared the jungle in any country, the Dekos come and rob us of it. Still if the Sahibs[26] nowadays did not help them, we should soon drive them to the other side of the Ganges. At the time of the insurrection[27] we had intended to make the Ganges our boundary; but

---

[23] It is not possible with any certainty to identify the countries mentioned. Skrefsrud thought that the expression "the country of the seven rivers" might be identified with the present Punjab. Others will identify Cae Campa with the country to the northwest of the present Chota Nagpur. As regards the last mentioned, the same name might have reference to two different countries. [24] lit. The Lady of the Sacred Grove. Every Santal village is to have a sacred grove (jahẹr) in its vicinity, where possible, a part of the original forest, consisting of sal-trees and at least one Mahua tree. More further on. [25] Deko is the name used by the Santals for a non-Santal of the better class, especially Hindus. A Mohammedan will not be so called, if he is recognized as a Mohammedan. [26] i.e., the European courts. The Santal's ideas of justice are not regulated by written laws. [27] The Santal insurrection of 1855, was not aimed against the Government of the day, but was a misguided attempt to get rid of the money-lenders. The Government naturally had to intervene. This insurrection marks the beginning of a new era for the Santals, according to their own estimation in many ways a beginning of deterioration. The mention of the insurrection here is an anticipation.

(what could we do) when the Europeans helped them. In olden times we had possession of the country on both sides of the Ganges river. They sing:

The Ganges river became full,
The Soṛa river became overflowing:
Do, my parakeet, come back.

Seeing whom shall I come back?
In my companion my soul is,
In my comrade my breath is.

*

My elder sister, my devotee,
The Ganges river is full to its banks.
My elder sister, my devotee,
The Soṛa river is overflowing.

My elder sister, my devotee,
We two will weave a net of thread;
My elder sister, my devotee,
We two will knit a four-cornered net.

My elder sister, my devotee,
We two will catch in the net a large prawn;
My elder sister, my devotee,
We two will drag in with the hand-net a young mạṅgri fish[28].

Having fought with the Dekos in Campa we were vanquished; they took the Campa fort. Thereafter we gained the victory and took our fort back. At that time the two Deko brothers talked with their sister:

My elder brothers, Ịndạn Siṅ, Mandan Siṅ,
My elder brothers, we have lost the Campa fort;
My younger sister, don't cry, don't grieve,
My younger sister, we shall sell our wristlets,
My younger sister, we shall sell our golden ear-rings,
My younger sister, in any case we shall get the Campa fort back.

We ourselves also were fighting and were killing each other. They sing:

Get up, get up, do get up, my companion,
Be watchful, be watchful, do be watchful, my companion,
The Kọeṇḍa people are cutting and killing each other.

---

[28] A common fish, Clarias batrachus.

Get up, get up, do get up, my companion,
Be watchful, be watchful, do be watchful, my companion.
The Badoli people are hitting and killing each other.

For what purpose are they cutting each other, my companion,
For what purpose are they killing each other, my companion,
For what purpose are they hitting and killing each other, my companion?

For the sake of a boundary they are cutting each other, my companion,
For the sake of a landmark they are killing each other, my companion,
For the sake of a landmark they are hitting and killing each other.

Up to Campa we and the Muṇḍas, the Birhoṛ, the Kuṛmbis and others were called by the name of Kharwar[29]. The Birhoṛ were outcasted because they for some cause or other ate Hanuman monkeys. Also the Muṇḍas separated themselves there, and the Kuṛmbis gradually became somewhat like Dekos. Some Kharwars joined in marriage with the Dekos called Siṅ[30]; therefore their descendants became Siṅs. Up to the present time these Siṅs are landlords in the old country. Also among the Birhoṛ some became Siṅs. Among these also until to-day some are landlords in the old country. In olden times, people tell, one Siṅ had illicit intercourse with a daughter of a Kisku king, and the girl bore the child out of wedlock and threw it away in the forest. Some wealthy Mạrṇḍis picked this child up and brought it home with them. The child grew up with them, and they named him Mandọ Siṅ. When this boy grew into maturity he became a great and valiant man; as regards intellect or fighting strength, nobody was able to compete with him. He became divan[31] with a Kisku "king". One day he said to the king: "Please, find a bride for me". Having called the council together the king asked them; but nobody would give him, this bastard, a girl to be his wife.

Because of this Mandọ Siṅ became very angry; he said: "If you will not give me a daughter to be my wife, I shall forcibly apply sindur to every girl of yours and defile them". Having heard this the people of the country became awfully afraid and said: "Come along, let us run away". At that time most of them fled; only a few people remained, because they coveted property.

Some people say, it is told, that this Mandọ Siṅ or some other Siṅ was a friend of the Muslims. They fought so fiercely, it is told, with our ancestors, that the sun was shadowed by the shooting of arrows, and when at sun-rise it became light again, the Muslims were angry and said: "Which fellow is it who is coming, a fellow more mighty than we, come,

---

29 Kherwar is nowadays the more common pronunciation. Some present-day Santals who have wanted to effect a kind of reformation have styled themselves Kherwars. 30 Possibly Rājputs. Siṅ means a lion; Paharias and many Bhũyas in the Santal Parganas like to style themselves Siṅ. 31 Minister, General manager.

let us cut him down!" Then they mounted on each others' shoulders to reach him; but he kicked them, so that they fell down — thud thud. From that time the Muslims have no hair on their head; they have only a chin-beard. We feel more angry with the Muslims and abhor them more than all other races.

From Campa the ancestors fled to Toṛe Pokhori Baha Bandela[32]. There they stayed for a very long time. Somehow or other also the Dekos entered the open country there in great numbers. Then the country-people came together at the foot of the tope sarjo̱m, labaṛ atnak̓, the bent Mahua tree; having spread out Lotus-leaves (to sit on) and drinking the water of the Ke̱re̱ spring, they, whether for twelve years or for twelve days, legislated and ruled, viz., from this day, when we have ceremonies in connexion with birth, with the giving of full social rights, with marriage and wedlock, with dying and death, we shall act and follow such and such customs. There our ancestors, who knows for what reason, upset the rules of the ancient ancestors. Much was mixed up for us with what the Dekos have. In a former age our ancient ancestors did not cremate their dead ones, nor did they take them to the river; they buried them. At marriages they did not apply sindur to the bride either. All this we have learnt from the Dekos[33].

Then they broke up from there and passed through Toṛe Pokhori Baha Bandela, who knows whether along the embankment or over the Lotus-leaves, and came up at the foot of the Icak̓ tree[34], that is to say, the men, and the women came up at the foot of the Mahua tree. Then they saw that neither had had their foot-soles wetted, nor had the Lotus-leaves been broken; therefore they said: "We have ruled well; let these very rules and customs remain ours for ever and always." They remained there for a very long time.

Then they fled from there also, who knows for what reason. Some people say, because they feared the Muslims. As they passed along they came to the Baṛi baḍwak̓ forest. No one was willing to go in there in front of the others; therefore they said: "We shall no one go in front of the others, we shall go in a row beside each other." Then they would cross the forest. At the Jona Jospur plain they came out and gathered there; and they asked each other: "How is it, have we all come through and out or not?" There also they tried to remain; they were in no way able to stay; therefore they went to Khaspal Belaoṅja. Whilst living there they were scattered, some to Sir, some to Sikhaṛ[35] and some to Nagpur. From that time we have mostly been under the Dekos. Only the Kharwars and Birho̱ṛ who have joined in marriage with Dekos have landlords of their own; as for us we have lost the name of Kharwar, who knows why. Some people say

---

[32] The place mentioned is generally taken to be situated somewhere to the northwest of the sources of the Damuda river. The first part of the name seems to be that of a dug tank (pukhri). [33] That the Santals and their ancestors have introduced Hindu customs, adapted to their own needs and ideas, is easily ascertained. [34] Woodfordia floribunda, Salis. [35] Some of the places mentioned are probably in the present Choṭa Nagpur. Sir is said to be to the southwest of Sikhar, and this lies in a southerly direction from Manbhum.

they have made us to be Santals, because we for a long time lived in the Sāt[36] country on the other side of Sikhạr.

We cleared all the forests of the Sikhạr king, and under him some of us became owners of many villages; but from there also the Dekos drove us away and took our sites and agricultural land. In Sikhạr we learnt from the king to celebrate the Chata festival[37].

From Sikhạr some of us came to Ṭuṇḍi[38]: Where shall we stay? — and a place there is nowhere. The ancestors had forbidden us: "Don't cross the Ajae river[39], and those who will cross, for them nip off at once even the child in the womb; for there is the country of the Muslims[40], the defiled country". But because of the difficulty of getting food we have come, we have not obeyed the words of the ancestors. Then we have gradually come to the Santal Parganas. We have come feeding and we exist like the silkworm. And some day we shall again go somewhere, who knows where. Some people have gone past Rajmahal to the other side of the Ganges. Who knows why Ṭhạkur is punishing us in this way.

Additional matters from other sources.

Kolean's report of the creation and the wanderings of the people ends here. As it may be of some ethnological interest, and also help to the proper valuation of the statements, some information derived from other sources follows, in literal translation.

One story of the creation begins as follows: The sons of man (i. e., the Santals) say, it is told, that at first this earth did not exist; it was sea, and it was dark; but the spirit of Isor (God) was flying round over the water, and Isor was alone. (The expressions used show that the narrator must have been in contact with Christians.) From heaven above, it is told, Isor came down along the gossamer thread to bathe; having bathed he again passed up along the same gossamer thread to heaven. It is told that Isor or Chando (the Sun) has no parents; and when the sun rises we call this to be born, and about the setting of the sun we say: Now he has entered the body of his mother; but the parents of Chando or Isor are sarag (heaven) and patal (the nether world). As he was coming down and passing up one day, some thought or other came to his mind; he had just put his clothes down and had had his bath. Then he created those that stay with him; he created Jǫlmae rạni (the water-mother queen), Kạlibhańj rạni, Bintoria rạni, Jhimoli rạni (the earthworm queen) and several others that stay with him. Thereupon he created the Five-the Six, Jahẹr era (the Lady of the sacred grove), Gosãe era (the Goddess of the sacred grove), thereupon Marań buru and Mahadeb to stay with him.

---

[36] See Santal Dictionary, s. v. Santal. [37] See Santal Dictionary s. v. Chata. [38] In the Manbhum district. Kolean hailed from this part. [39] The Ajae river runs in a North and South direction through the western parts of the present Santal Parganas district. The majority of the Santal people now live East of this river. [40] The expression is intended to frighten the people and prevent them from crossing the river. As a matter of fact there were very few Muslims living in the country to the East of the Ajae.

When he afterwards came down to bathe and was sitting there rubbing himself, he rubbed out, who knows how much dirt from his collar-bone; he was pressing this with his fingers and of this he made two very beautiful birds and put them down near his clothes. When he had bathed he brought up with him a little water in the hollow of his hands and was sprinkling this on his clothes; some water was spattered also on the two birds, and this became their gift of life. They at once flew upwards. And, it is told, as he saw that they were very beautiful, he sang (in corrupt Bihari):

The Hãs Hạ̃sil birds are flapping their wings,
Up to heaven, father, they went,
:/: In the heavens they are strangely flying round. :/:

And, it is told, because he has told also us of this wonder, we sprinkle flour-water (refers to part of the ceremonies at the name-giving festival), and after this the midwife tells us the race and sept or country. When the two birds became tired of constantly flying, from high up they caught sight of Mahadeb floating on the water; then flying down they alighted on him, because they did not find any other place to alight on. Every day they alighted on him, and by constantly doing this they worried him, and by letting droppings fall on him they covered him with filth.

Then Mahadeb was thinking in his mind: Why did you, Ṭhạkur Jiu, make these two birds? Look here, by constantly alighting on me they have worried me, and by dropping dirt they have also covered me with filth. I shall at once tell Ṭhạkur Jiu this. He did so and said this to him. When Ṭhạkur Jiu heard this he said to Mahadeb: Wait, let them alight for a while and also let them drop filth; we shall first have a talk about these two. Then he called together those he had created first and told them all about the two birds. He said to them: Well, I have made these two birds; where shall we place them? for we have no place for them to stay. They then said: To give these two a place to stay we shall bring up earth. And they said: Well, whom shall we get hold of to bring up earth? Again they said: Who is master of the water? They said: Rạghu boaṛ (the same as raghọp̃ boaṛ); they asked him and sent Maraṅ buru to fetch him. Here they sing to a buạṅ melody:

O dear, dear, do go to him,
O dear, dear, to Rạghu boaṛ.
O dear, dear, he will bring up the earth,
O dear, dear, he will make the earth appear,
O dear, dear, he will bring up the earth.

Then Maraṅ buru called and brought Rạghu boaṛ. They asked him: How is it, are you master of the water? He answered: Yes, I am. They asked him: Would you be willing to bring up the earth? He said: Yes, because if you tell me to do so, I might bring it up. Then, it is told, they decked him out like he was at first; when they had done this, he became very glad and started singing to a Sọhrae melody:

> Father, deck me out, Father, give me a cloth round my loins;
> Father, like the large prawn, Father, let me become grand.

Then, it is told, the boaṛ at once with a great display entered the water; who knows how far away the earth was, he went along and reached there and took some earth on his back. When he was carrying it up, all the earth was dissolved and flowed away. He brought only some dal (Panicum stagninum, L.); this they kept. They said to him: You were unable to bring up the earth. He answered: Quite so, Father, it has not been done through me. Then they asked him: Who is, besides you, a master of the water? He answered: The master of the water is the sọlẹ icạk̓ (a name for the large prawn). Then they sent Maraṅ buru to fetch him. Here follows a song like the first to a buạṅ melody, only with sọlẹ icạk̓ for rạghu boaṛ.

The prawn was brought, and now follow the same questions and answers. They then said to him: Come then, give up your head. For some reason or other they asked for and kept his head. The prawn entered the water, reached the earth, used his two claws, and took earth on his back; but it was all dissolved and flowed away; but in one claw he brought along the roots of the dhubi grass and in the other claw the roots of sirom. This they also kept. They asked the prawn: Above you who is master of the water? He answered: Above me is Ḍaṭọ kũạr master of the water (Ḍatọ kũạr, the crab prince, is another name for dhiri kaṭkọm and heard in karam binti). They did not give the prawn his head back; therefore prawns have no heads even nowadays.

Maraṅ buru was asked to fetch the crab, and here follow the same questions and answers, and the same result. In one claw the crab brought the root of the karam tree, in the other claw the root of the Lotus. They also asked for and kept his head; therefore crabs have no heads even nowadays. They asked him who was master of the water above him, and he named Kạchim kũạr (the Tortoise prince).

Maraṅ buru was sent and fetched him. (They sing the same as previously, only with Kạchim kũạr as the name.) When they asked him whether he would bring the earth up he answered: No, Father, I shall perhaps not be able to bring it up; but if somebody will bring it up I might keep it. Then they asked him who was master of the water above him, and he answered that it was Jhimoli. Maraṅ buru was sent to fetch her. (Again they sing the same song with Jhimoli named.)

When Maraṅ buru had brought Jhimoli rạni (the earthworm queen), and they asked her whether she would bring the earth up, she answered: Yes, I might bring it up, but who would keep it? They said to her: We have got a person who will keep it. Then these two took counsel together, and Jhimoli said: When I bring it up perhaps enemies will eat me?

They arranged to prevent this; they made the stem of the Lotus hollow and made her enter into this; they made Kạchim kũạr lie on his stomach on the water of the sea and placed the posterior of Jhimoli on the back of the Tortoise. Jhimoli commenced to eat down in the water and was voiding excrements on the back of the Tortoise. She voided a tremendous heap. Then when Kạchim kũạr became tired of lying on his stomach, he suddenly moved, and all the earth was dissolved and flowed away. Then they said: Oh, Oh, the earth was brought up, but as the Tortoise did not remain standing, it was lost. And they said: Let us chain him. Then, it is told, Chando from somewhere brought a chain; they fixed an iron post and chained his four legs. The Tortoise then said: Don't chain all my four legs; let me have one leg free, so that I may scratch myself with it. They therefore let one leg be free. It is told, when Kạchim kũạr sometimes scratches himself, the earth is moved. They tethered the Tortoise to the iron post, and as the Earthworm again ate earth she voided excrements on the back of the Tortoise, and this time the earth remained there.

When the earth had been brought up, they yoked the bull and the cock together to level it. They harrowed it level, and where here and there rubbish remained, these places became mountains or hills.

In the earth which was brought up they sowed grass and planted the root of the karam tree, and they arranged a garden to plant different things, fruits of all kinds and trees. Among all the trees the karam at once became very high, and when the Hãs Hạ̃sil birds saw this they left Mahadeb, flew to the karam and alighted there. They found their food in pools, but came to the karam to rest.

As time passed they had intercourse with each other and found a clump of sirom grass to lay their eggs. Having made their nest in the clump of the sirom grass they got two eggs. As they were sitting on these they became fecundated, and a voice was heard from their inside. Being frightened by this the two birds left off sitting on the eggs. Maraṅ buru then said to them: As you know, I saw that you had laid eggs there; why are you not sitting on them? They told him: We were sitting on the eggs; but there is a kind of sound in them; fearing this we are not sitting. Maraṅ buru then said: Well then, come along, we shall hear whether you are telling me the truth or not. Then they all went there and listened. The voice was like this (a song, buạṅ melody):

O dear, dear, in the sea,
O dear, dear, dal grass came into existence.
O dear, dear, on the dal grass,
O dear, dear, sirom came into existence;
O dear, dear, on the sirom,
O dear, dear, the Hãs Hạ̃sil birds are making a nest.

When Marañ buru heard this he said to them: O, don't be afraid of this; sit diligently on the eggs, you two. And by their continued sitting on the eggs two human beings came into existence, and they sing to the same melody:

O dear, dear, with what to support the two,
O dear, dear, with what to keep the two?
O dear, dear, with milk to support the two,
O dear, dear, with cream to keep the two.

Marañ buru told Chando this, and Chando gave Marañ buru milk and said to him: Do support the two human beings, and take care of them. Then Marañ buru was given over to the two, and he supported them, until they grew up. He taught them to work and instructed them. But where the two birds went and what happened to them, we do not know. But where the Hãs Hạsil birds were borne, and where they laid eggs, and where the two human beings were born, this place we call Hihiṛi Pipiṛi.

Marañ buru taught the two human beings to dig out medicines, to collect and prepare the stuffs for fermenting beer, to cut trees, to sow millets, to offer the first fruits of these, to invoke the spirits of the sacred grove and other matters. There seven boys and seven girls were born, and when mankind multiplied, Marañ buru gave them races and septs.

Because the human beings fell into sin, Chando became angry, and he destroyed the first born human beings by fire-rain. But he saved two human beings, keeping them in a stone-cave. Chando made the two human beings go to the Hihiṛi Pipiṛi country. He taught them the invocation in connexion with offering the first fruits of millets, and he made them prepare the sacred grove. At the foot of the trees of the sacred grove he made them fix a stone; at the stone he made them put down the ears of the iṛi millet (Panicum Crus-galli, L.), and he taught them the invocation (as follows):

Please take it, thou Five, here as thou seest, we offer thee the first fruits of the millet; afterwards also we, like the crows, like the kites, shall eat, shall take into our mouth; do not let stomach-ache, headache be created, be formed, Father my Ṭhạkur.

In the same manner they also make invocation to The Six, Marañ buru and Gosãe era.

In connexion with preparing the beer-fermenting stuffs they offer a cake made of a little flour and make this invocation:

Please take it, Pilcu haṛam, we are preparing the fermenting stuff for beer; may it become very savoury for us, that it may be drunk, be got quickly down.

In this way they invoke Marañ buru, the Six and Jahẹr era. They put down a little to taste it, and when the beer is ready brewed, they make the following invocation:

Please take it, Pilcu haṛam, we have brewed tasted beer, may it become savoury for us like neat spirits, that it may be drunk, be got quickly down.

Marań buru said to the two: Do drink this beer, all of it. He himself lay down there in this place, and he was singing to himself (a song in corrupt Bihari).

Other gurus have a more circumstantial lore, detailing traditional incidents and attempting to explain ethnological, also religious matters. The rôle played by Marań buru is different from what is otherwise taught; he is here appearing as a kind of factotum of Ṭhạkur, a spirit that should be in charge of mankind and be their guide. We shall later, when we reach what is told of the bongas, hear something quite different.

Kolean does not mention how mankind were divided into separate races. Other gurus have a story partly relating to this, partly also to the formation of sub-septs. The story runs: After the destruction of all mankind, except one pair, Ṭhạkur guided this pair back to Hihiṛi Pipiṛi. Here they got children and these were divided into septs. Gradually this division proved itself to be insufficient; they could not all get proper mates. Seeing this Ṭhạkur said to Marań buru: Do persuade these men to go to the Khaṇḍerae forest to hunt; otherwise they will again turn as bad as they were. As we (it might be noted that Ṭhạkur here constantly uses the inclusive plural) did not call what they did good, we exterminated them, the earth became empty, and we also repented. Therefore we shall not exterminate mankind, rather we shall again separate them into many septs. Marań buru did this, and all men went to this forest happy in mind. He then divided each sept into twelve, and from that time they found opportunity of marrying. Marań buru was given over to mankind, and he is ruling.

Then something again occurred to Marań buru: He said to Ṭhạkur: Again mankind have become very numerous; we cannot get further in the old way; therefore I think we shall make mankind into different races. Ṭhạkur said to him: Very well, see to their wants, that they may live well and not be exterminated from the earth, and so that they will remember us; make them work so. Then he again acted on a thought and stirred up the mind of the men. He gathered them in a plain near a river. Here he made them cook all kinds of flesh, viz., ox-meat, buffalo-meat, the flesh of goats and sheep, of fowls and pigs, of fish and camels. He arranged all this cooked meat in twelve leaf-cups, and having selected one principal man among each of the original septs he called these aside and said to them that they should look at the leaf-cups. When they had done this he took them away as far as the length of three or four plough-furrows; then he said to them: Now run along from here, and whichever leaf-cup any of you may like, take that and eat. Start running from here all of you at the same time, and any one who can gain on the others, let him.

They ran from there, and the man who reached there in advance, he took the leaf-cup with ox-meat and ate its contents. At this time, it is told, he separated the Santals and the Dekos. They who ate ox-meat became Santals, and they who ate the flesh of goats, of sheep, and of fish became Dekos. At that time their language was also altered; they who got the Deko language were spread in all directions from there, that is to say, they emigrated hither and thither. Those who got the Santal language all stayed together. (The story of this running competition is commonly heard among the Santals, both to explain the sub-septs, and also the different races. It might be mentioned that some Santals tell that their language was much influenced by Hindi and by what they call Kortha, a local dialect of Hindi, when they were living in peace with the other races after their having assisted king Rama to vanquish king Rabona.) It is told how they came to Jarpi and from there to Cae Campa.

As they felt very constrained to live in one place, they commenced to settle down on separate high-lying places (i. e., founded separate villages). At this time they had no difficulties; they were providing themselves with all they needed, also with salt and oil. They were themselves making all implements of iron, also made thread, wove their clothes, prepared everything. The comparatively poor ones were occupied with these kinds of work; they did not pay any rent, they had no money-lenders and people of that kind. They had no bongas, and nothing is told of festivals, whether they had such or not. All were called "kings" (raj, landholders), and the villages, where they had settled, were called gaṛ (forts).

All forms of their traditions agree, that in Cae Campa they stayed for a long time and ruled the country; their septs are mentioned as having separate occupations and got corresponding surnames. The Kiskus were called rapaj (collection of kings); the Murmus Ṭhạkur (because they were acting as priests), the Sorens sipạhi (soldiers), the Hembroms kũạr (princes, or nobility), the Marṇḍis kipisā̃ṛ (collection of wealthy people), the Besra bayar (lit. uncastrated buffaloes, lascivious ones), the Ṭuḍus mandạṛiạ (drummers who play the dancing drum), the Hãsdak̓s hasa panderae (? cultivators), the Chõṛẽs cacar-hat̓ (the dirty ones) and the Baskes cooks. (Cf. what Kolean has told. As a curiosity it may be mentioned that some present-day Santals have taken up some of these designations as their family surnames, e. g., there are some of the Hembrom sept who style themselves Koomar, i. e., kũạr, and some of the Kisku sept who call themselves Rapaj.)

It is told that the Murmus at this time ordered that the Jom sim festival should be observed once yearly, each year in a separate village, and there all should foregather.

In Campa the relations between the ancestors and the Dekos came, according to the traditions, to a head. The Kiskus and the Marṇḍis were fighting each other; some Dekos used this as an opportunity for entering and robbing the people. The Murmus took up the matter and commenced to fight the Dekos, but were vanquished; finally the Dekos occupied the whole country; most of the people ran away, but some remained and gradually became Dekos.

Some of the gurus explicitly state that a number of the lowcaste Hindus known to the Santals (they enumerate the Doms, Kamars, Bhũyas, Tilis, Hadis, Bauris, Kunkals, and others) originally belonged to the Kherwars, especially to the Kisku and Baske septs. It is also told that those who left the Kherwars and became Dekos spread in all directions.

We are here touching on one of India's problems, and a few words may be permitted. First as regards the wanderings of the Santals, as they may be observed at present and probably are a repetition of what has happened in earlier times. The Santals are among the very best of clearers of jungle in India, themselves originally a forest people. But they have not reached the stage of being really good agriculturists; it must also be remembered that they have very little understanding of the use of money; they may be said to know the value of a pice, but do not know the value of the rupee. What often follows is this: they get into the hands of the moneylenders who will do all they can to get hold of the fields cleared by the Santals, who frequently will not know or think of any other way of getting out of their difficulties than by emigrating to some other place, always towards the rising of the sun. Combined with this we have their backwardness as agriculturists: they have little idea of getting all that is possible out of the lands they have cleared or are occupying. They are a prolific race; the time comes when they have not enough land to support themselves. The result is, that either the whole family, or some of them, will go away, either to find fresh jungle to clear and occupy, or to work for others as labourers. It is in their blood to seek fresh fields; as they often are heard to say, they have a wish "to see land". Now if the whole family does not move away, some will stay; those who stay will gradually get under the influence of the more civilized neighbours and may ultimately become attached to these.

After this digression a little more about the traditions. As regards M a n d o̱ S i ṅ (by some also called M a d h w a or M a d h o̱) some have a very detailed story, something like a folk-tale. A servant girl is stated to have been with child by some of the young men of "the kings", who threatened to kill her if she revealed anything. She bore her child in the forest and left him there, but came every day to suckle him. This went on for two months; then one day the mother did not come quickly; the child became hungry and commenced to cry. Some Kiskü girls heard this, found the child and brought it home with them. They were convinced that the child was that of the girl; nothing was said about this, but they asked the girl to take charge of the child, saying that they had adopted it. The child grew up, became very intelligent and clever in all kinds of work. The king gave him office, and he gradually became indispensable. After some time the king asked him whether they had given him a wife; and as this was not the case the king ordered him to bring all the principal men to him; he wanted to ask them the reason for this. In spite of orders and persuasion they would not come and would not be brought, although the king sent elephants, horses, etc., to carry them. The king became angry and ordered Madhwa to go and apply sindur to all the daughters of these men, to the girls he might care to make his wives. He consequently went to these men and asked them whether they would give hime a daughter of theirs for a wife; otherwise he had the king's order to apply sindur with force to every daughter of theirs and thus to defile them. Frightened at this they promised him a wife, but asked for time to consult with each other. All the people of the land came together, but no one was willing to give a daughter, because they did not know to what sept he really belonged. So they decided to run away; but as they needed carts to get along, they appointed a day when they said they would give him a wife, giving them sufficient time to get the carts made. Madhwa believed them, and at this time they gave him the name of Madho̱ Siṅ. When the fixed day came, they ran away during the night.

It is told that some, because of their covetousness, and because they would not leave their wealth (cattle), did not follow the others, but made friends with Madho̱ Siṅ and gave him a daughter of theirs to be his wife. These belonged to the Bedea So̱re̱n sept; this is mentioned as the cause of their being lost to the Santals; they became Dekos.

There are some very elaborate, partly fanciful tales of what happened at Toṛe Pokhori Baha Bandela, where the ancestors adopted so many Hindu customs.

Some of the traditions have a number of details in connexion with the wanderings from Sikhar on, naming many places where they stayed for some time, also mentioning that many became Dekos (as they call it) by entering into marriage relations with these; such people originally belonged to the Ṭuḍu and Baske septs.

The traditions generally end with lamenting the present deplorable state of the people; they are living under the feet of the Dekos; they are unable to stay anywhere, are very poor, and so on. As a consequence they have forgotten their old customs; they have no longer any regular guru-training; and besides this they have no records (written), their records are all "in the mouth"; therefore so much has been lost, mixed up and brought into disorder. Especially since the Santal insurrection of 1855 much has been lost. Curiously enough, one of my informants tells that nowadays much is learnt from old women, who in the evenings may be heard relating traditions and folk-tales. This explains much, and enhances the value of Kolean's story. This is now continued.

II. CHAṬIAṚ, CEREMONIAL CLEANSING

a. Janam chaṭiaṛ, ceremonial cleansing after birth[1].

Children are named after (i. e. born into) the sept of their father, not after that of their mother. When a child is born in a village, this village becomes ceremonially unclean; therefore they do not perform any bonga-worship until the uncleanness has been blotted out. And where a child is born, this house becomes unclean; therefore until the uncleanness is wiped out, no inhabitant of the village will eat or drink in this house.

When a boy is born, they shave on the fifth day, and if it is a girl on the third day. On the day of shaving the father of the child calls on all, (also) poor people, to be shaved. They come together at his house; when all are come they set a barber to do the shaving. First of all he shaves the village priest, thereupon the field priest, thereupon the village headman, the deputy headman, the headman of morals and his deputy and the messenger of the village headman, and thereupon all the men of the village and last of all the father of the child.

Now the barber calls for the new-born child. The woman who has worked as midwife carries the child in her arms out to the door, bringing along two leaf-cups, one leaf-cup with water and one to put the hair in. The barber shaves the child[2]; when this is done, the midwife puts this hair in the leaf-cup; thereupon she binds two threads on the arrow with which she cut the umbilical cord when the child was born. Now the child's father fills oil in the leaf-cup and calls on the men of the village to come along with him to a place where they can go down to the water. They go along. When they come back after having bathed, the midwife takes along with her oil and turmeric and the arrow on which the two threads are bound, and calling on the women of the village to come along she takes them to the watering-place to bathe. They go there. At the place of bathing the midwife throws one thread together with the child's hair into the water and lets it float away, after she has made five marks of sindur at the descent to the water. This they call to buy way down to water. The other thread and the arrow she washes and brings with her back to the house, when all of them have bathed. Arrived to the house the midwife immerses the remaining thread in turmeric(water), and this she makes into

---

[1] The word is possibly to be connected with H. chaṭhi, the sixth (day after birth, when the house is cleaned, the child named, and so on). [2] The whole head.

a loin-string round the waist of the child. After this the child's mother sits down under the eaves of the house and takes the child in her arms; and she takes some atnak leaves[3] together with her child in her arms.

Now the midwife kneads some cow's dung with water on the eaves, and lets also some dung-water drip down on the child's mother; and receiving some dung-water in her left hand she daubs her head with it and sucks a little in. The child's mother then goes inside and lays the child down on a bedstead. Now the midwife mixes flour in water in three leaf-cups; the flour-water of one cup she sprinkles on all the four legs of the bedstead and thereupon throws this leaf-cup away. After this she sprinkles the flour-water of another leaf-cup first on the village priest, after him on the field priest, after him on the village headman, after him on his deputy, the village headman of morals and his deputy and on the messenger of the village headman, on their breasts. And after these on all the men of the village, on their breasts.

Thereupon she sprinkles the flour-water of the remaining leaf-cup, first on the wife of the village priest, after her on the wife of the field priest, after her on the wife of the village headman, after her on the wife of his deputy, after her on the wife of the headman of morals and on the wife of his deputy, and after her on the wife of the headman's messenger, and after these on all the women of the village, on their breasts.

Now the husband and wife of the house ask each other: Whom shall we name? Then they say if it is a boy: We shall name father, or in case it is a girl: We shall name mother. The first born boy gets the name of his father's father, and the first girl gets the name of her father's mother. The second born gets the name of his mother's father, and the second girl the name of her mother's mother. Those who come afterwards get the names of the brothers and sisters of the father and mother.

Now the midwife comes out into the courtyard, and telling them the name she greets them one after the other and says to them: From to-day please call out to him using this name when hunting and chasing, in case it is a boy, and if it is a girl: Come along you, if you will go and fetch water.

Thereupon they bring gruel with nim[4] in leaf-cups out to the courtyard. They give it first to the village priest and the other village officials in the order mentioned, and after these to all the men of the village. Afterwards they give the village priest's wife and so on all the women. Now the defilement is wiped out, and the child has come in among its relatives. Five days later the barber and the midwife again shave the child alone. Then all is finished.

What the midwife by customary right gets is as follows: When a boy is born, she gets a piece of cloth, three cubits long, and one maund (i. e., nearly 40 kg) paddy and one wristlet for cutting the umbilical cord; and if it is a girl, she gets a piece of cloth, three cubits long, twenty seers of paddy and one wristlet for cutting the umbilical cord.

---

[3] Terminalia tomentosa, W. & A. [4] Melia Azadirachta, L. (Melia indica, Brandis).

b. When a child is born out of wedlock.

In case a girl without being married gives birth to a child, her father and brothers inform the village headman and his deputy. These two call the village people together, and when they have gathered they ask the girl who is the father of the child. The village people then seize the man the girl names, and even if he denies responsibility, his word will not be accepted. But if he is able to prove that other youngsters are also implicated, then the child is born in the bidhuạ-state[5]. If only one person is proved to be responsible, he will have to take the girl and keep her as his wife; but if two or three persons are proved to be implicated, they will have to pay some money; then they shave off the hair of the child's head in the name of the Jọg Mạńjhi (custos morum of the village), and the child gets his sept. Or if the Jọg Mạńjhi is a relative, they will shave off the head-hair in the name of the Jọg Paranik (the deputy custos morum) or of any man in the village. Of the money that the young men have paid, the child's mother will get some, to nurse the child until it gets strong; the man in whose name they shave off the head-hair gets some, and the village people get the rest of the money. If the child's mother is unable to name anyone as father, then also the child becomes a bidhuạ, if the male relatives of the girl are unable to buy a man to stand as a husband for her. But if they are able to buy her a husband, the child will get this one's sept, and they shave off the head-hair of the child in his name. To buy a husband the male relatives of the girl will have to pay twenty rupees. This money the man who stands as husband gets. If they are unable to procure a husband, they will shave off the head-hair for the child as a bidhuạ in the name of the village Jọg Mạńjhi or his deputy, or of any man in the village, and the child will get this man's sept. At this time the male relatives of the child's mother will have to pay, and the man in whose name they shave off the child's head-hair will get the money. Formerly, before money was introduced, one pair of bullocks, one cow with calf (in milk) and one bundle of paddy had to be paid. This the man who stands as husband gets.

If a Santal man has had illicit intercourse with a girl of another race, or a Santal girl with a man of another race, and a child is born, in this case we outcaste such ones for life, and such people will run away from among us.

c. Caco chạṭiạr, the ceremony when a Santal is given full social rights.

There is no fixed time for the caco chạṭiạr[6], only that it must be performed before marriage, and children cannot be married unless they have gone through this ceremony. When a man has a number of children, he will have this act performed with

[5] The Santal word, bidhuạ, is used about one who has no recognized father. [6] Caco is the Santal word for toddling, a child's first successful attempt to walk. As the name implies, the caco chạṭiạr may be performed with a child, as soon as it is able to move about.

them all at the same time. If a child should die before having been through this ceremony, they do not cremate such ones and do not carry their bones to the Damuda river.

A man wants to have the caco chạṭiạr for his children; he brews beer and procures oil and turmeric to anoint the village people. Then he calls the village headman and his deputy and pours beer out to these two. They ask him: Look here, you, what beer is this that you are giving us? He says: This, father, is intimation-beer; I am minded to do so and so, that is to say, I am going to have caco chạṭiạr for my children. This happens in the morning. After having drunk the beer the village headman and his deputy send the Goḍet to call the village people[7]. They come; when they are assembled, the village girls first anoint the village priest and his wife sitting on a mat; thereupon they anoint the field priest and his wife, after them the village headman and his wife, thereupon his deputy and this one's wife, the custos morum and wife, his deputy and wife, the messenger and wife, and finally they anoint all the (men and) women of the village. Now they serve beer round. First they give the village headman and his deputy, thereupon all the people. When one round has been served they ask the father of the children: For how many is this? He answers: For so and so many. Then so many children as are to have the caco chạṭiạr, so many rounds of beer they serve, each round four leaf-cups to each. Then they ask the father of the children: How many iṛi and how many erba of yours have shot into ears[8]? He says: So many iṛi and so many erba have shot into ears. They say in reply: Very fortunate. Then they ask him: Whereabouts are the countries? The children's father then names the countries where the grandparents of the children live. Then they call for the namesake-beer. Now the grandparents of the children give the village people beer that they have brought with them from their homes. Thereupon the village people dance singing:

Along here, along in this direction are Nilgai tracks,
Along here, along in this direction are Nilgai hind tracks.

Track, track the Nilgai tracks,
Follow, follow the Nilgai hind tracks.

On the tank embankment are Nilgai tracks,
On the river bank are tracks of the Nilgai hind.

Tie on him (her), O mother, a golden bell,
Fasten on him (her) O mother, hollow sounding bells.

---

[7] Nowadays the Jọg Mạńjhi is generally asked to call the people together; the people sit in rows on straw spread out for the purpose.

[8] i. e., how many girls and how many sons have been born to you? iṛi is Panicum Crus-galli, L., fig. used about a girl; erba is Setaria italica, Kunth., fig. used about a boy.

All then drink this beer.

Thereupon they commence the recitation. How the world was created, and how the Santals have from that time come, feeding like the silk-worm, to the different countries, all this they tell, in order that the children may not forget it. When enumerating this they reach the words "they were scattered here and there", they mention Hikim pargana, the first overchief in the Sikhar country; they say: Hikim pargana said to them: Come along, we shall settle down; I have spied out for us virgin forest, virgin soil. The ancestors said: Come along, let us help him; we shall clear jungle, burning and felling; we shall support ourselves and get a living. Having come together there they joined in marriages; they cleared the jungle, burning and felling; they kept the iṛi and erba seed hidden away in gourd-shells, big and small; what they had sown as iṛi grew up into erba ears; what they had sown as erba grew up into iṛi ears. What they had cleared by burning they would watch, the iṛi and erba ripened; now birds might eat it; then they said: Come, we shall keep watch. The fowls cluck, the lizards nod, and the birds also chirp. Consequently at this time two persons keep watch, husband and wife. They had cleared the jungle at the junction of roads, at the cross-road. They both keep watch; while keeping watch they climb a slanting dry p̱o̱p̱o̱ṛo̱ tree[9] and play; and by the grace of Ṭhạkur the broken grain, the husked grain was not spilled, was not scattered; it came well down from the dry p̱o̱p̱o̱ṛo̱ tree. And when it 'trod' the earth it became religiously, ceremoniously unclean.

On the day of the pestle, on the day of the mortar we are first; on the day of fire, on the day of flame we are first, at the dug hole with percolated water, at the pool water we are first; at the day of fetching firewood, at the day of fetching leaves we are first; those of you who would not go, these also we made go; let this especially be your grief. (The village people here answer: Those who are grieving have gone to Somae's narrow sloping valley[10], to the fine sand to be crocodile herds.) Now we humbly beseech you village people, from to-day, when we are having the cleansing at birth, the social initiation, we have run into debt, we borrowed at the Suṇḍi house, the Hạḍi house[11]; then we provided, collected (the needful), and then we asked you, invited you to come. Consequently you came on your legs, we received you with our heads, as regards sitting and standing, as regards this also we overlooked and left it half-done: high seats, a high verandah, as regards this also we are lacking and in want. Now we beseech you, on the day of marriage, the day of wedlock, on the day of cleansing at birth, the day of social initiation, the day of dying, the day of death, we shall work and earn to squeeze out the beer, we shall work and earn to draw water, we shall work and earn to stitch the leaves

---

[9] P̱o̱p̱o̱ṛo̱ (or more commonly p̱õpṛõ or p̱o̱pṛo̱), Gardenia latifolia, Aiton. Here fig. about the wife.

[10] Somae sokṛa, acc. to tradition, a place near the sources of the Damuda river.

[11] Suṇḍi is the beer-brewing Hindu low-caste; Hạḍi the Hindu low-caste scavenger.

together. We are imploring you, the village people, we were like crows, we have become white like paddybirds; you village people be witnesses.

Now they drink beer, and commencing to sing chaṭiar and doṅ songs they dance. Then all is finished.

Song.

O, the sirom ear had been formed.
Of the woman such and such a girl was born.

O, the marãṛ bush[12] had blossomed,
The boy so and so was born.

The plump one, the stout one,
The little parakeet, the little starling,
The sucking boy, the sucking so and so,
Bring the two down at once,
The little parakeet, the little starling.

c. Of the burnt-mark.

The ancestors of old said that if any one did not get the burnt-mark, in the other world they would put in their arms a caterpillar big as a log; therefore all boys will diligently stand the pain. Some persons take only one burnt-mark, some three, some five, and some take seven burnt-marks. They get the burnt-mark on the left arm. The burnt-marks are made in the following way: They make a roll of a rag like a cigar. They set fire to this at the top end and put it down on the spot where the burnt-mark is to be. It burns slowly down. When it is burnt out the person who makes the mark quickly presses the ashes down on the spot. Then a blister forms and it becomes a sore. When this heals the burnt-mark is there.

d. Of tattooing.

Women do not take burnt-marks; they let themselves be tattooed, in order that in the other world they shall not put a caterpillar big as a log into their arms. They are tattooed on the breast. There are no special figures, only something indefinite, to look beautiful. First they draw with a bit of wood and soot-ink, and afterwards they prick with a needle along the pattern. When tattooing is done, they smear turmeric on, and they go and bathe.

[12] Erythrina indica, Lam.

III. ALL IN CONNEXION WITH MARRIAGE

a. The marriage-broker.

When anyone is in need of getting a wife for his son, he gets hold of a marriage-broker[1]. He says to him (her): I say, find out a bride for us somewhere. The marriage-broker answers: What kind of girl? The boy's father says: Such and such a one. The marriage-broker says: I remember some that is so; wait, I must first ask them whether they are agreeable or not. The boy's father says to him: Well then, come back here when you have made inquiries, after so and so many days.

Thereupon the marriage-broker goes to the house of the friends concerned and asks them, saying: I intend to bring some friends to you, will it suit you or not? What do you say? They answer him: What kind of friends? you are giving us quite a fright. The marriage-broker says: Good friends, of course, there is no cause for fear. Then he speaks plainly to them, saying: Have they shut in this girl anywhere or not? They answer him: No, she is unoccupied. The marriage-broker then says: In that case I shall bring some friends to you. They answer him: Well, that is so, you will bring some friends; of what sept are they? The marriage-broker tells them: Of such and such sept. Then they ask him: Of what village? He says: Of such and such village. They ask him: Who are they? He says: They are so and so. Then they say: Well then, provided they are pleased with us. The marriage-broker then says to them: At such and such a day I shall conduct them here, please be at home. They answer him: Please, this time, let it be somewhere outside, otherwise there might perhaps occur something shameful, if we should not be pleased with each other.

The marriage-broker then goes to the boy's father and says to him: The friends said, All right, please bring them, but this time somewhere outside. I have fixed a time for them after so and so many days; then we shall go.

b. Omens.

When the fixed day comes, the marriage-broker comes there and in the early morning takes them along, viz., the boy's parents and a couple of the village people. They start. If they, within the boundary of their own village, or of the girl's village, see fire, an

---

[1] see Santal Dictionary s. v. raebar.

axe, firewood on a woman's head, a snake or a jackal crossing the road in front of them, it is a bad omen, and they return home. But if they, within the boundary of their own village, or of the girl's village, see a full vessel, a cow, a new earthenware vessel, a pack bullock, or the footmarks of a tiger, these are excellent omens[2] for them; therefore they go in to the Jo̦g Ma̦ńjhi of the girl's village. (This in connexion with omens is nowadays only custom, because the boy's father tells the village headman in advance, viz., on such and such a day we shall, in the early morning, go to have a look at a vessel; warn the people of the village that they must not at that time touch anything that will hinder. The marriage-broker also tells the headman of the girl's village that the people of his village may behave in the same way.)

The marriage-broker says to the Jo̦g Ma̦ńjhi: We have come to see a vessel; you, please, show us this piece. The Jo̦g Ma̦ńjhi then goes to the house of the girl's father and tells them: The friends have come. They reply: Very well. Then the Jo̦g Ma̦ńjhi says to the girl: Come a couple of you girls to our house; some visitors have come to us; you pour out water[3] for them, we have no one to do it. The girl's parents then say to their daughter: Do go, girl. Then some three girls go; when they arrive there they go round and bow to all who are gathered. The girl concerned keeps her place as the middle one of the three, in order not to be ashamed. The marriage-broker then whispers to the boy's parents, saying: Look at the one in the middle. When they have greeted all, the girls will stand there for a moment and then go home. When they have left, the Jo̦g Ma̦ńjhi asks the marriage-broker: Well, how is it? Are you satisfied or not? The visitors answer: Yes, it is all right, so far as we are concerned; we are pleased; the question is whether they also will be pleased.

The Jo̦g Ma̦ńjhi then goes to the home of the girl's parents, who ask him: How is it, Jo̦g Ma̦ńjhi, what did the friends say? Are they pleased or not? The Jo̦g Ma̦ńjhi replies: The friends have said it is all right, they are pleased. The girl's father then says to the Jo̦g Ma̦ńjhi: Please, bring the friends here, they must drink some water before they leave. The Jo̦g Ma̦ńjhi returns to his own house and says to the visitors: Please, Sir Marriage-Broker, the friends are calling us, we shall drink some water before leaving. The young man's party say: No, not so, it is well as it is; shall we not drink later on? Surely we shall. If the girl's father has brewed beer or something, the Jo̦g Ma̦ńjhi speaks earnestly to them: Come along, you need not sit down, I shall not keep you for many moments. They consequently understand that they have brewed beer; then they go. The Jo̦g Ma̦ńjhi takes them along. The girls are there. As soon as the visitors arrive, they, i. e., the girls, bring them bedsteads, stools, pieces of wood to sit on. Pouring out water for them they again salute them. When this is done, the girl's parents greet the

---

2 Omens seem to be paid less attention to now than formerly; Kolean's remarks, put within parenthesis, are significant. 3 Visitors from a distance get their feet washed. It is an act of courtesy.

visitors, and they ask each other how they are faring. Thereupon the girls wash the feet of the visitors. Thereupon they take them inside; now they give all there beer and food. When they have had food and drink, they say good-bye to them. Some people will not the first time go to the home of the girl's parents; they return straight from the house of the J o̜ g M ạ ṅ j h i.

When they have come back home, the young man's father says to the marriage-broker: Well, come back here after so and so many days. When he comes on the fixed day they give him beer and say to him: Please, bring the friends here in their turn. The marriage-broker then goes to the girl's home and says to them: Please, the friends are calling us, when are we to go? The girl's father says: Wait a little, I must call these and these. He then calls the village headman and his deputy and the J o̜ g M ạ ṅ j h i; if he has beer or something, they drink and have a talk. The girl's father says: The friends are calling us; please, what day are we to fix for the marriage-broker? They fix the fifth day from then. The marriage-broker returns and tells the young man's father that the friends will come after so and so many days. The young man's father brews a couple of earthenware pots of beer.

On the fixed day, early in the morning, the people of the girl's side, her parents and a couple of others go to have a look at the prospective bridegroom. The marriage-broker conducts them thither. If they, inside the boundary of their own village, or of the village of the young man, see fire, an axe, firewood on the head of a woman, a snake, or a jackal crossing the road in front of them from the left side, it is a bad omen; consequently they return home, and there will be no marriage; but if they, inside their own boundary, or the boundary of the village of the young man, see a full earthenware pot, a cow, a new vessel, a pack bullock, or the foot-marks of a tiger, this is a very good omen for them; consequently they go in to the J o̜ g M ạ ṅ j h i of the young man's village. The marriage-broker says to the Jo̜g Mạṅjhi: Please, Jo̜g Mạṅjhi, we shall look up the friends, don't keep us long here. The Jo̜g Mạṅjhi then goes to the young man's home and says to his parents: Friends have come to us; I shall take the young man with me for a short while. The young man's parents send him along with a couple of his comrades. The Jo̜g Mạṅjhi takes them along. They arrive there and greet the visitors. The young man goes along between two others. The marriage-broker now whispers to the parents of the girl, saying: Look at him in the middle. They do so; if they are not pleased they privately say to the marriage-broker: Our girl will surely not be pleased, he is too old, or they will name some excuse or other, and they will quietly return home. If they are pleased, they will also tell the marriage-broker this. The marriage-broker tells the Jo̜g Mạṅjhi this, and he informs the parents of the young man. Hearing this the parents of the young man say to the Jo̜g Mạṅjhi: Please bring the friends here, they will go home when they have drunk some water. He brings them, and when they have all greeted each other, they make the young man once more salute the parents of the girl and their companions. Now the girls of the house wash the feet of the visitors, and they take them inside. First they drink beer; thereupon they give them food. When they have eaten, they say good-bye to them. They return home; this is now finished.

c. Seeing house and home.

Now the girl's people go to see the young man's house and home, that they may know how their circumstances are. On this occasion the uncles and aunts of the girl on both father's and mother's side, the headman of their village and his deputy and a couple of the village people go along with them. The marriage-broker takes them straight to the house of the parents of the prospective bridegroom. Here they place bedsteads, stools, and wooden slabs to sit on before them, and they sit down. Then they bring water in loṭas[4] and brass-cups, and they salute them one after the other. Thereupon they bring wooden slabs, water and oil in an earthenware lamp-vessel, and after the visitors have placed their feet on a wooden slab they wash their feet and anoint them with oil. When they have been washed the Jo̱g Mạṅjhi goes inside the house, brings oil out in a small earthenware vessel and one handful of tooth-brush twigs[5] and says to them: Do come along, we shall go to the water. He takes them along there. Here they bathe, clean their teeth and rub themselves in with oil. Thereupon they return to the house and again sit down on the bedsteads, as before. The people of the house now take mats inside and say: Please bring water for the friends in a loṭa; and this is done. The visitors now wash their hands; they take them into the house, and they sit down on the mats.

The Jo̱g Mạṅjhi then says: Please bring the beer. This is done; first they give the village headman, thereupon his deputy, and thereupon all who are there, they give each four leaf-cups of beer. Again the Jo̱g Mạṅjhi says: Please bring us beer in brass-cups, each of us once; give the friends. Thereupon they give all of them beer, and the village headman says: Please, Jo̱g Mạṅjhi, call a girl and let her pick up and throw these leaf-cups away. She does this, and they bring a brass-cup and water in a loṭa, thereupon all of them get their hands washed over the brass-cup.

Again the Jo̱g Mạṅjhi says: Please bring leaf-plates; and these are brought. First they place one before the village headman, and thereupon one before his deputy, and thereupon before all who are there. The Jo̱g Mạṅjhi says: Listen, one of you young men come here, give us some parched rice and some flattened rice[6]. First he gives the village headman, thereupon his deputy, and thereupon all who are there. Now the Jo̱g Mạṅjhi says: Please, honoured friends, let us wet the parched and flattened rice. They do this, and again the

---

[4] The loṭa is a small metal vessel, generally of brass. [5] Like the Hindus the Santals are very careful with their teeth and constantly brush them with a small twig, chewed into a brush. The word dạtạuni, tooth brush, is Hindi. [6] see Santal Dictionary s. vv. khạjạṛi and tabe̱n.

Jog Mạṅjhi says: Please, bring some molasses. When this is brought, they give the village headman and his deputy and after them all who are there.

The Jog Mạṅjhi then says: Honoured friends, as you see, we are drying people; otherwise in olden times they were saying, the rich people dry paddy and husks, as for us, we are drying you friends; for this, honoured friends, be especially grieved. Then the visitors answer: The grieving ones, Sir, have all gone in advance, to Somae's narrow valley, to the fine sand they have gone to herd crocodiles. Thereupon they eat, and when this is done the Jog Mạṅjhi again says: Listen, we have cut and cleared the threshing-floor, please, bring us again some parched and flattened rice. They bring this and give to all who are there. The Jog Mạṅjhi then says: Please, bring the friends some water from the closet of the ancestors[7]. Then they give them each one brass-cup full of beer. They finish eating and drinking.

Now the Jog Mạṅjhi calls out: You wife of the eldest son (if there is no such one, he will call some other girl), come here, pick up these leaf-plates and throw them away; bring some water in a loṭa, and pour some out in a brass-cup for all of us; we shall wash our hands and mouth. When they have washed themselves, they give each of them two leaf-cups of beer. They then come out from the house, enter the cow-shed[8] and sit down on bedsteads. The Jog Mạṅjhi says: You, wife of the eldest son (if there is such a one there), please bring a hookah[9] and tobacco. She brings this, and they hand it over to the visitors.

The Jog Mạṅjhi now goes into the house and says to the father of the young man: Look here, Sir, what shall we give the visitors to eat with the rice? He answers: Some of you call my eldest son. They call him; he comes and says: Why have you called me, father? His father says to him in reply: I say, my son, bring the biggest castrated goat. He goes and brings it.

The Jog Mạṅjhi then says: Do bring some water in a loṭa. They bring this and pour the water on the head of the castrated goat; thereupon they kill it.

They ask the visitors to sit down and take food. When they have given everybody rice and curry, the Jog Mạṅjhi says: As you see, Sirs, you are our friends; as for us, we are drying the friends; our ancestors of old, the rich ones, they would dry paddy and husks; as you see, we are drying you, our friends; let this especially grieve you. The visitors then reply: Yes, Sir, the grieving ones have gone to Somae's narrow valley, to the fine sand to herd crocodiles. Now they eat; when they have done, they wash and chew tobacco with lime.

Before they say good-bye to them, they again take them inside and give them beer. When they have drunk, they come out to be said good-bye to. They stand in a row, and while in this position they salute each other. Thereupon they see them off, and they go away.

---

7 See Santal Dictionary s. v. bhitạr. 8 During day-time, when no cattle is there, the cow-shed is commonly used for visitors. Bedsteads are placed here to sit down on. 9 See Santal Dictionary s. vv. hukạ and thamakur.

d. Betrothal.

The marriage-broker goes and comes. They fix a day for the betrothal[10]. They perform the ceremony of betrothal with the bride-elect first. On the fixed day the marriage-broker takes the young man's father, his father's younger and elder brothers, his mother's brothers, his father's sister's husband, the village headman and his deputy and a couple of the people of the village along to the girl's home. The Jo̱g Mạṅjhi of the prospective bride's village meets the visitors at the end of the village street with water in a loṭa and conducts them to the bride's home. Here they place bedsteads, stools, and wooden slabs before them, and they sit down.

The girl's parents and their brothers now come out from the house, and pouring out water for them they greet the visitors. After this they act as it was done in the young man's home, wash their feet, take them out to bathe, and when they have come back after bathing, they give them beer and parched and flattened rice. When they have eaten, the visitors go into the cow-shed, where they sit down.

As in the young man's home, they also here bring a castrated goat and pour water on its head. The Jo̱g Mạṅjhi now says: Honoured friends, here are some vegetables[11], cut it down for us. The visitors then kill the castrated goat. The Jo̱g Mạṅjhi calls out: You, eldest boy, do come here, cut this castrated goat up for us. They do so, cut the meat into bits and prepare the rice and curry. The visitors now say: Please, Jo̱g Mạṅjhi, be quick and expedite us.

The Jo̱g Mạṅjhi then says: You, eldest boy, do spread out the mats for us thus. He does this and the Jo̱g Mạṅjhi says: Honoured friends, we shall get off the bedsteads and sit on the mats. They sit down on the mats, and the Jo̱g Mạṅjhi says: Please, now bring the beer. They drink each two leaf-cups, just so much.

The Jo̱g Mạṅjhi then says: Please, Sir, now bring some water by the hand of the bride. They bring beer in a brass-cup. The bride-girl first brings a brass-cup full of beer and a loṭa with water to the village headman and bows to him. After him she brings the same to his deputy and bows to him also. Thereupon she gives the bridegroom's father one brass-cup beer and water in a loṭa. When he has drunk the beer, he puts the brass-cup down, and taking hold of the bride's upper arm he makes her sit on his thigh; he puts a brass necklet on her and kisses her mouth. Now those of the bride's side sing:

> Please, my good mother, let me have one loṭa with water
> To place before my father-in-law, when I greet him.

This they sing while the prospective bride gives the water to the bridegroom's father. When he makes the bride sit on his thigh they sing:

---

[10] See Santal Dictionary s. v. cikhnạ.   [11] Fig. about the goat.

Look at her, so and so,
Know her, so and so,
If you are pleased with her, place her on your thigh.

The bride-elect comes off from the thigh of the bridegroom's father and bows to him; once again she gives him beer. After this she gives all of them beer and water in a loṭa. And they sing:

Who are they who take water round in a gourd-shell, in a spout-vessel?
Who are they who received the water in the gourd-shell, in the spout-vessel?

Who are they who sought, who are they who got the good omens,
With the water of the gourd-shell, of the spout-vessel?

So and so are the people who take round the water of the gourd-shell, of the spout-vessel;
So and so are the people who received the water of the gourd-shell, of the spout-vessel.

So and so are the people who sought, so and so are the people who got the good omens
With the water of the gourd-shell, of the spout-vessel.

Instead of the words "so and so" they name the septs of the prospective bride and bridegroom. As is known, persons of the same sept do not marry, only when they are of different septs.

When all have drunk they say to the Jo̱g Mạṅjhi: Listen, Jo̱g Mạṅjhi, please go at once inside and see whether the rice and curry are ready or not as yet. He goes in and sees that they have it ready. The girl's father then calls out to the wife of his eldest son: O daughter-in-law, bring water in loṭas and cups. She does this and from the loṭa pours water into the brass-cup for one after the other of them, to wash their hands. Now the Jo̱g Mạṅjhi calls out: O eldest boy, please, you there, bring the rice and curry, the leaf-plates and the leaf-cups. Bringing these they place them first before the village headman, thereupon before his deputy, and afterwards they give to all who are there, to one after the other. Now the village headman makes the ceremonial recitation to the visitors: The wealthy ancestors dried the paddy and the husks; we, Sirs, are drying you; please be especially grieved at this. They answer: Yes, Sir, we certainly intend to eat; only when a great many things are brought near shall we be able to eat, straw-bits to wit, water to wit, leaves to wit, firewood to wit; only when all this is brought together, when it is cooked, when it is finally prepared, when all requirements are in order, then only we shall be able to eat.

When they have done eating and drinking, they wash themselves, and coming out into the courtyard they chew tobacco. The Jo̱g Mạṅjhi then says: Look here, Sir, when shall we see the visitors off? They say to the Jo̱g Mạṅjhi: Please go at once in and see whether there is room or not. He does this, there is room. Then they take the visitors (viz., the village headman and his deputy and the father of the prospective bridegroom and with him two-three people) inside and spread out mats for them to sit on. When they have sat down, the Jo̱g Mạṅjhi says: Please, bring the beer. They do so and give it to the visitors; when this is done, the fathers of the bridegroom and the bride sit down together in one place, and they bring them beer at the same time. Both of them then say: Please, co-parent-in-law, let us drink this beer. While they are drinking they say: Let us salute the friends. They both salute every one of the visitors. Thereupon the two co-parents-in-law take hold of each other's hands and move them three times backwards and forwards between them; they raise them up towards their heads; thereupon they butt each other's shoulders three times, and when this is done they again move their hands backwards and forwards between them and raising them towards their heads they say: Saheb! At this moment they sing:

Pleasure, pleasure, pleasure, o mother,
Pleasure, look what enjoyment!
On both sides the co-parents-in-law
Are tied together with chains,
On both sides the co-parents-in-law have
great enjoyment.

The girl's father then says: Listen, my co-parent-in-law, now this is your house. And the bridegroom's father says: The house far away is yours, my co-parent-in-law. Thereupon both co-parents-in-law say to each other: My co-parent-in-law, when you somehow were wandering about in villages and hamlets, were coming hunting and chasing, up to this time in the plains and open country, in the forest and jungle, you have drunk water from the dug-out holes in the rivers, from the pools; now from to-day please cease doing this, there is the shade of a pole with creepers, water in a gourd-bottle, the nest of a Finch Lark, please come straight here with a rush; don't turn to the right or to the left; when you somehow come wandering in this direction, come in here on your way past; you will drink some water on your way; you will also visit the children on your way. Talking together they finish the beer.

The visitors then say: Sir Jo̱g Mạṅjhi, please make haste and send us off. Then they go out into the courtyard. The people of the bride's side stand on one side, and those of the bridegroom's side on one side, opposite to each other; they salute the visitors one after the other; when they have been said good-bye to they go home. At this time the Jo̱g Mạṅjhi says: Honoured friends, as you know, you plucked hill-vegetables for us, you are surely forgetting the battle-axe, leaving it here; look here is yours. And he gives them the shoulder of the goat; they take this along with them.

In the same way the father of the bride and their party also go and give the bridegroom the sign of betrothal.

e. Handing over the money.

The marriage-broker goes and comes. The bridegroom's father says to him: Do find out what the friends have in mind and bring us word. He goes, and on returning he says: They have said yes. The father of the bridegroom then calls the village headman and his deputy, the Jọg Mạṅjhi and two-three of the village people together and gives them beer. The village headman then asks him: What beer is this? The father of the bridegroom says: This, Sir Headman, is marriage-broker beer; my intention is that we should hand over the money[12]. They finish the beer.

They then tie knots on a string, for five days or seven days. The marriage-broker takes the knot-string to the people of the bride's side. If these think the day too near, they want a longer time, and what they say will be done.

When the fixed day comes, the bridegroom's father calls the village headman and his deputy, the Jọg Mạṅjhi and the Goḍet and says: The day for handing over the money has come; come along, we shall go as the bridegroom's party. Then these people say: There are small and big people in the village; let us first call and bring them. Then they send the Goḍet to call them together. They come and ask the bridegroom's father: Look here, Sir, will there be enough oil and turmeric or not? He answers: There will be enough. Now they make the village priest and his wife sit down beside each other on a mat, and the anointing girls[13] anoint them with oil and turmeric. Thereupon they anoint the village headman and his wife, after them the Paranik, the Jọg Mạṅjhi, the Jọg Paranik and the Goḍet together with their respective wives. After this the parents of the bridegroom sit down on sheaves of thatching-grass and are anointed. Thereupon all the women of the village, big and small. Now the Jọg Mạṅjhi says: Please, bring the bridegroom, we shall anoint him. The bridegroom's mother then says: There is no conductor[14] of ceremonies. If the young man has no elder sister, then his elder brother's wife or even a (younger) sister will do for this. Again, they say, there is nọ follower[15] of the bridegroom, where shall we get such a one? Then they say: There is the son of his father's younger brother; he is younger than the bridegroom; we shall make him be the bridegroom's follower. If

---

[12] The payment of money is intended to be a proof of legal possession. [13] The anointing girls are — on both sides — three spinsters whose work is to anoint the bridal pair and others with oil and turmeric at the preliminary and the actual marriage operations. [14] The ạk̇curić, lit., the one who leads round, has always to be a near female relative of the bridegroom. [15] The follower (lumti), also called the "best-man", is always a real or, if none such is available, an imaginary younger cousin of the bridegroom.

there are no cousins (sons of father's brothers), a son of some other man will do, provided he stands in the relationship of cousin.

Now they bring a loṭa which they hand to the wife of the bridegroom's elder brother and say to her: Please, take the bridegroom round. The anointing girls take the mat in their arms, and the wife of the bridegroom's elder brother guides them, and having taken the loṭa with water she pours out a little round about. They go round three times; thereupon the anointing girls spread out the mat, and the bridegroom, his follower and the conductor of ceremonies sit down on this.

The Jo̧g Mạṅjhi then says: Please say to the bridegroom's mother that she may come. She comes; now they have oil and turmeric in a leaf-cup, and they say to the Jo̧g Mạṅjhi: Tell the bridegroom's mother that she should smear some oil and turmeric on the cheek of her son. When she has done this, the Jo̧g Mạṅjhi says to the anointing girls: Now his mother has prepared the way, please, anoint the bridegroom. They do this; and the marriage-broker says to them: Make yourselves ready, it is becoming night; come along. They are now on the point of starting.

They then ask the marriage-broker: Will you take us along the highroad or along a path? He says: I shall take us along the highroad. They take with them two rupees and a brass-necklet, further a kettle-drum and a Ram's horn[16]; drumming and blowing the horn they go on. When they reach the village, they stop at the end of the village street. The marriage-broker goes in advance to the bride's home and says to them: See, we have come, please meet us with water, and show us where you are putting us up. Now some people in the village may have an empty house[17], and they say to the Jo̧g Mạṅjhi: Do go and find out and bring us word. He finds such a place; and carrying a loṭa with water on a leaf-plate on the palm of his hand turned upwards he goes to the bridegroom's party and says to them: Come along, you of the bridegroom's party[18], I shall take us to the lodgings. Then they go there. The bridegroom's party say to the Jo̧g Mạṅjhi and the Goḍet: Please, get us firewood and leaves, two earthenware cooking pots for the rice, one earthenware small vessel, some wooden spoons and ladles, and show us where we can get water; where shall we find it when it is night? And also get us a flat basket, please, to pour the cooked rice out in. They bring them all this.

Thereupon the bridegroom's party pour out the fatigue removing beer; they give the Jo̧g Mạṅjhi and his companion and also drink themselves. The Jo̧g Mạṅjhi and his companion then say to them: Do prepare your food, and when we get ready we shall call you.

---

[16] See Santal Dictionary s. v. Hindi Ramsiṅga. [17] i. e., where there is nothing that the presence of strangers might contaminate. [18] It might be noted that the word, here and elsewhere, translated "bridegroom's party" stands for those who represent the family and especially the village community of the bridegroom. The word (bạriạtko) is of Aryan origin, which may be of some significance.

In the bride's home they pour out and squeeze out the beer; thereupon they send for the bridegroom's party. When they come, they salute each other; thereupon they make them sit down in the courtyard on straw; the village people also sit down. The Jọg Mạńjhi brings water and tobacco to the visitors and says: Do bring us the beer. They do this, and they drink the beer. The Jọg Mạńjhi then says: Listen, you the father of the bride, how many rupees will you take as bride-price? we shall let the bridegroom's party know. Those of the bride's side and those of the bridegroom's side do not verbally speak together. The Jọg Mạńjhi on the bride's side makes two leaf-cups. In one leaf-cup he puts twenty cowries, and in one leaf-cup he puts three twisted threads; one of these is half white and half red, and two of them are mostly white with one strand of red thread.

Now he calls on the marriage-broker and says to him: Look here, marriage-broker, this is yours, take it. He takes the two leaf-cups to the bridegroom's party. They do not take up the thread, but taking out one cowry they hand the leaf-cup back to the marriage-broker, saying: Do take it to the bride's father. He does this, and they look at it, saying: There is one wanting. They add one more, and handing it to the marriage-broker they say to him: Do take it to the bridegroom's father. They again take one out and send the leaf-cup back. They do the same three times or five times. Then they do not take any more, and now they talk. If the bride's father gets a bride-price of three rupees, the bridegroom's father keeps two cowries; if the bride-price becomes five rupees, he keeps three cowries, and if they give seven rupees as bride-price, he keeps seven cowries. When the bride-price paid is three rupees, the bridegroom's people get nothing in return. When it is five rupees, they get one cow and one brass-cup and for the bridegroom a cotton shawl and a loin-cloth, and the village people on the bridegroom's side get a castrated goat, one earthenware pot of beer and five half-seers of rice, together with salt and turmeric. This they call "bride-price recompense". And if the bride's people receive seven rupees as bride-price, they will have to give a cow with calf, one brass-cup and one brass-plate and for the bridegroom a cotton-shawl and a loincloth; and the bridegroom's people get as "bride-price recompense" a castrated goat, one pot of beer, and seven half-seers of rice.

Thereupon the bridegroom's party put a brass-neckring on the bride, and she gives them beer. After this they hand two rupees of the bride-price over into the hands of the Jọg Mạńjhi, and with these in his hand he salutes all there. This money they call: Track covering[19]. The Jọg Mạńjhi gives this money to the bride's father. Having saluted the others the bridegroom's party then go to their lodgings. After a short while they again send for them to come and partake of the feast. They act as they did at the time of the betrothal. When they have eaten, they go to their lodgings to lie down. The following

19 See Santal Dictionary s. v. Pańja tẹn.

morning they again send for the bridegroom's party. They give them beer, and the bride's mother gives the marriage-broker five seers of flattened and parched rice and ties it up in his cloth. All now go out into the courtyard and salute each other; they say good-bye to the bridegroom's party. And these come home, well and good.

f. Of the marriage itself.

The marriage-broker goes and comes. On both sides they get together what is needed for the marriage. When the money has been handed over, the marriage takes place, sometimes the same year and sometimes also after a lapse of one or two years.

When they feel like being able to have the marriage, the bridegroom's father says to the marriage-broker: Do bring us a knot-string[20] from the friends. He consequently goes to the bride's home and says to them: Please let us tie the knots. The bride's father then calls the village headman and his deputy and the Jog Mạṅjhi together and gives them beer. When they are drinking this the village headman asks him: What beer is this? The bride's father answers them: The marriage-broker has come; say for how many days shall we tie knots for him? They count the days and possible hindrances. When they have done this, they tie nine knots.

Thereupon they twist thread as signs for a twelve cubits long red and white striped cloth for the mother of the bride, and for an eight cubits long cloth for the bride's maternal grandmother, and a seven cubits long cloth for the bride's paternal grandmother. They give the knot-string and the twisted threads to the marriage-broker, and he takes them to the bridegroom's father.

When the bridegroom's father gets this, he calls the village headman and his deputy and says to them: You see this, they have sent us the knot-string; what are we to say? They say: It is well, let us also tie knots in reply to them. They drink the beer and also tie knots, five strings, one for the bride's father, one for the headman of the bridegroom's village, one for his deputy, one for the Jog Mạṅjhi, and one for the relatives of the bridegroom's father. The knot-string for the bride's father they at once send by the marriage-broker.

When three days remain, the bridegroom's father calls the village headman and his deputy and says to them: Listen, Sir, as you know, the day is getting near, let us set up the marriage-shed[21]. They answer him: All right. The bridegroom's father then says to them: Please get hold of five young men and five girls for me. The Jog Mạṅjhi then

---

[20] To ensure keeping correct time, or to know the day of certain coming events the Santals tie knots or rather loops on a string, one knot for every day remaining. It is done in connexion with marriage and b h a ṇ ḍ a n (the last funeral ceremonies). It is always an uneven number, seven or nine, and occasionally eleven knots. The string is taken to the parties concerned, who keep it and, as the days pass, release one knot each day; when the last knot is opened, they know that the day has come. It is to them a practical way of keeping time.

[21] See Santal Dictionary s. v. m a ṇ ḍ w a. The word is Hindi.

calls the young men in the village together, sending the Goḍet, and says to them: Do set up a marriage-shed for us here. Thereupon he brings the village priest. When he has come, the village headman says to the bridegroom's father: Please give the priest three fowls, one speckled and two white ones, three half-seers of rice, one pot of beer, and the necessaries for making a sacrifice. The priest takes all this to the sacred grove or somewhere in the open field and sacrifices the fowls in the name of the marriage-shed. He makes the following invocation: Here then, Jaher era, in connexion with so and so setting up a marriage-shed I am giving thee, handing thee a sacrificial fowl; mayest thou with pleasure, with favour, accept this, receive this; mayest thou caress this, deem this big; we are now going to such and such a village to be a bridegroom's party; on the road, in the forest may no sudden fear or alarm happen to us, no stumbling, no fall, no spells, no enchantments; to the right, to the left may you toss it away, spatter it away, Father my Ṭhạkur. We shall eat, we shall drink, do not let stomach-ache, headache arise, be caused. With the friends may there be no strife, no quarrel, no evil, no enmity, no loss, no destruction, Father my Ṭhạkur. While reciting this invocation he offers the speckled fowl to Jaher era. Thereupon he sacrifices one white fowl to The Five (Mõṛẽko Turuiko)[22], making a similar invocation. Lastly he sacrifices the remaining white fowl to Marań buru, and to him also he recites an invocation in the sạme way. The village priest has brought a couple of men with him; they make a hash of the fowls and eat them, and the pot of beer they brought they also drink; thereupon they return home.

The Jo̱g Mạńjhi then again goes to the marriage-shed and asks the young men: Have you finished the marriage-shed or not as yet? They answer him: Yes, we have finished it. The Jo̱g Mạńjhi then says to them: Dig a hole in the middle of the marriage-shed; we shall put a Mahua tree down there. He next asks them: Have you finished digging the hole or not as yet? He says to them: Enlarge the hole down below in the ground. When they have done this, the Jo̱g Mạńjhi says to the bridegroom's parents: Bring three branches of raw turmeric and five cowries and three tips of dhubi grass. Grind the turmeric, mix three grains of sun-dried rice into the turmeric. They collect this and cover it up in a bundle, and where they have enlarged the hole, there they put it down. When this is done, they plant the Mahua tree in the dug hole, and when they have planted the Mahua tree they wrap a straw-rope round it up to the top.

Thereupon the Jo̱g Mạńjhi calls the woman, the conductor of ceremonies, and says to her: Plaster this with earth and make it smooth, and whitewash it with flour, and grind some red-ochre stone; when this is done, paint figures on the marriage-shed post, and paint pictures of the bride and bridegroom in front. The conductor of ceremonies does this.

Thereupon the Jo̱g Mạńjhi says to the young men who set up the marriage-shed: This is finished; now before anything else have some food and strengthen yourselves. He goes

---

[22] See Santal Dictionary s. v.

into the bridegroom's house, brings out oil and toothbrush twigs and gives this to the young men and says to them: Do go and have a bath. They consequently go and bathe and brush their teeth. Coming back to the house they sit down. The Jo̱g Maṇ̇jhi brings an earthenware pot of beer out from the house of marriage, pours the beer out and gives it to them, and they drink. Thereupon he brings out one big flat basket with rice and one small earthenware pot with curry. Further he brings leaf-plates and a loṭa out; handing them the loṭa he says to them: Do pour out water for yourselves; wash your hands. They do this; the Jo̱g Maṇ̇jhi then says: I say, one of you, please give us the rice, and one of you the curry. Then they all eat, and when they have had food, he says to them: Twist some strings with fringes, some of you young men twist the strings, and some of you fetch mango leaves and insert them in the strings; tie the strings in the four corners of the marriage-shed. They do this. Again the Jo̱g Maṇ̇jhi says to them: Fix strings in three places in the village street[23], one string outside the headman's house, and one at each end of the village street. They do this and finish all, so far as they are concerned.

Thereupon the bridegroom's father says to the Jo̱g Maṇ̇jhi: Please call the village headman and his deputy and all the married ladies of the village and bring them here, to anoint them with oil and turmeric. He does this himself, and they come. When they have sat down, they first give each of them two leaf-cups of beer. After this the Jo̱g Maṇ̇jhi calls the anointing girls and says to them: Do anoint them for us with oil and turmeric. They do this; first they anoint the village priest and his wife, thereupon the priest of the outskirts and his wife, thereupon the village headman and his wife, thereupon his deputy with his wife, next the Jo̱g Maṇ̇jhi and his wife, next his deputy and his wife, thereupon the Goḍet and his wife, and thereupon all the married ladies of the village. This they call the marriage-shed oil and turmeric. When all have been anointed, the parents of the bridegroom sit down on thatching-grass sheaves, and they are both anointed. Lastly they anoint the bridegroom sitting on a mat between his follower and the lady conductor of ceremonies. At this time they sing[24]:

Turmeric, turmeric, perfect stuff,
Who is she who anoints me with turmeric,
Consecrating me to become a man?

Turmeric, turmeric, perfect stuff,
Mother anoints me with turmeric,
Consecrating me to become a man.

---

23 These strings are arranged so as to run across the street.

24 The song is, like many others sung during the marriage ceremonies, in a corrupt form of Bihari; these songs are often very difficult to understand. As a matter of fact, it has in many cases happened that no Santal has been able to tell what they really mean.

When they have anointed the bridegroom, they anoint his follower, and last of all they anoint the conductress of ceremonies. When they have again drunk two leaf-cups of beer each, they separate and go home. But from this day until the marriage is finished the young men and girls dance day and night.

After three days the time for going with the bridegroom comes. The father of the bridegroom then at cock-crow pours out one earthenware pot full of "intimation" beer, and calling the village headman and his deputy, the Jog Mańjhi and his deputy he gives them beer.

While they are drinking, the village headman asks the bridegroom's father: Look here, what beer is this? We do not find the malted grain. "Malted grain" is a metaphorical word, viz., the explanation of the matter, why he has brought them there. The father of the bridegroom then says in reply: Help us to-day to follow the bridegroom, the day fixed has come. The village headman then says to the Jog Mańjhi: Do call the village people together. He sends the Godet, who brings all there. They give beer to all. The bridegroom's father says to the Jog Mańjhi: Please get hold of five men for me. He brings them, and the bridegroom's father says: Do bring food out for us the bridegroom's party, rice, curry, salt, and five pots of beer; when it is light we shall send forerunners in advance; and at the same time they take along one goat and one pot of beer, three half-seers of rice (if the bride-price is five rupees, then five half-seers of rice), three branches of the root of turmeric, tobacco, salt, and oil in a small earthenware vessel, the last mentioned things are obligatory presents, that is to say, they call them materials for offering to the bongas.

When the forerunners have had food, they take all the things mentioned along in advance. When they reach there, one of them goes to the house where the marriage is to be held. Here also they have set up a marriage-shed and have worked as in the bridegroom's village. The man says: How is it, Sir, we the forerunners have come. The bride's father then says to the Jog Mańjhi: Please show them where to stay. The Jog Mańjhi then takes the forerunners to where they have made sheds for the bridegroom's party. He gives them earthenware pots for water and cooking, a flat basket, wooden ladles, firewood, leaf-plates, and leaf-cups; thereupon he returns to the house of marriage.

After they have sent the forerunners off, the people of the bridegroom's village, men and women, go to have "water-marriage". The bridegroom's mother takes a flat basket along. In this there is sun-dried paddy, sun-dried rice, a bunch of d h u b i grass, one egg, oil, and sindur and one ball of thread. The wife of the bridegroom's father's younger brother carries a sword, and his paternal aunt carries bow and arrows. Two anointing girls carry on their heads narrow-necked earthenware pots resting on pads of thread, having covered them up with clothes for the bride; these two pots they call omen-pots. A brother-in-law of the bridegroom they have made best-man[25]; he takes a kodali along, and the Jo̦g Mańjhi himself takes beer and leaf-cups along. The other people are only onlookers. They who have the flat basket, the sword and the bow and arrows in their hands, go dancing, until they reach the way down to the water. When they arrive there, they dance three times round. At this time the best-man digs a small basin near the water's edge, and making an opening he lets the water come into the small basin. When this is done, the Jo̦g Mańjhi plants three arrows in three corners of this basin; he winds thread five times round and puts one egg down near one of the arrows. He puts one cowry near each arrow; when he has done this, he applies sindur to the arrows. Thereupon he pours out as a libation one leaf-cup of beer to Maraṅ buru, one leaf-cup to the deceased village headman, and one leaf-cup to Pargana haṛam (the bonga). The remaining beer they drink.

Now the bridegroom's mother, his father's younger brother's wife and his paternal aunt dance three times round the place, and the two anointing girls follow round after these, and after these two all the others there. After this she who has the bow and the arrows in her hand shoots an arrow into the water, and she who has the sword, cuts the water; thereupon the two anointing girls draw water. After this all of them return and go into the marriage-shed.

The Jo̦g Mańjhi then says to the best-man: As we dug a basin there at the water-fetching place, dig one also here in the courtyard. He does this, and the Jo̦g Mańjhi plants three arrows at the three corners; on these arrows he winds thread five times round and says: Look here, you two girls, place the two omen-pots here. They do this.

The Jo̦g Mańjhi now says: Come here you three anointing girls, and take hold of the marriage-shed post. The bridegroom they also bring there. The Jo̦g Mańjhi ties the left hand little finger of the girls fast to the Mahua post, and gives each of them in their right hand one paddy grain, and from this paddy grain he makes them remove the husk with one hand without breaking it. They do this, and the Jo̦g Mańjhi looses them. Thereupon he takes a thread five times round from his right ear and to the little toe of his right foot and twists this. Now he calls out to a young man: Do bring some mango leaves, three. When he has done this, he says to him: Now bring three tips of dhubi grass and three sun-dried rice-grain, whole, not broken ones, and wet them a little with turmeric water. The young man brings the three rice-grains that the anointing girls unhusked and the dhubi grass. The Jo̦g Mańjhi then wraps the rice-grains and the dhubi grass up in the mango leaves and ties it with the thread he has twisted on to the bridegroom's right hand.

---

25 The Santal word is the same which they use for a brahmin (babṛe̥), generally a relative, especially a brother-in-law. When the bridegroom performs the binding act by applying sindur to the forehead of the girl, he rides on the shoulder of this man.

The Jog Maṅjhi then says to the best-man: Please shave the bridegroom; and he does this. For shaving he gets two half-seers of flattened rice, two half-seers of rice, salt, and tobacco. Thereupon they take the bridegroom to the water in the marriage-shed. And they bring out two yokes and find a sword. They make the bridegroom sit down on the two yokes and make his father stand in front of him, holding the sword resting on his head. The Jog Maṅjhi pours water with a loṭa from the omen-pot on the sword, and the water drips down on the head of the bridegroom, who is sitting behind his father's back. Thereafter they take the sword away, and the conductress of ceremonies bathes the bridegroom with the water of the omen-pot.

Now the bridegroom's party make themselves ready; they take food and drink beer in the bridegroom's home. While they are eating and drinking the anointing girls anoint the bridegroom, put necklaces and a solid neck-ornament on him and also apply eye-paint to his eyes. At this time they sing (in corrupt Bihari):

> How far away, how far away is the house of my bride's father?
> How far away is the house of my father-in-law?
> From here is the Ganges river, from there is the Jabo river,
> Between these two, my boy, is the house of thy bride's father.

The oil and turmeric not spent in anointing they give into the marriage-broker's charge. The Jog Maṅjhi now says to the bridegroom's parents: Please bring out the cloths for the bride, the red and white striped cloths, the cloths for the bride's grandmothers, the (turban) cloth for the bride's youngest brother, sindur for the bride's parents, oil for the bride's parents, Neem, ricinus leaves, and a little husks. They bring these things out to him, and he arranges them in a flat basket, and giving it into the marriage-broker's charge he says to him: Here are your things, see.

Next the best-man asks for five Sal-leaves, a small packet of sindur, and one handful sun-dried rice. They give him this, and he ties it up in his clothes. Thereupon the best-man puts a turban on the bridegroom, and the bridegroom's party all go out. The bridegroom's mother arranges a loṭa with water and molasses in a leaf-cup, and his father ties money up in his clothes. They go to the Maṅjhi than. Here they spread out a mat, and the bridegroom's mother sits down on it. She lets the bridegroom sit on her thigh. When he has sat down, she gives her son molasses into his mouth. She washes his mouth and gives him a little water to drink. The bridegroom now takes a rupee into his mouth, and his mother sucks him a little. His mother holds out her hand, and the bridegroom lets the rupee he has taken into his mouth fall out into his mother's hand. This they call sucking money, and this is the mother's right.

The bridegroom, the best-man, the bridegroom's follower, and the anointing girls now bow to the Maṅjhi haṛam (the deceased one), and a small pot of beer, that they have brought there, this they also offer to him. The anointing girls now carry the bridegroom on their hip to the end of the village street and set him down there, and from there they return home. The marriage-broker conducts the bridegroom's party to the bride's home, carrying a kettle-drum along. Nowadays they go taking with them big drums, trumpets, horns, tubas, cornets, palanquins, rockets, catherine-wheels, bombs, guns, and so on, that is to say, wealthy people do this; but such things were not used formerly, and we did not employ Doms to drum.

When the bridegroom's party reach the bride's village, they call a halt at the entrance to the village street. The marriage-broker goes to the bride's home and says to them: We have arrived; if there is anything you have not got ready, finish it quickly. They answer him: We are ready. The Jọg Mạńjhi now at once sends the Goḍet to summon the village people. They come there; they anoint themselves with oil and turmeric, beer they also drink, and all married women apply sindur[26] to themselves, but not spinsters, divorced ones, or widows.

Now the Jọg Mạńjhi makes the Goḍet carry a vessel with water on his shoulder, and he himself carries a loṭa with water, standing on a leaf-plate, kept on the palm of his hand turned upwards; they both go to the bridegroom's party, who have been dancing in the meantime. Seeing the Jọg Mạńjhi they stop. The Jọg Mạńjhi and the Goḍet say: Please, friends, drink water. The Jọg Mạńjhi hands the loṭa with water to the bridegroom's party; they receive it with both hands; thereupon they salute each other, and the bridegroom's party drink.

Thereupon the bride's mother, carrying on the up-turned palm of her hand a loṭa with water and a leaf-cup with molasses standing on a brass-plate, conducts the bride's party and the anointing girls on the bride's side and the women of the village to the end of the village street to meet the bridegroom with water. When they have reached there, she says to the marriage-broker: Bring the bridegroom here, we shall give them molasses to eat and water to drink. When the bridegroom's party and the bride's party have greeted each other and thus become one party, they dance. The marriage-broker says to the bride's mother: Look here, this one is the bridegroom. He salutes his mother-in-law and also a couple of the women. When the other women and the anointing girls see the bridegroom, they sing a number of abusive songs:

To-day, they say, to-day he will come, to-morrow, they say, to-morrow he will come;
How big a wealthy man's son is he, that we must wait until midnight?

Thy mother made friends with a dog,
Thy mother made friends with a cat.
Fie, fie, to a bastard,
My daughter I do not give.[27]

---

[26] The sindur, the blood-red vermilion, is applied to the forehead at the parting of the hair, just enough to show that the lady has a husband living. A Hindu custom.

[27] These two verses are in a kind of Bihari; the following verses are all in Santali.

Formerly they say, young and nice, young and nice, they say,
Well, I saw him, he has teeth standing out,
Face like that of a goat to be sacrificed, ill-shaped forehead.

Your mother's love, young man,
Your father's predilection, young man,
You have become wrinkled, young man, like a garden fig.

The mother and father of the bridegroom, they say,
Have gone to the town to sell oil,
To trade in salt they have gone;
Oil, O no oil trade,
Salt, O no salt trade;
To the blacksmith's working place to blow the bellows they have gone.

Formerly, they say, go to the town with a fine little oil pot,
I saw him, I looked at him,
He is standing there with a hideous face like a holed pumpkin ladle.

Instead of "young man" here they use the bridegroom's name, singing his praise. The bride's mother then washes the bridegroom's feet; thereupon she rinses his mouth and puts molasses into his mouth; after this she again washes his mouth and gives him a little water to drink. In the same way she feeds also the best-man and the bridegroom's follower.

Now the anointing girls carry the bridegroom and his follower on their hip to the place outside the first house in the village street; the Jo̜g Mạṅjhi goes along with them carrying the loṭa with water on the palm of his hand. The bridegroom's party and the bride's party follow after them dancing. Where the anointing girls have set the bridegroom down in the village street, here the woman of this house comes out and gives the bridegroom, his best-man and his follower molasses and water in their mouth. In the same way they treat them at every house. When they reach the outside of the bride's home, the bride's mother again feeds them. From there they go along the village street, and outside every house the women there feed them. Thereupon the Jo̜g Mạṅjhi takes them outside the village, to where the bridegroom's party are to be encamped, and says to them: Here are your lodgings: please stay here. The bridegroom's party now eat their own food and drink their own beer.

The Jo̜g Mạṅjhi then goes to the bride's home and tells them, i. e., all the women, to get ready; he says to them: Come along to bathe the bridegroom. They bring out one leaf-cup with oil, one leaf-cup with turmeric, one pot with water, one mat, one wooden slab to sit on, and one piece of loin-cloth and one cotton shawl for the bridegroom, and the Jog Mańjhi conducts them to the bridegroom's quarters, taking dancing-drums and kettle-drums along. When they reach there, the Jog Mańjhi says: Bring us our bridegroom. The bridegroom stands up, and the marriage-broker leads him by his hand to the women, who spread out the mat, and makes the bridegroom sit down on it. Three elder sisters[28] of the bride rub the bridegroom in with oil and comb him.

When they have finished this, they take away the mat, place the wooden slab there and make the bridegroom sit down on it; they have brought with them one vessel full of water, and with this water they bathe him. When they have done this, the Jog Mańjhi says: Listen, you, how will the bridegroom throw the "afterbirth"[29] away? The women of the bride's side then give the Jog Mańjhi the loin-cloth and shawl, and he gives it to the bridegroom, who takes this on and covers himself after having taken off his wet clothes. The anointing girls then say: He has thrown the afterbirth away; what shall we boil it in? The bridegroom's party then give them a pot of beer. Carrying this on the head they take it to the Jog Mańjhi's house, and having put it down there they separate.

Thereupon the village headman calls the Jog Mańjhi and the Godet and says to them: Please call all the village people, big and small, together; come along, we shall see the application of sindur. They call them together, and when they have come, they say to the marriage-broker: Make yourselves ready; come along, we shall see the application of sindur. When they have come, the village people say to the Jog Mańjhi and the Godet: Please find and bring some mango leaves, five leaves. They get these. The bridegroom's party are staying in the village street outside the bride's home and are dancing there.

The people of the bride's side then say: Please, you of the bridegroom's party, come all inside. They go inside and are given beer, which they drink. Outside the best-man has taken the bridegroom up to ride on his shoulder. At this moment the marriage-broker says: The younger brother of the bride is crying awfully to get a cloth. The village people then say: Bring him riding on somebody's shoulder. A brother-in-law of the bride then takes him on his shoulder and brings him out. They bring this one and the bridegroom together in the same place; they hand both of them water in a loṭa and five mango leaves, and they, i. e., all the people of the bridegroom's party, say to them: Now, bridegroom, sprinkle water with the mango leaves on his head three times. And all the people of the bride's side say to the young man: Now, you also, young man, sprinkle three times on the young bridegroom. They both sprinkle on each other. Thereupon they say to the bridegroom: Do put a turban on him. He does this, and they say to him: Now, kiss him. He does this; thereupon they blow chewed rice out of the mouth at each other. Thereupon they put the young man who got the turban down on the ground.

---

28 Women who are, or are counted as sisters. 29 Here fig. about used clothes that are to be taken off.

Now they say: Please bring the bride. Inside the house they make the bride take on the bridal cloth and make her sit down in a flat basket. The Jọg Mạñjhi then says to the bridegroom's party: Honoured bridegroom's party, this one you see here is for you. They carry her out into the village street outside the house to where they have the bridegroom riding on the best-man's shoulder. There they keep her lifted up, opposite to the bridegroom. Between these two the bridegroom's party now hang a cloth as a curtain. The Jọg Mạñjhi on the bride's side puts a loṭa with water into the palm of the bride's hand, and the bridegroom's party do the same to the bridegroom and say to him: Now, young man, sprinkle water on her head with a mango leaf, three times. The bride's people also say to her: Now, you also sprinkle water on the bridegroom's head with a mango leaf, three times. They both do this.

Thereupon the best-man hands five Sal leaves to the bridegroom; in the uppermost of the leaves he has wrapped up some sindur. The bridegroom's party then say to him: Now remove the covering cloth from the bride's head. He does this, and he keeps the sindur in his left hand above the bride's head. The bridegroom's party say to him: First let a little fall down on the ground. He does this, and they say to him: Now with the little finger of your right hand smear five times on the bride's forehead. When he has done this, they say to him: With your left hand take hold of the bride's neck and plaster all the sindur on her. He does this; then they cry Horibol[30].

Thereupon the best-man puts the bridegroom down on the ground, and his party say to him: Now take your bride on your hip and down. He does this, and then the bride's elder sister comes and ties together the clothes of bride and bridegroom.

After this the bride's mother and those with her, the three sisters-in-law[31] (wives of brothers), go inside into the house and arrange on a brass-plate a little dhubi grass, a little sun-dried paddy, sun-dried rice, three balls of flour and three balls of cowdung, and turmeric in one leaf-cup, and oil in one leaf-cup they also put on this brass-plate; they come out from the house to the village street outside, where the bride and the bridegroom, and the duenna[32] on the bride's side and the best-man and the follower on the bridegroom's side are. The bride's mother waves the brass-plate three times over the heads of the bride and the bridegroom, of the best-man and the two followers[33]. After this she also three times waves over their heads the dhubi grass, a little of the sun-dried paddy, and of the sun-dried rice that is on the brass-plate; then she scatters the dhubi grass and the paddy and the rice behind their backs. And mixing the oil and turmeric together she smears some on the bridegroom's two cheeks; and he also takes oil and turmeric up from

---

30 Horibol, the Bengali form for Hạribol, i. e. "call on Hari". 31 The wives of the bride's father (her mother) and of two of his brothers or cousins. 32 The lumti kuṛi or lumti buḍhi, who follows her to her new home and returns when all ceremonies have been performed. As a rule the bride has more than one such follower, generally three, sometimes even five. 33 See Dictionary s. v. cumạuṛa.

the leaf-cup with his hand and in his turn smears some on his mother-in-law's two cheeks. After this the bride's mother does the same to the bride and the best-man and the two followers, and they also in their turn do the same to her. The two wives of the brothers of the bride's father also act in the same way.

Thereupon two of those who performed the waving ceremony go into the house, and one of them takes some glowing embers out in an earthenware lid, and the other one takes a wooden pestle and brings it out to the street outside. They place the lid with the glowing embers before the bride and the bridegroom. The bride's mother then takes the pestle in her right hand and waves it over the lid with the glowing embers, and with her left hand she salutes the glowing embers; thereupon she takes the pestle in her left hand and waves it ceremoniously, and with her right hand she salutes the glowing embers; again she takes the pestle back in her right hand and waves it ceremoniously and salutes the glowing embers with her left hand. Then they give the pestle to her two sisters-in-law. They also both act in the same way, one after the other. Having acted in this way the last one stabs the glowing embers in the earthenware lid to pieces with the pestle and then carries the pestle quickly inside. All this they call "purifying"[34].

Thereupon she who tied the bride and the bridegroom together brings water in a loṭa and washes their feet, and, taking hold of the bride with her left hand, she leads the two into the house; what is left of the water in the loṭa that she has in her right hand, she pours it out, as she goes along, and the best-man and his party follow after the two. When they reach the door, the bride's younger sister blocks the way for them, and if she is unable to do it otherwise, she shuts the door. This they call the "shut door". The bridegroom gives her one anna; then she opens the way for them.

Inside the house they spread mats for them, and bride and bridegroom and their followers sit down on these. Now the anointing girls come and anoint them with oil and turmeric; when they have done this, they wash their hands. Thereupon they give them food. The bride's younger brother forcibly takes the rice from the bridegroom; he gives him one mouthful into his mouth; thereupon they eat together from the same plate. When they have eaten, they again wash them. Thereupon the conductress of ceremonies (they also call her Mrs. Best-man) who tied bride and bridegroom together, unties their clothes that were bound together. Thereupon the bridegroom and the best-man and the young follower go out and into the cowshed.

After this the bride's father takes his co-parent-in-law and the marriage-broker and the Jog Mańjhi into the house to drink rice-gruel. The bridegroom's father has, as you know, been fasting since he came away from home. They give them beer and food. They now go out and into the cowshed. The bridegroom's party are staying in the village street outside the house.

---

34 See Dictionary s. v. pạrchạu.

Now the village headman and the Jo̱g Mạṅjhi go inside the house. They give them each two leaf-cups of beer. They ask the bride's father: Let us take the bridegroom's party into the marriage-shed. Here they everywhere spread out straw for them. They call them; they come and all are standing there. The Jo̱g Mạṅjhi on the bride's side speaks to the village headman on the bridegroom's side, addressing him by name, and says: You, our so and so village headman, Sir! He answers: Sir! The Jo̱g Mạṅjhi says: Please, let us put our bodies upright like a grain-basket, let us set down the end of the spine. Now the bridegroom's party all sit down. Thereupon they bring one loṭa with water and put it down in front of them, and one leaf-cup with tobacco.

After this the bride's people ask the village headman on the bridegroom's side: You, our so and so Headman, Sir! He answers him: Sir! They say: When we sit down in one place, it is as if we live in one place. Now as regards soul and sept, body and skin, is it well with us or not? The bridegroom's party answer: As you see here, Sir, since it has been asked, inquiries have been made, our souls have grown like hills, our breasts have become broad like bamboo mats, our legs have grown five cubits longer, our beards have grown like buffalo horns: Sir, by your blessing we have become well. Those on the bride's side then say: By the grace of Ṭhạkur we shall get what is well. Then they sing:[35]

O mother, don't go to your father's house,
O father, don't go to the king's court,
They are coming, O mother and father, my bridegroom's party.

Let them come, my daughter, let them come,
At the entrance, my daughter, there is a fine Sandal tree.
We shall place before them, my daughter, golden seats,
We shall give them to eat betel nuts.

Come, friends, sit down, friends,
In our courtyard, ladies.
Let first the prince, so and so prince sit down,
After him let the ten friends sit down.

Bring, O sister, one loṭa with water,
Bring, O sister, one bowl with tobacco;
Hookah and tobacco, it is the proper act.

Now they bring them beer; they drink two leaf-cups each. Thereupon the village headman and the Jo̱g Mạṅjhi go inside to the bride's father and get each two leaf-cups of beer. When they have drunk this, the village headman says to the bride's father: We

---

[35] In corrupt Bihari.

have given beer to the bridegroom's party; how is it, shall we, while they are sitting there, ask them for the remaining brideprice money or not? If there is not much beer, he will say: We shall settle it now, while they are sitting there.

The village headman and the Jọg Mạṅjhi then both go out. The village headman says: We are to give these friends beer, you, Jọg Mạṅjhi, bring it out from the house. The Jọg Mạṅjhi fetches two men and takes them into the house. There they give them each two leaf-cups of beer, which they drink. The Jọg Mạṅjhi says to them: I say, you two give these friends beer; give to all who have come, big and small. They say to him: Please, Jọg Mạṅjhi, get us two earthenware narrow-necked pots. He procures this for them and gives them a basket full of leaf-cups.

Commencing with the village headman and his deputy they give to the bridegroom's party and to all the village people, and they drink. Now the Jọg Mạṅjhi says: Please, honoured bridegroom's party, we wish to see the remaining brideprice money; do take it out. Then they sing:

Bring out, young man, bring out
Money, fine like the puṭhi fish.
Bring out, young man, bring out
Gold, like fish-blood.

Hand over, young man, hand over
Money, fine like the puṭhi fish.
Hand over, young man, hand over
Gold, like fish blood.

Who are you sitting there?
Money, fine like the puṭhi fish.
Who are you there with the others,
Gold, like fish blood?

So and so is sitting there,
Money, like the puṭhi fish.
Big people are together there,
Gold, like fish blood.

Now the marriage-broker gives the remaining one rupee (or three or five rupees) into the Jọg Mạṅjhi's hand and says: Here, Sir, is the rest of the money. Commencing with the village headman he goes round and salutes all there. Thereupon the marriage-broker takes out a piece of women's clothing, two cloths for the bride's grandmothers and one cloth for her mother. Seeing these they measure them, how many cubits long they are;

they are of the proper length. The bride's mother then puts on the red and white striped cloth, and the mother of the bride's father and the mother of her mother put on the two grandmothers' cloths. And they sing:[36]

Mother took the fine cloth,
Father took a handful heavy rupees,
Brother took the bullock.

For one seer of rice
They bought sindur;
For all my life I shall be bound.

Soiled and torn will the fine cloth soon be,
Spent or stolen will the handful heavy rupees be,
Gone and broken will the bullock be.

For one seer of rice
They bought sindur;
For all my life I shall be bound.

Thereupon the marriage-broker brings out a goat that is to be (later) sacrificed, a pot of beer that is to be (later) libated, one half-seer of rice for each rupee of the brideprice, three bits of turmeric, a little salt, a little oil and a little tobacco, and gives it all to the parents of the bride. Thereupon he salutes all there, one after the other. The women who have got cloths, take the goat up in the lap and salute all, one after the other. Having tied the goat to the post they pretend to milk it. Then they bring a small earthenware vessel, and in this they put the malted grain of the beer; they bring leaves, and pretending that it is milk porridge of rice they divide it among the bridegroom's party, who pretend to eat it, and the women wash their hands.

Now the village headman says to the Jọg Mạṅjhi: Please bring a loṭa with water. He brings it and takes it from the village headman to his deputy and thereafter to the bridegroom's party. They do nothing with this loṭa with water. The Jọg Mạṅjhi only takes it to them. The village headman says to the Jọg Mạṅjhi: When you take the loṭa with water to the bridegroom's party, tell them that we shall pluck vegetables[37]. One after the other they salute the loṭa with water.

The father of the bride now smears cow-dung round the foot of the marriage-shed-post; after this he brings rice on a leaf-plate out from the house and puts this down on the cow-dung plaster. Thereupon he brings one small earthenware vessel with beer and four leaf-cups. Thereupon they bring a castrated goat from the house and let it feed on the

---

[36] In a kind of Bihari. [37] Fig. about the goat.

rice. They place a pole on its neck. The Jọg Mạṅjhi now takes the cord round the goat's neck and the pole, and calls out to the village people: Come here you. They come and pour water on the head of the goat. The Jọg Mạṅjhi calls out to the bridegroom's party: Please, honoured bridegroom's party, the vegetables are becoming old and tough; come and pluck them for us. Then they sing:[38]

Seize the sword, seize the sword, valiant cavalier,
A pair of fine castrated goats are tied here;
Please, valiant one, use the sword quickly.

One man among the bridegroom's party then stands up, and as they told him, he brings a sword along, and with this he beheads the goat. The Jọg Mạṅjhi goes into the house and brings out rice on a leaf-plate; on this they place the head of the goat. Again the Jọg Mạṅjhi goes into the house and brings out one pot of poured-out beer and two large leaf-cups and three to four ordinary leaf-cups.

The bride's father now pours out as a libation two leaf-cups of beer; when he has performed this, he calls the one who kept the goat and the one who beheaded it. When they come, the bride's father takes the two leaf-cups; thereupon he links the arms of both together and hands them each a large leaf-cup, and gives them each one large leaf-cup full of beer. They both drink this, and he says: Please salute each other, and thereupon salute the village headman and his deputy and all the people here. Both of them do this, and now they all say: Up to this we presume we have made all well; let us break up the meeting. The bride's people then say to the village headman on the bridegroom's side, addressing him by name: Please, you our so and so headman, Sir, like a grain-basket let us move our bodies a little. He answers: Sir, it is well, it is right. They then all stand up together, and after having saluted the bridegrooms' party go to their lodgings. But five of their number stay there.

Now the Jọg Mạṅjhi brings oil out from the house, and taking hold of two young men he says to them: You two please wash the feet of these friends. They do this; afterwards they again bring more water. The Jọg Mạṅjhi then says to the five of the bridegroom's party: Come along, we shall go inside. When they have gone in, they place wooden slabs before them, and they sit down on these. The Jọg Mạṅjhi then says to the two young men: Do bring beer and give the friends four leaf-cups full each. They give them this, and they drink it. Again the Jọg Mạṅjhi says to the two young men: Do, one of you, give them rice and one of you curry, until their stomach is filled. They eat.

After this the bridegroom's party get from the bride's parents the return presents for the brideprice, viz., one goat, five half-seers of rice, salt, turmeric, oil, and one pot of beer. Having received this they salute them; they lead the goat away, carry the beer pot on

---

[38] In a kind of Bihari.

the head, tie the rice up in their cloth, take the salt and turmeric in their hands, and they are off to their lodgings. This all of the bridegroom's party eat.

Now the Jọg Mạṅjhi takes the head of the castrated goat that they killed a while ago, and one seer rice to the bridegroom's party and says to them: You, the bridegroom's party, a while ago you went to pluck vegetables; as you know, you forgot the basket and left it; look here, we are bringing it to you. They cook a hash of the goat's head and the rice and divide it among themselves, and put five portions aside for the Jọg Mạṅjhi, who afterwards takes this away for himself. When he has given over the goat's head and left it with them, he takes five persons with him to the bride's home. These drink a pot of beer at the bride's paternal grandmother's; when they have done this, they go over to the bride's maternal grandmother and there drink another pot of beer; when this is done, they get one full pot of beer, twelve seers of parched and flattened rice, and one solid brass necklet and take this with them to their lodgings.

Thereupon the Jọg Mạṅjhi goes to the lodgings and gets the five portions of the hash. He says to all of the bridegroom's party: Come along to the village headman to pay the marriage-shed money. The bridegroom's party put a pot squeezed-out beer in a sling and first-class beer in a loṭa and take this along, and the Jọg Mạṅjhi conducts them to the village headman; and the bridegroom's party drum a kettle-drum as they go along. They reach the headman's house, where they spread out straw in the cow-shed, on which they let the bridegroom's party sit down.

The bridegroom's party then say to the headman: Please, Sir village headman, call the village people together; we cannot possibly do it alone. Then they call all the village people together, men and women. The Jọg Mạṅjhi then says: Please, Father headman, now, you know, you are mother and father, please ask the friends for us, how they are. The village headman then commences:[39]

Well then, Father headman, the two, husband and wife, a coveted boy, food and wealth, male and female servants, female agricultural servants and labourers, forefathers and ancestors, grandfathers and fathers, father's younger brothers uncles, nephews and nieces, younger brothers and daughters, a house with rice, a house with water, cattle and sheep and goats, the mother's property, the wife's property, clothes and ornaments, body and soul, earth below, cold water, (on the other side of) one river sixteen kọs, to this place we do not go and come: is it well with us all or not, Sir? The headman's deputy also speaks in the same way. Thereupon the village headman and his deputy ask the bridegroom's party, the friends: How is it, Sir, have you come to get as far as here, or how far are you going? The bridegroom's party answer: Up to here we have manifolded our steps,

---

[39] What the village headman starts saying is a rattling enumeration of what is deemed belonging to a prosperous family, partly Bihari, partly Santali words. The purpose of the following conversation seems to be the wish to have an agreed statement of what has led up to the marriage, and that it is in customary order.

Sir. The headman then says: There are different ways of wandering about; they wander in a forest, they seek for wood: this will do for a plough-beam, that will do for a yoke, this will do for a wheel, that will do for a stick, this will do for a plough, that will do for a plough-handle. We go about to villages; we look for vessels; this will do for a wide-mouthed earthenware vessel, that will do for a water-pot, this will do for a narrow-mouthed earthenware vessel, that will do for a small vessel. Now as for you, what kind of a vessel do you want?

The bridegroom's party answer him: As for us, Sir, we only want a vessel with a fissured bottom. The headman then says: Sir, there are no such vessels. You are buying and trading, what kind of vessel are you wanting? Do you want a diamond or a pearl? The bridegroom's party answer: We are wanting a diamond; but to-day the market is closed; we wonder at what market we shall get it. The village headman asks them: Do you wish the market after three days or the market after five days? The bridegroom's party answer: As for us, Sir, we know nothing of markets; we have taken hold of you, you will buy for us at any market. The headman says to them: Waiting get, watching get. They answer him: Well, we are here fasting, thirsting. The headman then says: The market is also closed, nothing is to be had; as is seen, you came too late; how did you come too late? The bridegroom's party answer: What shall we do, Sir headman? As we were coming along an uncastrated bullock was calving through the mouth[40], him we were looking at; there we became belated; we moved away from there; then we again caught sight of something, wild bees honey in the crook of a crab grass, where they have made honey[41]; we were looking at it there. When we moved away from there, then as we were coming along, we again caught sight of one thing, a black-plum tree[42] with ripe fruits; we threw a dove-tail axe[43] at it; twelve measures of black plums fell down; then we went to pick up the axe; this axe had fallen down on the head of a certain deer, so that we found it killed thereby. Then with what shall we bind it? They went to pull out some sun-grass[44]. When they were pulling out the sun-grass, they fell with their posteriors down on and killed twelve small baskets full of bush-quails. This is what we were looking at and thereby were belated.

Thereupon as we were walking along, there was a Blue-jay dancing the Jạtur dance[45] in the road; we were looking at it; in this way we were belated. Thereupon there was a king-crow that was watching seven fires; we were looking at him; in this way we were belated.

---

40 Said to be fig., about clothes being taken out of a vessel in which they were boiled. 41 Some Santals explain this as referring to a pot of beer, others say it refers to impregnation. 42 Eugenia Jambolana, Lam. 43 The smallest kind of axe, only used for cutting branches and small bushes. 44 Imperata arundinacea, Cyr. 45 Danced by men alone. It is said here to be a reference to the weaving of cloth, which is men's work among the Santals.

Now the bride's people ask them: Well, Sir, you are coming from so far away, which headman, which deputy is buying, is trading? At this time they sing:[46]

Tell us, tell us, brother,
Tell us your sept.
We don't know the sept, we don't know the tribe,
We do not know your sept.

The bridegroom's party answer: As for us, Sir, when they were talking of sept and tribe, we had gone to herd the goats, — yes, well then, we shall listen. The corporal is such and such a man (naming the sept of the young man's father), and the agent is such and such a man (naming the sept of the young man's mother). Now the bride's people ask: Well, Sir, how many flocks of bullocks have you broken in (to carry loads)? The bridegroom's party ask each other, how many brothers they are, viz., of the bridegroom, and they say to the bride's people: As for us, Sir, we have broken in three flocks (or if there are more brothers they tell so many). The bride's people then ask: How many bent sticks and mortars have we? The bridegroom's party answer: Sir, the mortars are so many. (They tell how many girls there are.) The bride's people then say: Sir, at which watering place[47] did you drink water? The father of the bridegroom answers them: Sir, we have drunk water at such and such a watering place. The bride's people again ask: Well, Sir, what are you trading in? The bridegroom's party answer them: As for us, Sir, we are trading in diamonds and pearls[48]. The bride's people say: The market is closed now, it is very far away, waiting get, watching get.

The bridegroom's party then answer: Yes, then we shall get it waiting, watching. The bride's people say: Take hold of the village headman, he will buy for you. What have you brought? Mustard or Sesame?[49] The bridegroom's party answer: We, Sir, have brought mustard. The bride's people then say: In our country, Sir, the mustard is very cheap, and the diamonds are very dear; only if you are able to buy it, only in that case will the headman procure it for you. There are both scales and jeweller's scales, there are both 36 grade weights and 30 grade weights; which do you like? The bridegroom's party answer: We, Sir, we will take it by the headman's balance, whatever will be shown as the proper full weight; we are satisfied with the diamond, we shall buy this one. Then they sing:

On the rock at the tank bank
The traders have camped;
You know, Father, there
They are melting gold;

[46] In a kind of Bihari. [47] A figurative reference to a son's marriage. [48] Diamond, fig. for a girl; pearl, fig. for a young man. [49] Again fig. speech. Mustard, tuṛi, Brassica campestris, L., stands for a boy or bridegroom, and Sesame, tilmiń, Sesamum indicum, L., stands for a girl sought in marriage.

You know, Father, there
They are casting wristlets;
You know, Father, there
Are those who buy and trade in diamonds and pearls.

The bride's people then say: Sirs, you have taken hold of the village headman to buy for you; in connexion with this something more is to be paid; you must pay this. The bridegroom's party say: How much will have to be paid, Sir? It is said, one four-anna bit, four annas are to be paid. The bridegroom's party answer: What shall we do then? if it has to be paid, shall we not give it, Sir? The Jọg Mạṅjhi then says to them: Out with it then. They now give into the Jọg Mạṅjhi's hand one rupee, the marriage-shed fee for the village headman. The Jọg Mạṅjhi receives this rupee and salutes the village people, and as he salutes, he says: This is the rupee to snap the foot-rope of the bed of the father's younger brother[50]. After this he also salutes the bridegroom's party all round. The poured-out beer and the squeezed-out beer of the bridegroom's party and the beer that the headman brought out, they have drunk up while they have been talking. Of the poured-out beer the village headman got two leaf-cups.

Now the village headman on the bride's side says: So far as this place is concerned, I presume we have done all well or how? The bridegroom's party answer: Yes, we are likely to have done it well. The Jọg Mạṅjhi stands up and says: Our so and so headman, Sir! (he addresses the village headman of the bridegroom's side by name) Come, we shall stretch the end of our spine a little. All there then stand up, and the bridegroom's party salute all the village people there, one after the other, commencing from the headman, and then go to their lodgings.

Now the Jọg Mạṅjhi calls out to three men among these: Honoured bridegroom's party, please come along with me some three men of you. He takes them into the house of the village headman. They sit down there, and they give them each two leaf-cups of beer, good beer. They drink this; thereupon they give them what is customary right: One pot of beer, a full one, twelve seers of rice, one solid brass arm-ring, one four-leaves-cup full of split peas, some three branches of the root of turmeric, tobacco, and salt. Of this rice the Jọg Mạṅjhi measures out again for himself one seer. Thereupon these three men also go to their lodgings, taking all these things with them.

Now the Jọg Mạṅjhi says to the bride's people: Come, we shall gather the people of the village, we shall have the waving ceremony. He then sends the Goḍet to call the village people together. He himself, keeping a l o ṭ a with water on a leaf-plate on the palm of his hand, goes to the bridegroom's party and says to them: Come along,

---

50 The father's younger brother is fig. for the village headman. The whole expression is said to imply that the last tie by which the bride is bound to her parental home is broken.

we shall see the waving ceremony. They make themselves ready and take with them one pot of squeezed-out-beer and one small pot of poured-out beer. This they call "Founding-still"[51]. Two men carry this along to the bride's home. When the bridegroom's party arrive there, they spread out straw for them to sit on in the temporary shed. The head-man of the bride's side says to the bridegroom's party: Please sit down here; we shall see the performance of the waving ceremony[52]. They sit down.

Now the Jọg Mạñjhi on the bride's side says: Please find the anointing girls and grind some turmeric; we shall anoint the bride and the bridegroom. The anointing girls anoint the bride and the bridegroom and those with them. Thereupon they give them food. At this time the bridegroom will not eat, and when they ask him, he will not speak. The bride's father then says to him: Do, my son-in-law, eat both of you, I shall give you both milk[53] to eat. And as he promises to give him a calf, he eats. When they have eaten, they get up. The anointing girls roll up the mat, and in the hem-end of their cloths they take the broken bits of turmeric. Now the conductress of ceremonies takes the loṭa with water and goes out into the courtyard; when she has gone out, they see that no figures are drawn at the Mahua post. The Jọg Mạñjhi then says to her: Please smear cow-dung there and draw figures with flour. She answers him: Give me something, then only I shall draw. The Jọg Mạñjhi says to the bridegroom's party: Please, honoured bridegroom's party, no drawing is being made here, as you see. They answer him: How is it that no drawing is being made; do exert yourself to make her draw. He answers them: I am exerting myself; it is not proper. They then say: Make her willing, we shall give (what is needed).

Thereupon the conductress of ceremonies plasters with cow-dung and draws figures, so that it may look nice. The Jọg Mạñjhi says to her: Now please, take the loṭa with water and lead the bride and the bridegroom three times round where drawings have been made. She does this; then the Jọg Mạñjhi says to the girls who are keeping the mats: Do spread the mat out on this drawing. They do this, and the Jọg Mạñjhi says to the bride and the bridegroom, the best-man, the two followers and the conductress: Please sit down on the mat. They sit down, and the Jọg Mạñjhi goes into the house and says to the bride's mother: Take out the lucky-pot[54]. The bride's mother and her followers, i. e., the wives of three brothers, take out the lucky-pot; and they also take with them one seer of paddy in a fold of their cloth; in front of the bride and the bridegroom they take the paddy out from the cloth-fold and put it down there, and thereupon they put the pot down on the top of the paddy. They put an earthenware lid on the mouth of the narrow-necked pot. After this they

---

[51] The translation is only an attempt. The word rendered as "still" (bhạṭi, a Hindi word) is the name of the oven or kiln used by Suṇḍis when brewing beer or distilling liquor, and is by Santals mostly used fig. about liquor. [52] Different from the previously mentioned ceremony, in as much as the waving is ended by giving a present; cf. Dictionary s. v. cumạuṛa. [53] Fig. about the gift of a calf (heifer). [54] Kolean here uses the word that is the common one in Manbhum (karwās ṭhili) and rare in the Santal Parganas, where sạgun ṭhili, omen pot, is mostly heard.

bring oil and pour this out on the lid. The mother of the bride twists a wick, and this they kindle.

Thereupon the Jo̱g Mạṅjhi says to the bride's father: Please bring us beer. He brings out the "Founding-still" beer. The Jo̱g Mạṅjhi then sets one young man of the bridegroom's party and one young man of the bride's people to serve out beer a second time. He gives these two young men leaf-cups, about two baskets full. The young man of the bridegroom's party gives the people of the bride's side the beer of the bridegroom's party, and the young man of the bride's side gives the beer of the bride's people to the bridegroom's party, both commencing with the village headman of each side.

The Jo̱g Mạṅjhi then goes into the house and says to the mother of the bride: Please perform the waving ceremony; we have started drinking the beer. The wives of the brothers then come out, and the women of the village are standing at the door. Now they commence the waving ceremony. The bride's mother is the first to do it. In a flat basket she has put sun-dried paddy, sun-dried rice, d h u b i grass, one pair of men's wristlets and a solid brass necklet. This basket she waves three times round over the heads of the bride and the bridegroom. Thereupon she takes a little paddy, rice, and d h u b i grass in her hand and waves it over them and then throws it down behind their backs. She then sits down in front of the bride and the bridegroom. First she puts one pair of wristlets on both the bridegroom's wrists, and puts one brass necklet on the bride's neck. Thereupon she salutes them, and they also both make their obeisance to her. Thereupon the two sisters-in-law of the mother also act in the same way; but they don't put any ornament on the bridegroom; instead of this they give him money. Thereupon the village headman's wife, his deputy's wife, and all the women of the village put ornaments on the bride or instead of this give her money, and the bridegroom they give money. The younger sister of the bride next washes the feet of the bride and the bridegroom, and she catches hold of the bridegroom's leg. The bridegroom then gives her one anna. Now they make the bride and the bridegroom stand up, they both go into the house, and the Jo̱g Mạṅjhi gives the money into the charge of the bridegroom's father, after having counted it.

Now the bride's father, the village headman, and the Jo̱g Mạṅjhi also all go inside. The village headman asks the bride's father: Look here, how much beer is there? The bride's father answers: There will be enough for the bridegroom's party. The village headman then says to the Jo̱g Mạṅjhi: Please go and find out the wishes of the bridegroom's party; the bride says, I will give my father and his ones water. The Jo̱g Mạṅjhi goes out and tells this to the bridegroom's party. They answer him: If there is any water, please bring us some, we shall drink. The Jo̱g Mạṅjhi again goes inside and brings the bride and the anointing girls out. Thereupon he brings out one pot of poured-out beer and says to the anointing girls: Do bring one l o ṭ a with water. They do this, and he conducts the bride and the anointing girls to the bridegroom's party. The bride then puts the loṭa with water down near the village headman of the bridegroom's party. The headman takes the loṭa with water and rinses his mouth. The Jo̩g Ma̩ṅjhi then hands to the bride a brass-cup with poured-out beer, and she gives this to the headman. He receives and drinks it. Thereupon he takes hold of the bride's upper arm with his left hand and makes her sit down on his thigh; he puts a wristlet on her and kisses her. The bride moves away, and turning round she salutes the headman.

From there the bride goes to the headman's deputy, who also acts in the same way. From him she goes to her bridegroom's father and from him to her bridegroom's uncles, who also all act in the same way. Afterwards she goes to all of the bridegroom's party; these do not put any wristlets or ornaments on her; they give her money. Now they break up the meeting; the bride goes inside the house, and the bridegroom's party go to their lodgings.

The Jo̩g Ma̩ṅjhi now asks the bride's parents: How is it, is the rice and curry ready or not as yet? They answer him: We have made all ready; do send for the bridegroom's party to come and eat the feast. The Jo̩g Ma̩ṅjhi then says to the Goḍet: You call and bring all our village people, also the poor ones, to partake of the feast; I shall send for and bring the bridegroom's party. They both do this. They have brought water out in the village street outside the house; all wash their hands. The village headman says to them: Come along, we shall sit down in the shed. They go in and sit down. The Jo̩g Ma̩ṅjhi sets the young men of the village to work, some bring out the rice, some the curry, some leaf-plates, and some leaf-cups; in front of the village headman and his deputy they first put down leaf-plates and leaf-cups, and afterwards in front of all of the bridegroom's party and the men of the village. Thereupon they give them rice and curry, one after the other, commencing from the headman.

Now the village headman says: So and so our headman, Sir, in olden times, they say: Rich people dry paddy and husks; as for us, Sir, I presume we are drying people, this especially make mention of to us. The bridegroom's party then answer: Quite so, Sir; do they not say: we say we shall eat, that is so; very much is required in connexion with this, there is water, leaves, firewood, straw-pins, whatever it is all called, only when all these things are brought near, then only we shall be able to get food. Those who speak of this have gone in advance to Somae's narrow valley, to the Kere pool, to the fine sand to herd crocodiles have they gone. Thereupon they eat; if they give the village people two helpings of food, they give the bridegroom's party three helpings. When they have eaten, they separate, that is to say, the men. Thereupon the women of the village eat. When they have had food, they also separate. The bridegroom stays in the bride's home from the time when the sindur was applied.

Thereupon the Jo̩g Ma̩ṅjhi calls some of the bridegroom's party to eat the present-food. They come, one man for each rupee of the brideprice. When they have come, they wash their feet, take them into the house and first give them two leaf-cups of beer each. Thereupon they give them rice and curry, as much as they are able to eat. This they call present-food, in exchange for the goat to be sacrificed and the other things that the bridegroom's party have given. When they have eaten, they go to their lodgings.

Now the Jog Mańjhi brings the bridegroom's father and a couple of elderly men among the bridegroom's party to drink the "rafter counting"[55] beer. They take them into the house, and the two co-parents-in-law find a place beside each other, and they give them both beer at the same time. They salute each other and drink. Thereafter they give to all. Now they sing[56]:

Look at the posts, look at the posts, my co-parent-in-law,
Look at the posts from the lucky forest.

Look at the roof-beams, look at the roof-beams, my co-parent-in-law,
Look at the roof-beams from the lucky forest.

Look at the rafters, look at the rafters, my co-parent-in-law,
Look at the rafters from the lucky forest.

Look at the wattle, look at the wattle, my co-parent-in-law,
Look at the wattle from the lucky forest.

Look at the thatching grass, look at the thatching grass, my co-parent-in-law,
Look at the thatching grass from the lucky forest.

Under the laths on the rafters
Who are the people sitting?
Who are the persons resting there?

Under the laths on the rafters
So and so persons are sitting,
So and so persons are deliberating.

Young father-in-law, big father-in-law,
We shall rejoice, we shall play together,
So long as life lasts, father-in-law.
The king of the netherworld will soon call out.

They finish the beer, and they also stop singing; they go to their lodgings, that is, the bridegroom's party go.

---

55 See Dictionary s. v. sener lekha handi.

56 All the verses are in a kind of Bihari.

Those among the bridegroom's party who wish now go to the young people of the village and dance with them under the marriage-shed the whole night; they drum the dancing-drum and sing a good deal. The old men of the bridegroom's side say to the young men of their party, before they go to dance: Dance, young fellows, just dance, but don't touch anything; they impose fines. People who go in a bridegroom's party cannot flirt with the girls of the bride's village; if they do, they punish them very severely. On the other hand even if a young man of the bride's people flirt with the girls of the bridegroom's village, they do not make much of this.

The next morning the Jo̱g Mạṅjhi goes to the lodgings of the bridegroom's party and asks them: How is it, honoured bridegroom's party, have you had your midday-meal or not? They answer him: A while ago we have had our meal and been strengthened, and your portion we have kept for you; please be quick and send us off. They then give into his charge the big and the small earthenware pots and his five portions of food. Thereupon the bridegroom's party at once send some forerunners off in advance to their home. The Jo̱g Mạṅjhi then conducts the bridegroom's party to the bride's home. The bridegroom's party dance in the street outside the bride's home.

The Jo̱g Mạṅjhi thereupon goes in and says to the bride's parents: Please anoint the bride and the bridegroom with oil and turmeric; find me five young men to follow the bride, and one elderly duenna. The anointing girls anoint the bride and the bridegroom; they bring the followers of the bride and the old duenna. Then the Jo̱g Mạṅjhi says: Well, let them eat and strengthen themselves. Thereupon they give the bride and the bridegroom and the bride's male followers and the old duenna food, and they eat.

Thereupon the Jo̱g Mạṅjhi says to all these: Well, make yourselves ready, I shall bring the bride and the bridegroom out. While they are making themselves ready, the Jo̱g Mạṅjhi says to the bride's parents: Please get me one wooden pestle, having covered the ferrule with leaves. They bring him this, and he gives it into the charge of the bride's brother. Now the Jo̱g Mạṅjhi says to the bride's mother: Please arrange molasses and water in loṭas and brass-cups and find a mat. The bride's mother answers him: We are all ready. Saying this she puts about one seer of paddy into a fold of the bride's cloth. The Jo̱g Mạṅjhi then says: Why, where is the beer for the Mạṅjhi haṛam? They hand him this in a small pot with a cover. Taking this in his hand he says to them all: Come along, let us go out. While they are going out, the bride turns round and shakes the paddy that was put in a fold of her cloth out in the door-opening of the house, salutes it and goes away. Thereupon they go to the Mạṅjhi than. The bridegroom's party also go there together with the others.

The bridegroom's party are dancing, and the Jo̱g Mạṅjhi pours out the beer as a libation to the dead Mạṅjhi haṛam. As he makes the libation to him, he makes an invocation: As is seen here, Mạṅjhi haṛam, I give thee, hand thee this for the sake of good-bye being said to the bride and the bridegroom. When going in the forest may there be no tripping, no stumbling, no widows, no women of ill omen; spells or enchantments may not be thrown on, may not hit them; on the road, in the forest may no stomach-ache, no headache arise, come into being; — before the year turns round also for these two, for the bride and the bridegroom may we old men cover leaf-cups below the bedstead: Thou going first, we going after thee, may the bride's and the bridegroom's parties, the bride's brothers reach there in good order. Thereupon all there, the bride's people and the bridegroom's party go to the cross-road at the end of the village street.

At the cross-road they spread a mat and make the bride's mother sit down on it. They then first bring the bridegroom and make him sit down on the thigh of his mother-in-law. She washes his mouth; thereupon she three times puts molasses into his mouth, and he eats it. Now the bride's mother takes the loṭa with water in her hand; she washes the bridegroom's mouth and then kisses him. Thereupon he gets off, and they bring the bride. Her also she treats in the same way. After this the two wives of the brothers of the bride's father also treat the bride and the bridegroom in the same way.

Thereupon the people of the bride's village stand in rows, on one side the men and on the other side the women. The bride's mother then says to the bridal pair: Do salute them, one after the other, commencing from the village headman. They do this, the bride with the anointing girls first, and the bridegroom with his best-man and his follower after them. They salute all the men and women. After this the bridegroom's party salute all the people of the bride's village, one after the other, commencing from the village headman. Then they sing[57]:

Start, dearie, go, dearie
To your own house, dearie,
The swinging chair, dearie, is very heavy.

In the Tilai tree (Wendlandia tinctoria, DC.) plain, dearie,
I have tied, dearie, the horse.
The swinging chair, dearie, is very heavy.

*

In the deserted village
Sugar-cane was planted.
How sweet is that sugar-cane?

We do not know whether it is bitter,
We do not know whether it is sweet,
We do not know, how it is.

---

[57] All the verses are in corrupt Bihari.

So and so people will know,
The village brothers will know,
The people of the country will know.

Thereupon the Jọg Mạńjhi asks the bridegroom's party for the customary dues: For finishing the painting two annas, for fireplace damages two annas, and as a "shepherding" fee one pice. The painting fee the conducting girl gets, she who made the drawings at the marriage-shed post, and the fireplace damages those get who cooked the feast-food, and the "shepherding" pice the Jọg Mạńjhi gets.

Thereupon the Jọg Mạńjhi calls out to the bridegroom's party: Come, we shall have a little talk together. He takes aside the elderly men, and they sit down in rows beside each other. The Jọg Mạńjhi then calls the village people. Of these he also takes out the elderly men, who sit down opposite to the bridegroom's party facing them.

Now the village headman of the bride's side commences to talk: Honoured bridegroom's party, there is one matter about which I shall talk: During the hunt or the chase, when there is distress and danger, there is not promise — well then, having had good omens, a bullock on the right-hand side, a woodpecker on the left-hand side, we have tied together, joined together the bonds; now then the Day-spirit, the Five mountain spirits, the ancestors of old sitting together, we have joined the bonds; the house of the bride's side the bridegroom has got, and the house of the bridegroom's side the bride has got; it has become an exchange of houses. Now you may happen to wander hunting and chasing, you may happen to go to market or some such thing, you may wander to villages and hamlets, well then, up to this time, due to lack of knowledge, you drank water from hollowed out cavities in rivers and from pools; now as is seen here, we have bought houses, from to-day then do not pass to the right or to the left; in the house there is a cup of water and shadow in a cowshed, please come to this. From twelve kilns you have selected a vessel; having tapped it and found it sound you bought it: Then if it is lazy, if it is slothful, if it is irregular and knotty, if it comes to grief, if it is lost, it is not our responsibility; — if it becomes tin, if it becomes copper, if it becomes a strumpet, a harlot, if it becomes a drug, a witch, it will be your look-out; as the quality of the house is, the people develop, as the quality of the cow-shed is, the cattle develop, — we have also taken the brideprice without giving anything in return, the bullock for the bride's brother, the cloths for the grandmothers, the cloth for the mother of the bride, these also we have received without giving anything in return: both bones and ashes have we sold. Head-blood, ear-blood, this we have not sold, this we shall follow up. Well then, if one full day or half-a-day the rice is burnt, or the curry is burnt, may you suffer it, may you endure it; if by exhorting and tutoring it will not get well, then so and so headman, please send us a man; if no man is to be had, please send us a crooked stick; and if a stick is not to be found either, please send us a dog; we shall take counsel together.

Now the village headman on the bridegroom's side says in return: This is true, Sir, this is not something done by us alone, the Day-spirit, the Five mountain spirits, the ancestors of old sitting together, having had good omens, a bullock on the right-hand side, a woodpecker on the left-hand side, we have joined the bonds, — it is true, we selected from twelve kilns, having tapped and sounded we bought the thing. We have removed your tame parrot from your stand to our stand: consequently if it becomes tin or copper, the person is our one; if it becomes lazy or slothful, it is our look-out; if it comes to grief, if it is lost, it is our look-out; if it becomes ditches and holes, it is our look-out; if it becomes a strumpet, a harlot, a drug or a witch, it is our look-out; if it becomes a thief, a stealer, it is our look-out; — both bones and ashes have we bought to-day. Head-blood, ear-blood we have not bought, this you can follow up. Yes, if then one day, half-a-day the rice is burnt, the curry is burnt, shall we not instruct and tutor her? And if she will not be instructed and tutored, we shall send you word and consult together.

Well then as for you also, when you somehow or other go in our direction, you also don't pass on the right or the left side of us; when you wander about hunting or chasing, to villages and hamlets, you men and male ones, don't pass on the right or the left side. Up to this time due to lack of knowledge you drank water from hollowed out cavities in rivers and pools. From to-day leave this, give this up. The shade of a pole with creepers on, water in a gourd-bottle, please come straight along to this. The house here is ours and the house there is yours.

Thereupon the Jọg Mạṅjhi takes hold of the bride's hand and takes her to the headman of the bridegroom's village and says to him: This person, Father, I am giving over to you. The village headman answers: Yes, Father, we have received her. Thereupon the bridegroom's party start to go home, taking the bride with them. At this moment the Jọg Mạṅjhi calls out to them: Wait, bridegroom's party, stop at once, you are forgetting to take the battle-axe. Then he hands them a goat's shoulder. Together with the bridegroom's party five brothers of the bride and one duenna go to the bridegroom's home. The duenna takes a mat along, carrying it in her armpit. The bridegroom's party are off, and the people on the bride's side return to their homes.

The goat given by the bridegroom they fell; they divide the raw meat in three parts. One part and the head the bride's father gets, and two parts the village people make into a hash and eat. And they drink the presented beer. They take up the Mahua post in the marriage-shed, and they take out the sun-dried rice, the raw turmeric, the d h u b i grass, and the cowries that had been buried there. They loosen these things and look how they have developed. If the turmeric and sun-dried rice have sprouted, the bride and the bridegroom are very fortunate. Afterwards the young people of the village get one flat basket full of cooked rice, one pot of curry, and one pot of beer. This they call dew beer, dew rice.

The Jọg Mạṅjhi then gives the anointing girls into their parents' charge, each with one portion food. And then all go to their respective homes.

Now the bridegroom's party reach their own village. The marriage-broker makes them stop at the entrance to the village street, and himself goes in advance to the bridegroom's home. He says to them: The bride and the bridegroom have come; come along, we shall meet them with water. The bridegroom's father then brings the headman and his deputy, the Jọg Mạṅjhi and his deputy, and the Goḍet of the bridegroom's village to his house and gives them two leaf-cups of beer each and says: Listen, headman, come along, the bridal pair has arrived; we shall meet them with water. The headman then says: Well then, Jọg Mạṅjhi, call the young people of the village. The Jọg Mạṅjhi sends the Goḍet and has them brought. The village headman says to the bridegroom's father: Please have ready one pot of beer in the house. Thereupon the village headman says to the Jọg Mạṅjhi: Do give these young men two leaf-cups of beer each. The bridegroom's father libates a little beer, and the Jọg Mạṅjhi gives some to the young men.

The headman then says to the young men: Take your cloths tightly round your loins and get hold of one pair af dancing drums. He says to the Jōg Mạṅjhi: Please get water in a vessel and one l o ṭ a. When they have got these things, he says to them: Come along, we shall bring the bride and the bridegroom, the bride's brothers, all of them. Then the young girls and men all go to the bride and the bridegroom at the entrance to the village street. The Jọg Mạṅjhi gives the l o ṭ a with water to the bride's brothers and after them to the duenna.

Now the bridegroom's mother washes the feet of the bridegroom, the bride, the bride's brothers, and the duenna and gives them molasses and water into their mouths. While this is going on, the women and girls of the village abuse the bride singing. In the same way as the bride's people met the bridegroom with abusive songs, just the same songs, only the name is changed. At this moment the Jọg Mạṅjhi says to the girls: Please take the bride and the bridegroom on your hips. Carrying them along they put them down at every house, and the women of each house wash their feet and put molasses with water into their mouths. When they reach the house of the village headman, the bride and the bridegroom, the bride's brothers, and the duenna make their bow to the dead Mạṅjhi haṛam at the Mạṅjhi than. And the women of the house wash their feet and give them molasses with water into their mouths. Last of all they reach the home of the bridegroom and stop outside in the street. The best-man's wife ties the ends of the bride's and the bridegroom's clothes together. Now the bridegroom's mother on a brass-plate arranges sun-dried rice, sun-dried paddy, d h u b i grass, three balls of flour, and three balls of cow-dung, in one large leaf-cup turmeric, in one large leaf-cup oil, one iron wristlet, sindur, and a comb, and she takes this outside into the street. With this brass-plate she performs the waving ceremony over the bride and the bridegroom and party three times. Thereupon she puts the brass-plate down, and keeping together in her hands a little dhubi grass, sun-dried rice, and sun-dried paddy she performs the waving ceremony three times over the bride and the bridegroom and party; thereupon she throws it down behind the back of the bridal pair.

Now she smears the turmeric water that she has put in a leaf-cup, mixed into a soft mass, on the bridegroom's cheek, and he also does the same to her. Thereupon the bridegroom's mother smears turmeric also on the bride's cheek, and she also does the same to her mother-in-law. Next the bridegroom's mother smears oil on the head of the bride and combs her a little, and she applies sindur to her; and she also smears oil on her mother-in-law and combs her a little and in her turn applies sindur to her. At this moment the bridegroom's mother puts an iron wristlet on the bride's left arm, and the flour-balls and cow-dung balls she at once throws away in three directions. Thereupon the wives of the bridegroom's father's elder and younger brothers also do the same.

Now the bridegroom's mother says to the marriage-broker: Give me the wooden pestle. He asks the bride's brother for this and hands it to the mother of the bridegroom. This they call the "gift pestle". Now the anointing girls on an earthenware lid bring glowing embers out from the house to the entrance door from the street. Now the three wives of the three brothers (first the mother of the bridegroom) take the wooden pestle in their left hands, wave it over the glowing embers on the lid and salute it with their right hands; thereupon they take the pestle in their right hands and wave it and make the salute with their left hands; again they once take the pestle in their left hands, wave it and make the salute with their right hands. She who was the last one to perform the waving ceremony stabs the glowing embers on the lid with the pestle, breaking them up, and the pestle she takes away and into the house. This act they call the purifying ceremony in bringing the bride and the bridegroom in.

Then they bring the bride and the bridegroom to the house-door; here they wash their feet over a brass-plate. Thereupon they are going to take them into the house; then a younger sister of the bridegroom shuts the door against them. Now they sing:

If you have strength, you so and so,
If you have maturity, you so and so,
Open, you so and so, the stone door.

If you have strength, you so and so,
If you have maturity, you so and so,
Open a little, you so and so, the stone door.

This they call the song of the closed door. The bride then gives her sister-in-law one anna, and she opens the door for them. They go inside, and the anointing girls spread out mats for them. The bride and bridegroom sit down there and with them the best-man, the follower, the girl conductor, and the duenna also. The anointing girls smear oil and turmeric on them. While they are doing this they sing[58]:

For whom, Father, is the elephant saddled?
For whom, Father, is the Maena-like queen?

For the young prince is the elephant saddled,
For the young prince is the Maena-like queen.

*

You went to the East, my boy, you came from the West;
Where, my boy, did you find, my boy, the Kiạ flower?

On the other side of seven seas, at the way down to the Ganges river
Father bought the Kiạ flower.

Now the anointing girls apply sindur to the bride and the bridegroom and their party, all who are sitting there; after having done this they wash their hands. Now they give the bride and the bridegroom rice cooked in milk, and to the others they give rice and curry. At this time the younger sister of the bridegroom forcibly takes rice from the bride; she puts one handful into the bride's mouth; thereupon they both eat their food together. When they have eaten, the anointing girls wash the hands of all. They go out gradually; the bridegroom stays with the brothers of the bride, and the bride with her duenna.

The Jọg Mạṅjhi then calls the bride's brothers. Two boys of the village wash their feet; thereupon the anointing girls pour out water for them. They wash their hands, and the Jọg Mạṅjhi says to the bride's brothers: Come along into the house, we shall have some gruel. They go inside; they spread out mats for them, and they sit down. First they give each of them two leaf-cups of beer. They drink this; thereupon the bridegroom's mother herself gives the brothers of the bride food; she makes them eat plentifully to make them pleased. Again the Jọg Mạṅjhi says: Please bring the beer. Again they drink, each two leaf-cups of beer, of the very best. The two boys wash them. Thereupon the Jọg Mạṅjhi takes them to a house open for all. When they have gone there, the Jọg Mạṅjhi calls the bridegroom's party. When they come, they give them beer and food. This they call "dust removing food and beer". All lie down to sleep.

When day dawns the bridegroom's father says to the Jọg Mạṅjhi: Please remember the bride's brothers, have they got up or not? The Jọg Mạṅjhi answers: They are up. Then the father of the bridegroom, the bride's brothers, the bride and the bridegroom, the duenna,

---

58 In a kind of Bihari.

and the village headman and a couple of the village people go to the cattle herd. And the father of the bridegroom points out a bull-calf to the brothers of the bride and says to them: This is yours, Sirs, look carefully at it, so as to remember it. The younger brother of the bride, or her elder brother, then slaps the calf on the back and salutes it; after this he bows before the village headman and all present. Now they sit down together, and the village headman says to the bride's brothers: In olden times, they say, standing on the top of a white-ant hill they yoked the bullocks of the bride's brother. As for us this one here is what we can furnish; let this especially be a grief to you. They answer: The grieving ones, Father, have gone in advance to Somae's narrow valley, they have gone in advance to the fine sand to herd crocodiles. The headman then says: Please, Sir, this we have cut off and separated, it may come to grief, it may stray, it may be lost, it may get away, it will be your look-out, please, drive it away with you. The brothers of the bride answer: Yes, Sir, let it remain a couple of days here in the meantime. After having saluted they go inside.

The Jog Mańjhi then says to the father of the bridegroom: Please give us oil and tooth-brush-twigs; we are going to have a bath. They give them this, and the Jog Mańjhi takes the brothers of the bride to the water. They have their bath, return and sit down. The Jog Mańjhi goes inside and says to those there: We have come; we are very hungry: do be quick. The anointing girls pour out water for the brothers of the bride, and they wash their hands. The Jog Mańjhi then takes these inside into the house and tells them to sit down on the mats, and they do so.

At this moment the Jog Mańjhi says: Please give each of us four leaf-cups of beer. This is done, and they drink it. The anointing girls wash their hands. They pluck up the leaf-cups and throw them away.

The bridegroom's mother now brings flattened and parched rice out in a flat basket. One of the anointing girls brings a loṭa with water. The mother of the bridegroom then says to the brothers of the bride: Take this, honoured brothers of the bride, wet the flattened and parched rice. They do this; one of the anointing girls with a small ladle pours molasses out to them, to one after the other. Thereafter they pour curds out to them.

Now the father of the bridegroom commences the recitation: Formerly, Sirs, the wealthy ones were spreading paddy and husks out on a bamboo mat; as you see, we are spreading out the bride's brother, to dry; be especially grieved for this. They say in reply: The grieving ones have gone in advance, Sir, to Somae's narrow valley; in the fine sand they are propping up booths and hovels. After this they eat. When they have had food, they give them beer in brass-cups. They wash themselves, and the father of the bridegroom says to the brothers of the bride: Now, Sirs, my daughter-in-law's brothers, take your leaf-plates with you; let the leaves be here. Then they go out.

The Jọg Mạṅjhi again goes into the house and says to the father of the bridegroom: What curry shall we give these friends? He answers: There is a castrated goat; we shall make curry of this for them. The Jọg Mạṅjhi then calls a young man from the village. They give him one brass-cup of beer; he drinks this, and the Jọg Mạṅjhi says to him: Look here, young man, tell all the village people, big and small: Come along, we shall make the bride's brothers pluck vegetables. The whole family, mother and children, all come and assemble in the bridegroom's home. The village people bring with them beer or rice as presents.

The Jọg Mạṅjhi brings a loṭa with water out from the house and keeps it on a leaf-plate held on the palm of his hand, and one man seizes the castrated goat. The Jọg Mạṅjhi then takes the loṭa with water to the village headman and his deputy, who salute it. Thereupon he takes it to the brothers of the bride, who also salute it. After this he takes it to the men of the village, who also salute the loṭa with water. And lastly he takes it to the women, who also in the same way salute it.

Now the Jọg Mạṅjhi gets hold of a battle-axe and gives this to the brothers of the bride. Having tied the castrated goat with a cord he pours water on its head; thereupon he makes it eat of the rice on a leaf-plate. He then says to the brothers of the bride: Come, honoured brothers of the bride, pluck vegetables for us. They stand up, and one among them seizes the battle-axe and makes a feint with it at the castrated goat; thereupon he puts the battle-axe down. One of the men of the village then seizes the battle-axe and cuts and kills the animal. The brothers of the bride do not kill the castrated goat, because they say the marriage will then be broken. The Jọg Mạṅjhi puts the head of the goat on the rice on the leaf-plate and takes it inside the house. He who, when the goat was cut, seized the pole, he smears the blood on some straw, and tying it to the pole he puts it down on the ground. Thereupon the father of the bridegroom pours some beer from the small vessel out as a libation where the goat was cut and killed. And in front of the bride-brother who made a feint at the goat, and the young man who seized the pole, he puts a leaf-cup down, having turned his hand upside, and he says to them: Please drink. They do this; thereupon he again gives them both one leaf-cup of beer each.

The Jọg Mạṅjhi then says to these two: Please salute each other; thereupon you will salute all here. They then salute each other like co-parents-in-law, and commencing from the village headman they salute all there. Now two young men from the village give all there two leaf-cups of poured-out beer and two leaf-cups of squeezed-out beer; when they have drunk, they keep quiet. The young people are dancing, and people who have work to do, work.

The father of the bridegroom then says to the village headman: Please, Sir, let us have the waving ceremony in good time. The headman then says to the Jọg Mạṅjhi: Do call all the village people here; we shall see the waving ceremony. He sends the Goḍet to call the village people together. An elder sister of the bridegroom, or if there is no such one, then a younger sister, acts as conductress of ceremonies in the bridegroom's home. In the same way as they drew paintings at the marriage-shed post in the bride's home, so she also paints in the same way; but she does not finish painting, until the father of the bridegroom promises to give her a calf.

The anointing girls now take the bride and the bridegroom into the house and make them sit down on a mat, and together with them the best-man, his follower, the duenna, and the conductress of ceremonies sit down. The anointing girls anoint them with oil and turmeric; however, the mother of the bridegroom first anoints them; when she has made way for them, the anointing girls anoint them. When the anointing is finished, the conductress, i. e., the wife of the best-man, ties the ends of the clothes of the bride and the bridegroom together. Thereupon they give them all food. At this time the bride will not eat, and when they ask her, she does not speak. The father of the bridegroom then says to her: Please eat, daughter-in-law, I shall give you a calf to get milk to eat. Then she eats. When they have had food, they get up.

Now the conductress, with a loṭa with water in her hand, conducts them out to the marriage-shed post. The duenna of the bride's side also is with them. Where they have made drawings, there they walk three times round, and the lady conductor also pours out the water in the loṭa all around over the place. The anointing girls now spread mats over the drawings; thereupon the bride and the bridegroom and their followers sit down on these. Then, as they acted when performing the waving ceremony in the bride's home, in the same way they also act in the bridegroom's home. All the women of the village give them, when performing the waving ceremony, wristlets, necklaces, rings, money. But the brothers of the bride do not give them anything. The brothers of the bride and all the village people drink beer during the waving ceremony. The beer is finished, and the waving ceremony is also ended. The younger sister of the bridegroom washes their feet, and at this time she catches hold of the bride's leg. The mother of the bridegroom then asks the duenna: How did you act at the bride's place? She says to her: We took one anna in money. The mother of the bridegroom then says: In that case let her loose. The duenna then gives her who has caught hold of the leg one anna, and she sets her free; thereupon the two salute each other. All stand up, and having gone round three times the bride and the bridegroom and their followers go inside the house.

The Jọg Mạṅjhi then says: Come at once here, you the father of the bridegroom, here to the house. With a couple of men he goes inside. The mother of the bridegroom calls the wife of the village headman and a couple of women and takes them inside. Thereupon, looking at the money, the brass necklets, and the different things that fell down at the waving ceremony, they count them. They give all this over in charge to the mother of the bridegroom. And they who give it in charge get beer.

Thereupon they start serving out the feast. As they acted in the bride's home in connexion with food, drink and recitations, in the same way they act also in the bridegroom's home. When they have had food and drink, those who wish it dance, and those who wish to lie down go to sleep.

When day dawns, the conductress boils the marriage clothes of the bride and the bridegroom, and when this is done, she dumps and washes them and brings them. They make the brothers of the bride and the duenna brush their teeth. When they have done this, they give them, the bride and the bridegroom included, stale food, flattened and parched rice. Afterwards they gather the village people to see the bride and the bridegroom being bathed and getting their hair washed. The wives of the village headman and of his deputy, of the Jọg Mȧṅjhi and of his deputy and of the Goḍet and of the village priest especially come. They then commence to bathe and wash the hair. They place before them two wooden slabs to sit on, one beside the other, and in one large leaf-cup they have made some hair-wash earth[59] wet. They have brought two tooth-brush twigs. They make the bride and the bridegroom sit down beside each other on the two wooden slabs. They make them sit facing the sun-rise. The bride sits on the right hand side of the bridegroom. The bridegroom then chews the tooth-brush twig; she, that is the conductress, gives this chewed twig to the bride, for her to brush her teeth. And the unused tooth-brush twig in the hand of the bride the conductress gives to the bridegroom. Now they both brush their teeth, and they wash their mouth and hands.

The bridegroom then takes a little of the hair-wash earth up with his left hand and smears this on the head of the bride; and the bride washes the bridegroom's hair with the earth in the leaf-cup. Having washed his hair she washes and cleans him. Thereupon the conductress washes and cleans the bride. The bride next washes the bridegroom's feet and smears oil on his feet. Thereupon she bows to him, and then he moves away. The duenna, the brothers of the bride, and the village people look at this sitting. After this the bride washes the feet of the village priest, the field priest, the village headman and his deputy, the Jọg Mạṅjhi and his deputy and the Goḍet, and after these she washes the feet of the bridegroom's father and maternal uncles and their ones. Thereupon she turns to the women, viz., to the wives of the village priest, of the field priest, of the village headman and of his deputy, of the Jọg Mạṅjhi and of his deputy and of the Goḍet, and to the mother of the bridegroom and her ones and the sister of the bridegroom's father and her ones, she washes the feet of all these.

Thereupon she washes the feet of the bridegroom's elder brothers, the brothers-in-law and younger brothers of the bridegroom with their ones, and she catches hold of the leg of each one, until they give her a wristlet or the like or some money. They give and

---

[59] The Santals use a soapy kind of earth for washing the hair

save themselves. Thereupon she and they pour water on each other and salute each other. After this she acts in the same way also towards the elder and younger sisters of the bridegroom. These also have to give something; then only she sets them free. Thereupon she and they pour water on each other and salute each other. The conductress and the bride now wash each other's feet, and they catch hold of each other's legs. Both give each other something, and they salute each other. Thereupon they give them all beer, which they drink.

Now the principal people and the brothers of the bride, the bride and the bridegroom, and the duenna all go inside the house. What fell to the bride they count and give in charge to the mother of the bridegroom. They now drink beer handed to them by the bride and the bridegroom, and they get food.

When they have had food, the village headman gives them a recitation; the bride and the bridegroom sit in front of him, facing him. He says: You bride, this here is your house and home; here are your big and small vessels; from to-day look well after what is yours; these two are your mother and father; give them what they may ask you for, and listen to them in whatever they may put you to do; this one here is your husband; when there is night, is darkness, stomach-ache, headache, tell your mother and father, and if these two do not do what you wish, tell your husband, saying, come and help me. Do not go out alone in night and darkness.

Thereupon the village headman says to the parents: This daughter-in-law has not come of her own accord; we have ourselves bought and brought her, she is a stranger here, — from to-day instruct and tutor her well and carefully; guide her in a nice way.

The village headman then says to the bridegroom: You also, young man, from to-day you will go hunting and chasing, or you will wander in the forest, you will find something or other; if you find a hollowed ebony fruit, a hollowed t a r ǫ p̉ fruit[60], resin, marking nuts[61], don't eat it alone, eat a piece, bring half a piece to your wife; — or if you kill a bird or something of that kind, eat one slice, take half a slice in a fold of your cloth along to your wife. And now, young man, up to this time in connexion with attending religious or social festivals, wherever you were at night-fall there you were at dawn, so look now, from to-day we have hung a p ǫ p ṛ ǫ bell on you; consequently where you two have your place, when it is time for lying down, come and find her there and lie down both of you. You also, bride, from to-day the young man may go somewhere or other; then when he comes from anywhere give him at once water and a tooth-brush twig; when you go with companions to draw water, to fetch leaves, don't talk and laugh with anybody else; this one is your man, don't look elsewhere.

The bride then answers: Yes, father, getting good omens, a bullock on the right-hand side, a woodpecker on the left-hand side, you joined the bonds; now, as is seen, you, the

[60] Buchanania latifolia, Roxb. [61] Semecarpus Anacardium, L.

people of the community, have planted me: these two here are my mother and my father in righteousness, and this one here is my righteous mate: he may come tired and hungry from anywhere; as soon as I see him, I shall pour out water and meet him with it; and my mother and father may come from anywhere tired and hungry, for them also I shall pour out water and meet them; if I do not act in this way, you, the people of the community, will blame me.

Now the village headman speaks jokingly, saying: The bride is exceedingly good; the way in which she has given us rice and curry and beer, this we have all seen; we have had food and drink; we believe it.

Now the father of the bridegroom gives the marriage-broker and the best-man their dues. The marriage-broker gets a loin-cloth, five cubits long and one four-anna bit and one anna for sandal-wear, and the best-man gets a loin-cloth, five cubits long. They now go out into the court-yard.

The Jo̱g Ma̱ńjhi enters the house and says to the mother of the bridegroom: Please give me oil and a comb. They procure this for him. They then spread out a mat in the cow-shed; on this they make the brothers of the bride sit down. Three young men from the village rub them in with oil; thereupon they comb them and poke a good deal of fun at them. The women of the village also treat the duenna in the same way, and they apply any amount of sindur-spots on her. The anointing girls make tassels of straw and plaits of hemp. The young men of the village make the plaits into hairknots on the brothers of the bride and tie them tight with the tassels.

The Jo̱g Ma̱ńjhi now brings a dancing-drum out into the court-yard. They drum and the oil-smearing young men take hold of the brothers of the bride to dance, and the women take hold of the duenna to dance. They are dancing and singing do̱ṅ songs:

Please, bride, tell your brothers to wait for the midday meal,
Eating off, a spotted back he is leaving for you, mother.

A thieving dog slinking about,
A brother of the bride greedily licking.

Who, girls, who, girls, is the thieving dog?
Who, girls, who, girls, is the brother of the bride?

With a ladle girls, beat the thieving dog,
With a vessel, girls, cover up the brother of the bride.

The duenna, the diarrhoea covering,
Some one importuning,
Some one importuning, mother, girls, in the house below the hill.

The brother of the bride, shaved and cracked,
Some one importuning,
Some one importuning, mother, girls, in the house below the hill.

Thereupon they go out into the street outside the house. They fix five days to take the bride and bridegroom away and back again. Again they take the duenna into the house. They put down for her one seer rice, one seer flattened and parched rice and on the rice one wristlet; thereupon she goes out into the street outside. The Jọg Mạṅjhi now brings out for the brothers of the bride five half-seers parched and flattened rice; their sticks and different implements and the quarter joint he also brings out.

Now the brothers of the bride say to her: Please, girl, don't grieve; in five days we shall come back and take you both away. As for you, brew beer in the meantime, and make five seers of flattened rice in the meantime. After this the duenna instructs and tutors the bride before leaving: Please stay here, girl, this here is your home, this here is your door to go out and in through; work all of you, eat diligently. Do not long for us; this is your home for life; both bones and ashes have we sold you; for one leaf-cup have we sold you, also for half a leaf-cup have we sold you; therefore you would not fit in with us. Do not grieve; in five days we shall come again.

Thereupon the bride and bridegroom and the brothers of the bride and the duenna salute all the village people, commencing from the village headman. When this is done, the brothers of the bride and the duenna stand on one side, and the bride and bridegroom salute them, and these two go alone inside the house. The bridegroom then takes out one small packet of tobacco and one small packet lime, and the bride a loṭa with water. They go both to the brothers of the bride. The bride gives her own real brother the loṭa with water. He drinks and gives her the loṭa back. Thereupon the bridegroom gives him the lime and the tobacco; this he puts in his waist-cloth. Thereupon they go.

When they have gone, the young girls and men in the village take the marriage-shed down, and as they acted in the bride's home, in the same way they eat and drink "dew beer" and "dew rice". They get no presents. Afterwards they dance.

When it becomes time for drawing water, the bride goes together with a couple of the village girls to draw water. She takes with her to the water-fetching place a little oil and sindur. There she makes five marks with oil and sindur downwards, and having drawn water she comes back with her companions. This they call to buy way down to water.

After five days the marriage-broker and two of the brothers of the bride come. After having saluted each other they "water" their feet, take them inside the house and give them beer. Afterwards they kill some fowls for them, and preparing rice and curry they give it to them. They lie down to sleep. When day dawns, they give them stale food, flattened and parched rice. For the midday meal they prepare rice and curry for them.

They eat this. The mother-in-law then combs the bride and ties up her hair and applies sindur to her. The bridegroom they also make ready. For the bride they bring out one large pot of beer and five seers of flattened rice. The flattened rice she ties up in a cloth. Thereupon she salutes her parents-in-law; the two brothers of the bride and the marriage-broker also salute them. The bride takes the beer on her head, and the cloth-bundle with the flattened rice she carries under her armpit: there they then are off to the old home of the bride. When they reach there, they wash the feet of the two, the elder and younger sisters of the bride do this. Thereupon they take hold of the bridegroom's leg. They set him free when he gives them money or necklaces; thereupon they pour water on each other and salute each other. They take the two inside the house and give them food.

When it becomes evening, they call the village headman and his deputy and their ones and all the village people. When they have come, the bride and bridegroom salute them. First the father of the bride offers the beer and the flattened rice that they call brought-along gifts to the dead ancestors and to Maraṅ buru. Then they bring out the beer and the flattened rice and give it to the village people, who eat and drink, dividing it between themselves. This beer they call "umbilical cord burying beer". The elderly men then talk together: Having got good omens, a bullock on the right-hand side, a woodpecker on the left-hand side, we have, as is seen here, joined the bonds, we have had a marriage — we have settled taking the bride and bridegroom away and bringing them back; beer and flattened rice we have also got sufficiently; in all respects it has been sufficient; please, you two, the bride's parents, let this especially be your grief. They both answer: Yes, Sir, they who grieve have gone in advance.

The bride and the bridegroom then stay there for two nights. The marriage-broker then says: I shall take them there. They make ready for them one pot of beer and five seers flattened rice. The girl carries this away on her head and under her armpit. After having saluted those there, they go together with the marriage-broker to the bridegroom's home. When they have arrived there, they call all the village people together. As they did with the beer and the flattened rice in the bride's old home, in the same way they also act in the bridegroom's home. They eat and drink, and here also they make formal recitations as in the bride's old home. Thereupon all go to their respective homes. Now the bride and bridegroom are settled for good.

g. Ṭuṅki dipil[62] marriage.

This is the marriage of poor people. The bridegroom does not go to the home of the bride, only the marriage-broker and a bridegroom's party of five go there. They do not make a marriage-shed, and they do not put the bridegroom's party up in outside lodgings.

---

[62] See Dictionary s. v.

The customary dues are as in a marriage with parties; eating and drinking and beer are also in the same way. After having had food and drink the bridegroom's party bring the bride to the bridegroom's home. Three brothers of the bride and a duenna go along with the girl. For "finishing the painting" and for "fireplace damages" nothing has to be given. The applying of sindur is done in the house of the bridegroom. Here they also act as customary at a marriage with parties. In connexion with taking the pair away and back again it is also as in other marriages.

h. Ghạrdi jãwãe[63] (house son-in-law).

People who have no son, or whose sons are small and not fit to do any work, such people keep house sons-in-law, when they have grown up daughters; and only a poor man or an orphan will stay as a house son-in-law. House sons-in-law have no brideprice or expenses to pay, nor have they any customary dues to give; the expenses are all on the girl's side. The marriage is performed for them like for other people. They serve for the bride five years with their father-in-law. They do not get any wages, only food and clothes. When they take in a house son-in-law, they show him a calf. If before the five years are gone, the girl does not pull together with her husband, he goes away taking the calf with him. At the time when the two are married the father gives also the girl a calf. And for five years she gets her reaping perquisites, and this paddy she gives out on interest to somebody. When five years have passed, they will, if they are pleased, stay on, getting wages; if not, they leave.

And if a girl's parents have no male children, and if the house son-in-law and his wife will take care of and feed the two (parents) until death, the two will get the house and household, all the agricultural and other land, and they will get half the cattle; the other half the brothers (or cousins) of the girl's father will get. The ghạrdi jãwãe and his wife have to bear the expenses in connexion with the final funeral ceremonies. If there are two or three house sons-in-law, they divide.

i. The marriage of widowers, widows, and divorced ones.

Widowers are not liked; therefore (girls) will not quickly agree to be married to such ones. They say: "As a widower snarled"; "a widower a worn-out broom, scraping, scraping, who will be fool enough to agree to be married to such a one"?

Divorced men are not liked either. They say: "A divorced man, a fickle fellow, who knows for how many days."

They also put blame on widows. They say: "A widow, a stallion, neighing, neighing."

Divorced girls are especially blamed. They say: "A divorced girl, the head of a maena, smooth, smooth"; "a divorced girl, a green Bulbul bird, they cry in a thousand ways";

---

[63] See Dictionary s. v.

"a divorced girl, a decoy partridge, they are leading astray"; "a divorced girl, a c o̜ ḍ g o̜ ć[64] fish, they do not remain in one place".

If a widower or a divorced man marries a spinster, her parents will take a brideprice of five or seven rupees for good, that is to say, the bridegroom does not get anything in return. The marriage is performed as between bachelor and spinster.

Formerly bachelors did not marry widows or divorced women, and also nowadays this is not in accordance with the rule; still nowadays a few men marry such persons, because the age has become depraved. Those who marry a widow or a divorced woman have to pay only half the brideprice, and the Jo̜g Mạṅjhi gets eight annas as marriage fee. The village headman gets nothing. Cloth for the mother, cloths for the grandmothers there is nothing of, and presents and the like are absent also; there is no bathing and hair-washing, no going and coming either. This is no real marriage, we call it a temporary hire. The name of such a marriage is s a ṅ g h a. The bridegroom does not apply sindur to the bride. Applying sindur to a flower, he with his left hand sticks this into the bride's hair. This is s a ṅ g h a (marrying a widow or divorced woman). No feast has to be given either, the bridegroom gives only a couple of people some beer.

Girls who get a child while being spinsters they call c u p i c h ạ ḍ w i, tail-divorced. Any one who marries such a girl, pays a brideprice as for a divorced girl. But the marriage is performed as a marriage with a spinster.

j. Running in.

If in any village a young man and a girl have become of one mind, the girl will inform the Jo̜g Mạṅjhi of this. Having found out what the young man wishes, the Jo̜g Mạṅjhi takes the girl into the house of the young man's parents. A couple of days afterwards the parents tell the village headman. They come together and have a talk. They ask the girl and the young man what they intend. If these two say they are willing and agree, they separate them and fix a day for the marriage. The village community gets five four-anna bits. The marriage is performed like other marriages.

If any young man and girl have sexual intercourse, and the young man afterwards is unwilling to marry her, the girl will run in to the young man, forcing her way in. If the young man professes to marry her, in this case their marriage is performed as with the above run-in girl. But if the young man will not agree to marry her, he will in accordance with the decision of the village council have to pay the girl three rupees, and the village council will fine the father of the young man and the father of the girl each five four-anna bits. When the girl has got the money, the Jo̜g Mạṅjhi will take her to the house of her parents.

---

[64] Ophiocephalus gachua, Ham. Buch.

k. Forcibly applying sindur.

To apply sindur to any girl without cooperation of the village community is called iputut. This is of two kinds. Sometimes a young man will apply sindur to a girl with her knowledge and consent, and sometimes they apply the sindur without right or reason. If a young man and a girl wish it, and they have agreed, while the parents of the girl are unwilling to bestow her on the young man, then the young man will forcibly apply sindur to the girl, after the two have talked together and decided on it. If a young man has fallen in love with a girl, and he has doubts: who knows whether they will bestow her on me or not, or whether the girl will be pleased with me or not, then the young man will apply sindur to the girl without telling her and without giving any warning. And sometimes it also happens that they defile a girl in anger, to make her become a divorcee.

People say, it is told, that only the spinsters they marry will they get in the next world — but not widows or divorcees —; therefore it sometimes happens when a man's first wife is a widow or a divorcee, that in order to get a wife in the next world, he will marry or apply forcibly sindur to a spinster, whether he afterwards keeps her as his wife or not; he has made way for himself in the next world.

When a young man is going to apply sindur forcibly to a girl, he puts sindur in a leaf in a fold of his cloth, and going to a place where they fetch water or to a plain where the hook-swinging or some other festival is going on, he without warning smears the sindur on the girl's forehead. If he has no sindur, it may be done also with earth or lime. Also during a festival or when they are fetching leaves and firewood or leaves, they forcibly apply sindur to a girl. If a girl has got sindur forcibly applied to her, she has, according to the law, become the wife of the man who did it. And if she does not stay with him, she becomes a divorcee.

When a young man has forcibly applied sindur to a girl, he will at once run away, fearing that the father and male relatives of the girl will thrash him. When the father and male relatives of the girl get to know that sindur has been forcibly applied to her, they become furious, and calling the village people together they go with bows and arrows to the young man's house to "follow the bloody tracks"[65]. First they go to the headman of that village and tell him. He says to them: Please act for us in accordance with custom. They then enter the young man's courtyard and beat every single water-pot into pieces, and entering the house they break their cooking vessels and the fireplace to pieces and scatter them, and if they find the young man there, they bind him and beat him, so that he lies there done for, they leave him only his life, — thereupon they lay him down in the middle of the courtyard and go to hunt for castrated goats or pigs. If they find goats, they kill two with a battle-axe, and if pigs, they shoot and kill two with bow and arrow. Thereupon they go to the cattle-herd to seize some cattle. They drive some three pairs

---

[65] A common expression used about the forcible application of sindur to a girl, is that a leopard has clawed her; this may be another way of showing their attitude towards the act.

of the very best bullocks or buffaloes to the house of the village headman, and the two killed castrated animals they also take there.

The village headman now calls the village people together to a council meeting, and they judge in the matter. They follow the matter up, to find out how it happened. They then also send a couple of men to the girl's home and ask her whether it was with her consent or forcibly that the young man applied sindur to her, and they take with them also from the girl's home a castrated animal (goat or pig). The three castrated animals the people of both sides eat, and the cattle the headman of the young man's side and the village council give in charge to the village headman of the girl's side, until the father of the young man pays the fine money. The girl's father gets sixteen rupees without giving anything in return, whether the young man gets the girl or not. And the headman of the young man's village gets five rupees from the father of the young man. This they call the head-saving rupees. Formerly they have sometimes beaten such a young man to death on account of the crime of forcibly applying sindur to a girl. And this they did not take up for inquiry. The village headman stands to shelter the young man; therefore he gets the money. Of these five rupees the headman gives two rupees to his village people as their share. A girl that has got sindur applied to her they, with a few exceptions, give in marriage to the young man. They afterwards marry the two over again as at the marriage of bachelor and spinster. And if they do not bestow the girl on the young man, she becomes a divorcee.

l. About getting a second wife.

In bygone days they were living satisfied with only one wife; none had two wives. And also nowadays, if they out of licentiousness get two or three wives, they do not call this good; and there are very few such people. But if a man's wife does not get children, then the husband may, both of them agreeing, take a co-wife. The first wife rules the household. And if the elder brother of the husband dies, then his younger brother can, even if he has a wife, keep his sister-in-law as a wife, and they do this in order that the children may not be alienated. And this they do not deem bad. But if some one's younger brother dies, then an elder brother cannot keep this one's wife. A younger brother's wife they honour equal to a bonga, — they do not even touch their bedsteads.

Those who commit the fault of getting two wives, will afterwards reap the fruit of this, because a first wife and a co-wife will not live in peace. People say: "A co-wife, needle pricks, they prick"; "a co-wife, ebony firewood, crackles"; "a co-wife, a hen with just hatched out chickens, at loggerheads, they are not reconciled"; "a first wife, kicked in going, kicked in coming, they will endure it"; "co-wives make a dull sound with a wooden slab rapping with the feet"; "a co-wife, the itching of the etka[66], cannot be endured".

66 Mucuna pruriens, DC., produces an intense itching.

m. Hirom bạ̃ihạ̃ (a solatium to the first wife for getting a co-wife).

When a married pair do not get children, or a man, only due to licentiousness, or for any reason, gets a co-wife, he cannot, without making his first wife agree to it, bring the co-wife into his house. If the first wife is not willing, she can, standing in the door, meet the co-wife, beating her. There is a customary rule about this. The first wife gets as a solatium for getting a co-wife five rupees or a calf. When she gets this, all three will sit down beside each other in front of the village council, facing the rising of the sun. Husband and wife make the co-wife sit between them on the right side of the man. The man then applies sindur to his first wife, and what is left of the sindur he applies to a ḍimbu flower[67], and with his left hand he sticks this into the hair of the co-wife's head. The first wife manages the house and household.

n. Elopement.

When a man and a woman run away to another country to live together, we call this an elopement. A woman who has a husband, or a related woman or girl, whom it is not permissible to marry, such ones they elope with, fearing the husband, or fearing to be outcasted.

If a man runs away with a married woman, they would formerly track them, until they found them, and then cut them down, and none would follow this matter up. Nowadays they make them pay double brideprice and give the woman into charge, and the headman of the village of the eloping man gets five rupees, because he saves his head. And if related persons elope, they outcaste such people. If they do not separate, they will remain outcasted for their whole life, and no one will eat or drink with them, and children of these will not find way down to water (i. e., to be married). If they separate they will "eat them into caste"; but there will be very heavy expenses. If relatives who are prohibited from marrying elope, the parents on both sides will also have to arrange and pay to be "eaten into caste again", they themselves alone; thereby they will be taken into society again. But if they permit the two who eloped to come to their homes, the whole family will be outcasted; and the village people will also be punished, otherwise people will not give them their daughters in marriage either, and will not marry theirs.

To strive after the possession of a married woman and to elope with another man's wife is somehow customary. If they elope with a person of another race, they remain outcasted for life, these two alone, and the parents get more punishment.

---

[67] Ocymum Basilicum, var. thyrsiflorum, L.

o. Divorce.

Formerly people were separated only for two reasons, viz., the woman's adultery and witchcraft. Nowadays, if husband and wife will not live in peace, they "tear the leaves" also for this reason. From the time that they have commenced to take co-wives, a wife also can demand divorce for this reason. If they are separated on account of witchcraft, a woman may be married again without having had "the leaves torn", otherwise only when this has been properly done. The customary rule of separation because of the woman's adultery has been mentioned above.

If anyone's wife has been established to be a witch by five witch-finders, her husband will, together with the village council, give her in charge in the house of her parents or of her male relatives, and even a child of hers he will rob her of and keep; and if she has a sucking child, he will afterwards bring home this child of his, paying the woman for its support. There is no punishment or the like for this act, only the village council will get food. And if afterwards a daughter grows up and is married, this woman will not get the cloth given to a mother.

Nowadays, when a divorce is due to their not living in peace, the guilty person will have to pay a fine. If a man leaves his wife without any fault of hers, he will not get the brideprice paid back, and he will himself have to pay damages. Any children will belong to the man, and he will have to give his wife a cow, one bundle paddy, one brass-cup, and a piece of women's cloth. And if she feeds a sucking child of his, she will, when he fetches the child, get separately for this sixteen maunds paddy and one cloth. If there should have been any expense in connexion with the child during fever or illness, this also the mother will get.

If husband and wife separate on account of the woman's fault, the man will get the brideprice paid back, and the woman will get nothing. Food for the village council sitting in the matter they will take from both sides, five four-anna bits from each.

When the wife demands divorce because the husband has taken a co-wife, the man will not get the brideprice paid back, and he will have to give a cow, one bundle paddy, a cloth, and a brass-cup.

They tear the leaves in the following way: The village headmen and the village people of both sides come together. They put a loṭa with water on the ground, and make the husband and wife stand with this between them, facing each other. The headman of the husband's village then says: Well, you so and so, we the people of our village, invocating the Day bonga, the Five mountain spirits, and the ancestors of old, having got good omens, a bullock on the right-hand side, a woodpecker on the left-hand side, we bound together, joined together the bonds like the laṛ climber, the bando climber[68]; for one day we did

---

[68] Laṛ here refers to the jọm laṛ, Bauhinia Vahlii, W. & A. Bando is Spatholobus Roxburghii, Benth.

not join you two together, but for ever and always, like stone, like rock, until very old and white-haired, — now there is no guilt of ours; then as you two do not suit each other, what can we village people do? Now both of you consider in your heart, take warning for yourselves, otherwise some day in the future you might say about us: these people caused us to separate. Now then, you so and so, if you really will leave her for good, make your appeal to the Day spirit, the Five mountain spirits, the ancestors of old, and tear the leaves, or else, do not tear them.

Thereupon they make him stand on his left leg, and facing the sun-rise they make him raise his hands in supplication. Thereupon they give him three Sal-leaves[69]. He takes these, and with a piece of cloth round his neck he invokes the Day spirit and quickly tears the three leaves along the mid-ribs from the stalk to the top. Thereupon he turns round and with his right foot kicks over the loṭa with water and makes renunciation. And commencing from the village headman he salutes all there. The woman also salutes them in the same way.

If the leaves are not torn straight along the mid-ribs when he tears them, people say, they are likely to meet again. And if the water in the loṭa does not all run out, then also they say, their affection has not been removed, perhaps they will again come together.

p. Outcasting.

Only because of two crimes the ancestors have made it a rule for us to outcaste people, viz., sexual intercourse with people of another race or with a non-permissible relative. If anyone misbehaves in such a way, the village headman calls the headmen of the neighbouring villages together and informs them. If it is proved, they inform the people of their respective villages saying to them: Don't eat and drink with so and so, or don't in the meantime get into marriage relations with them; otherwise you may be burnt by the same fire. But these people are not able to outcaste them; this is in the hand of the people of the country. Only when the matter is taken to the burnt forest, it is settled. At the council meeting during the hunt of the people of the country they publish the matter. If the Parganas, Dẹsmạṅjhis, Mạṅjhis, and the people of the country do not get proofs, they punish those who have started the matter severely; but if it is proved, they order: Well, we shall fix used leaves in the ground for them. The young men of the country then compose songs, and going to the village they sing praising them and mentioning the names and sins of those who have committed the crime. All the people of the country enter the village street, blowing flutes and drumming kettle-drums, and in the street outside the house of the miscreants they fix in the ground a post to which

69 Shorea robusta, Gaertn., the sacred tree of the Santals.

used leaves, a burnt log of wood and a worn-out broom have been tied. The people of the village will remain included in the pollution, until they give what is needed for propitiation. They worry the miscreant very much. They do not give him fire, nor do they let the people of this house draw water at the common water-fetching place. Great hardship.

If the village headman meets them with a loṭa with water before the people of the country enter the village street, they do not sing the songs; but in any case they perform the outcasting.

q. Taking into society again.

Outcasted people, who can be taken into society again, do their utmost to provide what is necessary, that they may become members of society again. When they have made the necessary provisions, they inform the village headman, who tells the Pargana. The Pargana informs the Parganas of twelve countries. On the fixed day they assemble in the village. Outside they call a halt. The outcasted people have killed pigs and goats and make a big feast. All is ready.

Thereupon the outcasted man, having a loṭa with water in his hand, goes to the end of the village street. There he stands with a piece of cloth round his neck, keeping the loṭa with water on the palms of both his hands turned upwards and making supplication, and he looks very miserable and humble. The venerable old Pargana then says to the Parganas of the country and to the collected village headmen: Come along, let us console his soul; he looks very much in need of mercy. He thereupon leads them to the outcasted man. When they reach him, the outcasted man makes his worship to the Day spirit (Siń boṅga) and says to them: O Father, I have sinned awfully, I acknowledge my fault, have mercy on me. Then the venerable old Pargana (formerly this was the right of the Murmu people) receives the loṭa with water from the hands of the outcasted man, and worshipping the Day spirit he says to the outcasted man: Because you have acknowledged your sin, we have taken over and taken on us all this (sin) of yours. Having rinsed his mouth with a little water he gives the loṭa to the others, to one after the other. All the leading men rinse their mouths with water from the loṭa.

Thereupon they enter the village. There the man washes the feet of all the leading men, in his courtyard. When he has done this, they sit down in rows beside each other to eat. The man thereupon pours rice out on the leaf-plates to them, one after the other. He sprinkles water on them; he gives them curry, and he puts down on their leaf-plates, for each of the Parganas five rupees, and for each of the village headmen one rupee, and for the headman of his own village he puts down five rupees.

Now they eat, and when they have done this, the venerable Pargana says to the people of the country: From to-day we have taken this man in among us as one of ourselves;

uncleanness and defilement all has been cleared away. Consequently from to-day we shall drink a cup of water of his, we shall also smoke a hookah-bowl of his, we shall also give him a daughter of ours in marriage, his daughters we shall also take; like water in a hollowed-out pit in the river, like water in a pool, we have made all clear and pure. Any one who from to-day mentions this matter anywhere or speaks depreciatingly, him we shall make pay one hundred rupees and make him give one hundred leaf-plates (of cooked rice) as a social punishment. Thereupon they dig a pit, bury balls of cow-dung there and press a stone down on it. Now they salute each other and separate.

IV. WHEN A MARRIED SON LIVES IN THE HOUSE OF HIS FATHER

a. Brothers living together.

Santals do not at once, when getting married, set up separate households; they stay in the house of the man's parents. If a man moves away to live in the house of his father-in-law, they blame him very much, and such a man will not afterwards get any share of the inheritance. Some people will, because they are annoyed beyond sufferance, perform the final funeral ceremonies for such a son. Nowadays a few men will give them a share of the original property; but this is only a favour; formerly they had no right to this.

Until the father makes his sons set up separate households, they work together, eat together. The parents of the young men look upon their daughters-in-law as their own daughters. Among his sons the father will love the oldest son most, provided he is good, and the mother will love her youngest child most. The young men with their wives honour their uncles and aunts like their own parents, and these look upon them as their own children.

The father guides, instructs and tutors his sons, and the mother does the same with her daughters-in-law and daughters. The younger daughters-in-law address the elder daughters-in-law as elder sisters and obey their word like that of their mother-in-law; the elder daughters-in-law address the younger ones, saying "girl" to them, and look upon them as younger sisters. When the parents have lost their strength, the eldest son and the eldest daughter-in-law manage the household, and they have to stand up when the young ones misbehave or commit any fault. If the elder ones while living let the younger ones manage, awful quarrelings arise. The old man mostly scolds his wife if the work and business don't go well, and now and then he will also upbraid his sons, but never his daughters-in-law. Those who really start quarrels, are the mothers-in-law and daughters-in-law, and the wives of the brothers, and through their quarrels brothers also become enemies. Santals say: "A mother-in-law, a bitter pumpkin, not tasty"; "a daughter-in-law, plugged ears, they don't hear"; "a daughter-in-law, a python snake, dragging themselves along, they do not move". Of the husbands of daughters they say: "A daughter's husband, crooked firewood, will be still more crooked"; "Another's child, a forest fowl, they will not become one's own".

An elder brother's wife and the younger brothers and sisters of her husband are great friends; they do not quarrel. Girls tell the wife of their elder brother everything, both good and bad, and the young men speak and laugh much with the wife of their elder brother; no one takes any notice of this.

Old men and their wives love their grandchildren very much; they carry them on their hips, they fondle them, and the wives of brothers also, if they live in peace with each other, carry the children of them all on their hips and fondle them, and when they have fever or are ill, they also nurse each other.

b. Separation of brothers.

When the grandchildren become very numerous, or when they do not live in harmony in the house together, the parents separate them. In connexion with the village headman and the village council the father divides the agricultural and other land, the cattle, big and small, all in equal parts, and gives it to them, and he keeps for himself one part, and the son with whom the old couple stays, with him their part will stay. When the parents lose all strength, the sons have to support them, because at the time when the children were unable to support themselves the parents supported them with great hardship. Daughters do not get any share. Generally, at the time when they are married, they give them each one calf. And at the time of separation, if they are spinsters, they give them a calf. And sons, who at the time of separation are bachelors, get a double share of the cattle, one share being for their marriage. The pieces of cattle that daughters-in-law have got from their father and brothers, and from their father-in-law at the time of marriage, these are not divided; but the cattle, that sons-in-law get from their father-in-law at the time of marriage, these are divided.

V. HUSBAND AND WIFE IN THEIR OWN HOME

a. Setting up a household.

When husband and wife have been separated from his parents, they set up a household for themselves. They ask the village headman to get a house-site. They give him beer and food. The husband cuts trees and brings them from the forest; he cuts thatching grass in the forest, or buys it from somewhere. He fixes nine posts in the ground; thereupon he puts up three roof-beams; at three places he fixes double cross-beams, he fixes forty rafters, and in three places, at the top, in the middle, and at the bottom of these, he puts cross-laths. Thereupon he makes the rafter-framework and after this thatches. Then he makes a wattle and daub wall; having done this he puts up something to keep separate the place for the ancestors. The wife then kneads earth and smears this on; afterwards she fills the house inside with earth and plasters all smooth, and she makes a fire-place. The husband makes a door, of wood or of thin bamboo-slips. In the house they have two bedsteads, a wooden mortar and pestle, a winnowing-fan, baskets, brooms, earthenware vessels, big and small, ladles made of wood or of pumpkin-shell, kodali axe, chisel, adze, sickle, knife, plough-beam, yoke, plough and plough-share, flute, bow and arrows, battle-axe, sword and dancing-drum and kettle-drum. Poor people have no battle-axe, sword, dancing-drum, or kettle-drum.

The sacred closet is for the ancestors to stay hidden in. Women belonging to other men are not permitted to go in there; and some people do not permit even their own daughters to go in there, that is, when they have been married. In this closet they make a small enclosure, and this is the real place for the ancestors to stay hidden in. In the closet money is also kept. On the backside of the house they have the homestead field; here they cultivate maize. And in front of the house towards the village street they have the court-yard. This they fence securely in on the four sides. They make two openings for going out and in, one is the homestead field door and one the village street door.

The man builds a shed for the cows and bullocks and buffaloes, a fold for the goats and sheep and a sty for the pigs. The fowls and the cat stay in the house, and the dog stays somewhere on the verandah, to guard the house.

b. The clothes of the family.

A man's dress is a piece of cloth, one cubit broad and five cubits long, this is to take round the loins; and to wrap oneself in they have a cotton shawl or an over-cloth, five cubits long and three cubits broad. If they are wealthy, they also wrap a turban cloth, some five cubits long, round their head. Poor people use a piece of cloth some two cubits long and half a cubit broad as a loin-strip, or they have a piece of cloth two and a half cubits long and one cubit broad as a loin-strip. And during the cold season they have a piece of cloth, some three cubits square, to wrap round themselves.

Women have only one piece, ten cubits long, of women's cloth; this they take round the waist and up over the back and breast.

Children stay naked, until they are eight years old; after this age boys get a loin-strip and girls a girl-loincloth.

Men arrange a hair-knot, and the women tie up their hair with a plait of cow's tail hair. All use a comb.

c. The ornaments of the Santals.

Formerly men and women, when they had reached some age, did not use ornaments. And the ornaments of young men and girls were only flowers. Nowadays all have ear-rings, whether women or men, whether boys or girls. Elderly men also use wristlets. Besides these, elderly men have no ornaments. Elderly women have wristlets, necklaces, and rings.

Young men have wristlets, necklaces, and rings, and when they dance they adorn themselves with hollow bells round the ankles, hollow ankle-rings, blue-jay feathers, and flowers. Girls adorn themselves with wristlets, anklets, curved anklets, thin toe-rings, great toe-rings, toe-rings with hollow bells, necklaces, rings, solid close-fitting necklets, solid neck ornaments, arm ornaments, upper arm ornaments, and flowers. On small boys and girls they put hollow anklets and small hollow bells.

d. Men's work.

From the month of Phalgun to the end of Baisak (i. e., from the middle of February to the middle of May) it is "sitting time". Then the men make implements for their own use and gather provisions for the household; then they make ploughbeams and yokes, ploughs, and clod-crushers, earth-shovels and cart-wheels, cart shafts and axles, neck-ropes and yoke-leather-thongs, hide-straps and ropes, spinning wheels and cotton-cleaning implements, handles for spades and pick-axes, axes and adzes, bedstead legs and frames, stools and wooden slabs to sit on, wooden ladles and spoons, bows and arrows, flutes, wooden pestles and mortars and weaving implements; they weave cloth and bedsteads, and they bring firewood and wood for the house, and they repair the house.

From Jheṭ to Bhador (i. e., from the middle of May to the middle of August) they do agricultural work. Then they plough from morning to noon, and later on they work making ricefield-ridges and so on. First they sow millets and jungle corn, later janhe̱ millet, maize, bajṛa, ko̱de̱, raheṛ, ghaṅgra, and sutri[1]. After this they sow paddy for transplanting. They hoe the maize (in this the women help them). They do the first ploughing for paddy-planting; thereupon they plough the second time, thereupon plough the third time; they also make ready the ricefield ridges; they make the fields muddy and harrow; then they pull the paddy seedlings out. (To plant the paddy is women's work.)

At this time they sow cotton and tilmiń oilseed[2] in the course of the month of San (middle of July to middle of August). In Bhador (middle of August to middle of September) they plough the fields for ho̱ṛe̱ć and surguja[3] and sow these. They harvest the maize. In this work and in hoeing the cotton the women help them. They harvest the iṛi, gundli, ko̱de̱, and erba millets[4]. In this work also the women assist them. The men thresh.

In the month of Dasãe (middle of September to middle of October) they plough the homestead field where the maize was, and sow mustard seed, and they harvest and thresh janhe̱ millet and the early paddy. In Aghãṛ (middle of November to middle of December) they dig and plane the threshing-floor, and together with the women they harvest the paddy, cut the bajṛa and tilmiń, cut the raheṛ, pluck the ghaṅgra and sutri, and pull out the ho̱ṛe̱ć and surguja. The women alone pull out the cotton. When the men have carted all this up to the threshing-floor, they spread it out on this, and joining cattle together they thresh. Having threshed out the seed they throw the straw away, having winnowed the grain they make a heap of it, and having twisted straw-ropes and straw-strings they put it into bundles. The other crops they beat out and put into bundles. Thereupon they cart all to their houses. In the month of Magh (middle of January to middle of February) they harvest the mustard and cut the thatching grass. Now the agricultural work is finished.

Besides all this work the men have all business with the money-lenders, and they pay the rent to the village headman. Men and women help each other to press oil in the oil-press. They do not make oil from the mustard and tilmiń; they sell this. They make oil from several kinds of fruit: kũiṇḍi, baṛu, kujri, bando, boṅga sarjo̱m, eraḍo̱m, lo̱po̱ṅ, ko̱ro̱ńj, nim, and others[5].

[1] Janhe̱ is Paspalum scrobiculatum, L.; bajṛa, Sorghum vulgare, Pers.; ko̱de̱, Eleusine corocana, Gaertn.; raheṛ, Cajanus indicus, Spreng.; ghaṅgra, Dolichos Catjang, Willd.; sutri, Phaseolus calcaratus, Roxb.

[2] Tilmiń, Sesamum indicum, DC.

[3] Ho̱ṛe̱ć, Dolichos biflorus, L. Surguja, Guizotia abyssinica, Cass.

[4] Iṛi, Panicum Crus-galli, L.; gundli, Panicum miliare, Lamarck; ko̱de̱, Eleusine corocana, Gaertn.; erba, Setaria italica, Kunth.

[5] Kũiṇḍi, the fruit of the Mahua tree, Bassia latifolia, Roxb.; baṛu, Schleichera trijuga, L.; kujri, Celastrus paniculatus, Willd.; bando, Spatholobus Roxburghii, Benth.; boṅga sarjo̱m, Ventilago calyculata, Tulasne; eraḍo̱m, Ricinus communis, L.; lo̱po̱ṅ, Terminalia belerica, Roxb.; ko̱ro̱ńj, Pongamia glabra, Vent.; nim, Melia Azadirachta, L.

e. Women's work.

The women are constantly working. Getting up at cock-crow they pound paddy. When day dawns, they plaster the court-yard with cowdung. Thereupon they draw and fetch water. They next give the gruel that is left from the previous day to the men and children. When these have eaten, they themselves take food. Thereupon they make up fire and put the midday meal food on the fire; they cook the rice, make curry; they pin leaf-cups and leaf-plates, ladle out the cooked rice, and when it becomes noon, they give the men and children their midday meal and afterwards eat themselves. From noon to the second time for drawing water (about 5 p. m.) they do different kinds of work, pluck vegetables, fetch leaves, and if they live near a forest, they go to fetch firewood, or they clear out the cotton seed in the cạrkhi[6], they clean the cotton with a bow[7], they make rolls of carded cotton on twigs, they spin on the spinning wheel, they wind the thread on their fingers, that the men may afterwards use it when weaving cloth. When it becomes the second time for drawing water, they go to fetch water, and then make preparations for the evening meal. Some two hours after it has become dark they eat. The women eat after the others. Meat they (i. e., all Santals) eat only now and then, mostly they eat cooked rice with vegetables and split peas. The spices for meat are turmeric, Anis seed, garlic, oil, and salt. The spices for fish are turmeric and mithi[8], and oil and salt; for vegetables and split peas only salt. They talk together about different matters while inside, thereupon they lie down to sleep. At the time of sowing and harvesting the women plant rice, hoe the maize, and when the paddy is ripe, they reap it. At the time of Dasãe they make the house and door smooth: so there, this is the work of the women.

f. Children's work and amusements.

Until they are able to tend cattle, small boys only run about and play. When they become fit for being cattle-herds, they tend cattle, also sheep and goats, together with the other village boys. In the morning they let the cattle out, and they tend them, two or three companions going together. They blow the flute, they hunt birds. At noon they take the cattle to a place where they rest, that they may themselves get food. When they have eaten, they drive the cattle out to graze, and when it becomes evening, they bring the cattle to the village and take them in. At noon grown-up people milk the cows; they give the milk to the children; what is left they keep and add to it day after day and make clarified butter of it. To make clarified butter they boil the milk; having boiled it they let it become curds; these they churn mixed with water; thereupon they skim off the

---

[6] See Dictionary s. v. [7] This bow is now fairly rare. It is made of bamboo; at one end, the end kept in the right hand, it is compact; the rest is split and bent and a catgut string is fixed so as to make it a bow. It is worked putting the bow-string down in the cotton and "playing" this with the thumb and index-finger of the left hand. [8] Trigonella Foenum-Graecum, L.

butter, and melting the butter they make clarified butter. The butter-milk they eat themselves; they also give a share of it to poor people.

Fairly small boys make carts of earth and amuse themselves pulling these round about; they also make small carts of wood for them. They make bows and arrows for them, and they play shooting lizards, grasshoppers and so on with these. When they have become a little more grown up, they play ṭir and kạti[9].

The work of small girls is to carry children on the hip, to pluck vegetables and to help their mother with something or other. When they become fairly big, they fetch water and leaves and do different kinds of work. When they are small girls, they play, pretending to prepare rice and curry from dust; when they have become a little more grown up, they dance the road-dance and they sing a good deal.

Until they grow up, boys and girls play together the following: hedel guḍu, bhela ṭap̔ ṭup̔, sui gutu, bhiṛkạị bhiṛkạị, kanṭhaṛ dare, cạlia̤, simić simić, kul kul, kaera saṛae sapae, tayo tayo, pusi pusi, duṛup̔ teṅgon, jhampa, bet̔ bet̔, šikṛĩć sikṛĩć, sutạm ọrọk̔, hon gujur, kitkitạ, ạitạu pã̤iṭạu, and others[10]

g. The sorrows and pleasures of married people.

Some married people live in great peace. The husband lightens the burdens of his wife, and the wife also does the same for her husband. In the evening husband and wife consult together about their work and business. When there is any need, the husband says to his wife: For the present prepare gruel for us feeling your way; at present it is a time of scarcity. And also the wife says to her husband: Exert yourself to procure foodstuffs for us, it is coming to an end; or, the clothes of the children are being torn, how will you provide them with clothes? or, Our son has grown up, will you not look about to get us a daughter-in-law somewhere? He might perhaps commit some offence somewhere and make it difficult for us; or, The children don't listen to me, when I give them an order, how much must I speak? Scold them, so that they become afraid; or, The children are ill, let some one feel their pulse. Such good married people at once listen to each other's words. They work and get their food with one mind.

But some women are very bad-tempered; they irritate their husband all day long; they nag awfully, they speak angrily, and easily become sulky. The husband has never any peace. He may talk with somebody or other about something; then his wife will at once impute something bad to him. If the husband is a little late coming from somewhere, the woman will get sulky, and if he asks for water or anything, she will at once speak

[9] Ṭir is a small piece of wood, some 15 cm long, thrown by one part and met with a stick in the air by the opposite part. Kạti is a small flat piece of potsherd or of wood used in a pitch and toss game.
[10] The Santals have an astonishingly large number of games, many more than those here mentioned; to describe these would require a separate paper.

angrily to him, she will meet him with abuse: Pour out yourself and gulp it down, did she not give you any? He may be thirsty. She will abuse and scold him, until she makes him angry. Now men cannot take it up with women as regards the mouth; therefore he becomes furious and thrashes her, so that she lies there done for. The woman will howl and abuse him foully: That woman you have, stab your woman! Bring her, let her cook, gnash it both of you, heaps of it; your stomach, is it not expanding? You blind fool, you staring wretch, die like a beast; did you not see me then? Your burst eyes! Were they in your neck? I will not stay here; do you imagine you are the only man existing? And the children howl uproariously; they run out and cry: Come here, Father, come here, Father, he is killing our mother. The village people then come and warn the two; and if such happens often, they fine them after having found out what the fault is. Some women are very lazy and squander everything. Some men also are very bad-tempered; without any reason they beat their wives; they find fault with the food and the work, when it is good; all day long they scowl at their wives, and they speak only roughly and harshly to them. And some men squander everything by beer-drinking. When the man or the woman, or both of them, continue bad in this way they separate, that is to say, some people do; but some people will not separate, because they feel pity for the children. Such people live in great trouble.

h. The sorrows and joys of father, mother, and children.

Parents will not beat their children wantonly, if they do not become angry; and they will rather themselves not take food, but, if there is any food, they will give it to the children. In the presence of the mother the father is unable to beat the children; their mother will protect them. And there is very little done in the way of punishing children; therefore they live as they like. If they do not obey when they have been ordered to do something once or twice, the parents will leave them alone and be done with it. And if they are beaten or the like, the children will run away sulky to relatives. These will not upbraid them and send them home; they let them stay; thereby the children get courage. The parents are forced to go to fetch them, and only by coaxing them are they able to bring them home. Also when grown up, the children will commit faults without fear, because they themselves are not punished; the parents are punished. The Santals have much trouble with their children, because the children are not kept in discipline. So long as they are small or live in the houses of their parents, children will not get what they deserve for their bad behaviour; but in their time they will get full retribution for not having respected their parents. Sometimes when they have become utterly worried, the parents will say to their misbehaving children: You young fellow, or you young girl, when we both are no more, you will not get enough water even to clean yourself, and you will be carried away like a whirlwind.

i. Male and female servants.

People who are short of help in their family take in servants. They ask somebody to find some for them (saying): Find a servant or the like for us somewhere. When they have found some they tell them, saying: At such and such a place I have found that there is one. Then the man who wants a servant, and the one who went to find one, go and bring the young man or the girl, and his or her parents. They give them food and beer; thereupon they talk about the wages, in case of perquisites then of these, in case of money then about this. Male servants get two rupees yearly as wages, and as regards perquisites they will keep for themselves daily one handful of all kinds of agricultural crops, as they are harvested. Servant girls get only one rupee in yearly wages, but as regards harvest perquisites they get the same as male servants. The male servants get a change of clothes for the rainy season, viz., a piece of cloth five cubits long and a loin-strip. When they have worked the full year, they get a loin-cloth, five cubits long and a cotton-shawl of five cubits. At the Sohrae on the day of bathing they get twenty breads; at this time they talk about continuing or leaving. Servant girls get, as a change of clothes for the rainy season, a loin-cloth of three cubits and to carry over the breast and shoulder a piece of cloth, four cubits long. And when they have worked the full year, they get a woman's cloth, ten cubits long, to dress in.

The male servant helps the master, and the servant girl helps the master's wife. If there are no servant girls, the male servant will at cock-crow help the master's wife to pound. A male servant, with whose work and doings the master's wife is pleased, lives in great comfort. But if the master's wife is displeased, then however good the master may be, the male servant will have trouble. His food she will give him stingingly, and she will also worry her husband to make him scold the servant. If the master's wife is pleased with the servant, she will not let him be scolded by her husband. If the master's wife has a grown-up daughter, they may sometimes keep a servant also as a house-son-in-law; but only when the master's wife is pleased; it does not happen because the master says so. If the master's wife is always good, servant girls have great comfort, otherwise they get no end of trouble.

If they take some boy in, only to tend the cattle, they give such a one one rupee the year, and as clothes a loin-cloth, five cubits long, and a cotton shawl, five cubits long, besides food.

When they engage hired workers during the time of agricultural work, whether they are men or women, they give them breakfast, the noon-meal, for the children one portion rice left-over from last evening, and two seers paddy or Indian corn, as wages.

j. Concerning fever and illness.

When husband or wife or the children get fever, they let some one feel the hand (pulse). When he has done this, he says: He is all right; let some medicine be crushed for the ill one, he will get well. Then they say to him: Do, Sir, please you give him medicine. He will then go to the forest, dig up and bring medicine; when he has done this, he pounds it for the patient; the juice he squeezes out into a leaf-cup; he then makes him drink it. He does this for him some three or four days. If the patient does not get well by this, the medicine giver says: By this all people recover; how is it that this one is not recovering; let the reason for this be found out from some one.

Then they get hold of an ojha. He makes divination. The person who wants divination to be made goes to an ojha with oil and Sal-leaves, hands these over to him and says to him: Please, Father, look into these leaves and this oil of mine. The ojha asks him: Who of you is ill? He says: My wife, or my child (as the case may be). The ojha says: What is your name? He tells him this. The ojha then asks him about his village. Having got the name of the village he pours some oil out on one leaf; thereupon he sprinkles the oil on the leaf three times on the ground, naming his patron godling. He then presses a leaf down on the leaf with oil, covering it, and he rubs it, pronouncing an incantation. Thereupon he puts it for a short while down on the ground. Having taken it up from the ground he salutes it, and separating the leaves he looks at it. The person who has caused the divination to be made, asks the ojha: What do you see, Father, disease or a bonga or people? The ojha answers him: So and so bonga of yours is feeling hungry, and some spell of an evil eye is also there. Ojhas will not at once mention witches. If two or three ojhas, of different villages, say the same, then the person believes it and having reached home he pours out water as a libation to the bonga they have named, and says: May he (she) recover; when he (she) has recovered, I shall fill thee, give thee as much as thou canst take.

Thereupon he takes hold of the ojha of the village. He makes divination to catch the bongas of the outskirts. He then says: The evil-eye-bonga is so and so. The man who causes the divination to be made says: Please reconcile him. Now the ojha asks for a little sun-dried rice. He gets this in a leaf. The ojha then makes the patient touch this rice with his left hand, and he exorcizes him (her) with the rice. Thereupon he goes to the end of the homestead field and prickles himself with a thorn in five places on his thigh; he smears the blood on the rice; thereupon he kneads and mixes the blood-smeared rice with the rice in the leaf. Thereupon he sows this out with his left hand to the bonga who has been caught. He now makes an invocation: Beware then, thou so and so, in so and so headman's house thou applied thyself, knocked thyself; to-day I caught thee, grasped thee with my hand like a fish, like a crab; from to-day mayest thou forswear, leave for ever this house; what is ill, what is diseased, may that recover, may it get well; what there is of pain, of suffering, mayest thou fasten, mayest thou make less; like water in a hollowed out hole in a river, in a spring pool, may he become pure, may he become well, Lord, Father my Ṭhạkur.

Thereupon he spreads out (rice) for the bongas of the places along the boundary. He then says to these: Here, O Lords, ye are here in these parts, in stumps and in roots, in water, anywhere, in recesses, in holes, ye who are moving, come near, and ye who do not move, be witnesses from a distance, favour it.

Thereupon he brings roots and crushes them for the patient. If the patient recovers by this, well and good; if not, the ojha says: I am unable to manage it; apply to the village headman and his deputy; somebody, who knows who, are instigating and entering into this.

k. Concerning relatives.

Among the relatives, excepting those of both parents (i. e., of husband and wife), they like those on the wife's side best. For the maternal uncles and their family and for the brothers of the wife husband and wife have much thought. They mostly visit these. When they are visited, they kill a good many fowls and pigs, and they give them much beer and food. And the two themselves also show them much hospitality. They also love and show hospitality to the brothers of the husband or the maternal uncles on the husband's side and their families, but not to such a degree. There is a folk tale: Once, who knows when, they tell, the maternal and paternal uncles of a child had come on a visit and met at the couple's house. When they had had their noon meal, it commenced to threaten to rain. At this time the woman took the child on her hip and fondled it in the court-yard; then she said: In the direction of the home of your maternal uncles, my child, heavy heavy clouds have arisen, it is black there; in the direction of the home of your paternal uncles there is a clear sky. Then the brothers of her husband came out and looked about; there were the same kind of clouds everywhere; consequently it dawned upon them: the wife wants to send us away, so that she may entertain her brothers. Thereupon, pleading something or other as an excuse, they quietly took themselves off; what could they otherwise do? Then her brothers were also on the point of going. But then she says to them: Don't, my elder brothers, go away, there is a pot of weak, weak beer, stay to-day. When it became evening, she poured out beer, and she made her husband kill a pig. She gave them any amount of meat, rice, and beer; they ate and drank abundantly.

The women do not turn their back to the relatives on their husband's side; they keep water for the children (i. e., arrange for their support), in order that when their father is no more, they may teach them to worship the spirits; but they have not much love for them, it is only for the sake of profit.

Every year in the month of Dasãe (Aug.—Sept.) husband and wife go round to visit their relatives, even when they live very far away, in so far as they know of them, provided they have grown-up sons in their home, otherwise only the man will go. The meaning of visiting relatives is this: that they may not be lost to each other.

Any time they are in want of resources, the relatives on the man's side and those on the woman's side will help each other, when they live in harmony with each other, whether it be in connexion with food or with draught-cattle. And when some among the relatives become orphans, or they are in straits, at such times relatives who have the means will take care of them, or they will divide their own land and fields with them. But such people who are rescued from poverty and difficulties, are mostly ungrateful; only a few people show gratitude. If these ungrateful persons put on just a little flesh, they will show you the thumb (defy you), they may let you go adrift. They will say: Do you imagine that you have supported me, until I have become full grown; why, I have been supported by my own strength. At any time when you are in need, they will leave you in the lurch. They grow up, then look, off they are. But such people will some day get their retribution, if not they themselves, then their children.

What women have really to rely on, is their father and male relatives. When husband and wife do not live in harmony, or when the husband worries and beats his wife, or somebody calls her a witch, then she will cry out to her father and male relatives, and they will stand up for her. This is their right, because on the day of her marriage they have stipulated for this. Without informing her father and male relatives they do not go to a witch-finder. And if these are not satisfied with one witch-finder, they will take them to five such places. Because of this the women have great trust in their father and male relatives.

1. When husband or wife dies.

If the mother dies before her children are married, then even if their father has got a second wife, the sons cannot demand a division. But if the sons at that time are married, they can, if they wish, set up separate households. The village council meet and divide the property; the father gets one part, and the sons one part each. In case the second wife has not borne the man a male child before he dies, then after his death the sons of the first wife can take possession also of the part left by the father. If they take possession of this, they will have to perform the final funeral ceremonies for their stepmother, when she dies.

If any woman becomes a widow without having borne any male child, the father or the male relatives of the man get all the property; the woman gets only one calf, one bundle of paddy, one brass-cup and a cloth, and she leaves and goes to the house of her father and brothers. In such a difficult position some people will keep an elder brother's wife; they will not let her go to the home of her father and brothers. Santals call this very good.

A person who keeps his elder brother's wife gets only his own share of the property of his deceased elder brother, he does not get all.

When the widow has daughters, then their grandfather or the elder or younger brothers of their father will take mother and children to themselves and support them, and the property will remain in their hand. When the daughters grow up, they will give them away in marriage, and as they would get presents from their father at the time of marriage, in the same way these also give them, and their mother they will support until she dies. If such a one does not stay there, she will get her customary right like a childless widow and go to her father's or brother's house, or she will go and live with a daughter.

A widow having sons will keep all the property in her hand. The grandfather of the children or the younger and elder brothers of their father have only a right to see that their mother does not squander anything. If the mother marries again before the children are married, their grandfather or the younger or elder brothers of their father will collect the children and all the property, and the mother of the children will by right get nothing. Some people will give her a calf as a present for the sake of a farewell feasting.

The law of inheritance is this: A man's father will get the property of a son. If he is not living, the full brothers of the man will get the property. In case these are not living, that is to say, if they have died, then the sons of these, that is to say, the sons of the man's younger and elder brothers will get it. And when these or sons of these are not living, then the dead man's uncles or their sons will get it. And in case there are no inheritors, the king of the country will get the property.

VI. VILLAGE LIFE

a. Searching for a village site and omens.

The Santals do not build houses for themselves away from others; they build villages, and there they live together in one place. To found a village three to four men will go with a leader and investigate a forest. When they, after having entered the forest, see any of three kinds of quails flying, they say: Some day in the future a village here will be deserted. But if they see these birds sitting quiet on their eggs, or they meet a tiger or see the footmarks of a tiger, they say: Some day in the future we shall become a very populous village and we shall be settled here. Thereupon, continuing to investigate, they select a place of this kind, viz., where there is dry ground, where there will be good highland and homestead fields, where ricefields can be prepared and where water is easily had. They are pleased with what they have seen and return home.

Thereupon they one day go to take omens. They take along with them two white and one speckled fowl, a little sun-dried rice, oil, sindur, and water in a new thin-necked earthenware pot. Where the leader intends to build his house, there he goes in the evening and makes five spots with sindur. Close to the sindur spots they drop some small heaps of sun-dried rice, and beside this they also set down the pot with water. Near this same place they tie the fowls in a row, just so far away that they cannot reach the rice. Thereupon they make an invocation: O Sun god (Siṅ boṅga) in heaven, like a bamboo mat thou art spread, the four corners, the four worlds thou hast covered, and ye, the Five the Six of the earth, in your name, as ye see here, in the virgin soil, the virgin forest we are seeking omens; this ye show to us, the milk as milk, the water as water; having judged, show it to us. Thereupon they go somewhere to spend the night.

Next morning they go there and look. If a big fowl-feather has fallen down, they say about this: A few grown up persons among us will die; and if small feathers have fallen down, they say about this: Children will die here in future. And if no feathers at all have fallen, this is excellent, no one will soon die there. And if the fowls have left droppings round about the place, they say about this: All in the village, well-to-do and poor, we shall support ourselves well. If they have left droppings in a heap in one place, they say about this: The headman alone will become wealthy. And if in two places, they say: The headman and his deputy will become wealthy. And if in three places, then also one of the villagers will become wealthy. In the directions in which the ants have carried off rice, in so many directions it will be necessary to bring up bongas. If the water in the narrow-mouthed pot has dwindled a little, they say about this: A couple of years we shall have a scarcity of water. And if the water has not dwindled at all, they say: We shall not have any scarcity of water. If the fowls have disappeared, if there is no rice, and the water in the narrow-mouthed pot has dried up, they say: This place is ill-fated; and they leave it; they will not found a village there.

But if there are good omens from the fowls, the rice and the water in the narrow-mouthed pot, then they dig a small four-cornered hole. On three sides of this they put the dug-out earth. With this earth they again fill the hole up. If it is filled with the earth on two sides, they say: We shall get full crops here; and if no earth is left (in filling the hole), they say: It is inauspicious here. Thereupon they seek omens in another high place inside the boundary that they have walked up, and in the name of another village headman. They continue to act in this way, until they get full good omens. They ultimately get this.

b. On settling down.

Now one day they return and make a shelter of sticks leaning against each other, for the leader. He, the leader, who is to become the headman of the village, cuts down the first tree. Nowadays, after they have investigated the forest, they ask the landowner for permission; formerly, before landowners made their appearance, there was nothing of this kind.

Together with the leader they now divide between themselves the homestead fields. On their respective homestead fields they each put up a hut for themselves, and each a pen to keep their cattle in. Thereupon they go back to their old homes and call on each other saying: When shall we start? They then take their children and all they possess with them and go to the new village. The time of moving is the months of Phalgun and Chait (middle of Febr. to middle of April). Now all of them clear the jungle for the homestead fields, and the trees they have cut down also serve them for house-timber. Any remaining timber, etc., they burn away. They build houses. Running along the middle of the place they keep a village street, and at the end of this they arrange a sacred grove.

c. Bringing up the bongas in the sacred grove.

To bring the bongas up in the sacred grove they get three to four men who are to become possessed[1]. They come together at the village headman's. The headman pours out water for the persons to be possessed, that they may wash. The men to be possessed then wash their feet and sprinkle water on their head. Thereupon they sit down in a row beside each

[1] See Dictionary s. v. rum.

other. They put a winnowing-fan in front of each of them. Thereupon they give each of them one handful of sun-dried rice in the winnowing-fan. The men who are to be possessed then with the right hand rub the sun-dried rice in the winnowing-fan; now the village people call out: Come, Lords, the Five, the Lady of the sacred grove, the Pargana, Maraṅ buru, Gosãe era, and Mạṅjhi haṛam, we are calling upon ye, invoking ye. Thereupon the four men become possessed and turn their heads violently round. Speaking through the mouth of the possessed men the bongas say sạhạk̓ (it is all right); thereby the village people understand that the bongas have taken possession of the inspired ones.

They then ask them: Now then, adored King, worshipped Lord, the landowners, the Muṇḍas with horses, with umbrellas, to the end of the lowland, to the end of the country they run about, hurry about, the spirits, the mountain spirits, be it five, be it twenty-five, with disciples, with pupils sitting, having seated themselves, in hurry, in haste, calling out, crying, the stone door having been opened, been opened a little, like a cow with calf, like a milch cow they come running, they come in haste: Well then, Lord Father, my Ṭhạkur, the race, the birth, when this is told, is shown, then only we shall know, shall recognize, it is this spirit, this mountain-spirit, then only below the Pipol tree, below the Banyan tree the principal stool, the principal wooden slab to sit on will be placed before him, be spread out before him, then only we shall worship him, pay homage to him[2].

The bongas then reply: Look then, be it five, be it twenty five with disciples, when you sit down with pupils, you have seated yourselves, when you have taken hold of, have seized a Mahle[3] winnowing-fan, when we discovered, found out about the cleaned rice, the mixed rice, like a cow with calf, like a milch cow I came running, I came in haste, what my race, my birth may be, I might show twelve shapes, show twelve meanings, what it is, is fully true, otherwise all is up. Wealthy people, stallions, at the back of the house, in the eaves, gold, silver they bury, put away; for what purpose should I bury, put away my race, my birth; what is, truly with happiness, with easy circumstances I may strengthen, I may apportion, it is fully up. Consequently, whoever I may be, in the Ganges river, in the Soṛa river my race, my birth, I may bathe, may wash my hair, with happiness, with easy circumstances I may strengthen, may apportion, it is fully up. Shopkeepers, pedlars for a seer of paddy, a basket of paddy they sell away, throw down oil, salt; as for me race and birth, whatever it may be, for a seer of paddy, for a basket of paddy I may sell it away, throw it down, with happiness, with easy circumstances I may strengthen, may apportion it, it is fully up. This is well and all. So look out, I am Jahe̜r era (the Lady of the sacred grove).

---

[2] So far as possible a literal translation of the here following invocations and answers is given; they convey very little meaning to the ordinary Santal, if they are at all understood. This, however, is not needed.

[3] i. e., made by a Mahle. The Mahles are workers in bamboo, besides being agriculturists and palanquin bearers.

The village people then say: Greetings, Lord! After this every single bonga, one after the other, speaks the same, only at the end they name their different names.

Thereupon the village people take the rice in the winnowing-fan up in their hands, and handing it into the hands of the possessed ones they say to them: Here then, Lord Father my Ṭhạkur, the broken grain, the rice grain have no eyes, have no ears. Having understood, having satisfied yourselves in your soul, in your breast, in your mind, in your body, tell us, show us, we are blind, ignorant human beings; when we speak, it stops in our throat, we are choked in the words; therefore do not keep it, do not let it stick in your soul, in your breast; in the house of Jolhas[4], in the house of Dhunias[5] stuck thread, stuck cotton is caught up, sticks; like split bamboo, like thread stretched out make ye a way, make ye a road, Lord Father my Ṭhạkur.

The bongas then answer: Look out then, brothers, younger and elder, sitting down, having seated ourselves we have understood, have satisfied ourselves as to water-country, salt-country, for whom it may be, in our souls, in our breasts we may put it, may stick it. Thereupon they say: Well that is all, it is good.

Thereupon the village people say: Please then, Lord, where shall we make a place of worship for ye, make a place for ye to stay? Now the bongas get up and go towards the forest. They find and take along some stones. Having brought them to the place they put them down, as they think well, at the foot of trees, three in a row beside each other at one place, each stone at the foot of a separate tree, one representing the Lady of the sacred grove, one representing the Five, and one Maraṅ buru. Again going to the forest they bring three stones. One representing Gosãe era they put down at the foot of a Mahua tree, one representing the old Pargana they put down at the foot of any tree, and the one representing Mạṅjhi haṛam they bring to the village street and put it down in the street outside the house of the village headman. Here they later on build a structure, the Mạṅjhi than.

They then sit down at the place where they first were. And the village people say: Please, Lord, by whose hand are ye pleased to be worshipped and offered to? Find a priest for yourselves. And they place a loṭa with water in front of them. The bongas then get up. The Lady of the sacred grove takes the loṭa with water, and the bongas call out: Ei (hallo there). Taking this loṭa with water along the bongas choose the priest for themselves among the men. Any one they like, on his head they pour out the water in the loṭa.

Now all the people stand up, and the man they have chosen to be priest puts the bongas (stones) nicely down, one after the other, and he plasters there with cow-dung, and he smears sindur on all the bongas.

Now they are going to restore the possessed bongas to consciousness. The priest gives the rice in the winnowing-fan into the hands of the possessed bongas. Then they say to

---

[4] Mohammedan weavers. [5] Mohammedan cotton-carders.

them: Please, Lords, the promise you gave is a promise, your promise is a golden promise, ours is a skin promise, please give us a hand-given promise, before you leave. A promise given is a promise, a promise of luck and good fortune, may they never become false and worthless. Thereupon the bongas, one after the other, give to the priest the rice they have in their hand. The village people then say: Please, Lords, it has been a long time, and it is very late, the horses, the umbrellas in the Siṅ forest, the Man forest[6], dig and fill their stomach with hasa vegetables, with ḍimbu vegetables[7]. Then the possessed men regain consciousness. The rice mentioned the men who were possessed take. And having reached the village they enter the headman's house, where they give them food. This is the way in which the bongas are brought up in the sacred grove.

d. The assistants of the village headman.

Thereupon all the men come together at the Mạṅjhi (the village headman). He has brewed beer. Now as he deems the men in the village fit, in accordance with this he chooses some to assist him in the village; he appoints them to positions: You become our Paranik, you become our Goḍet. And if there are sufficient people, he will at the same time also appoint a Jọg Mạṅjhi and a Jọg Paranik. And one for whom it is possible to offer his own blood, he will appoint to be Kuḍạm Naeke. He gives them beer; they drink and then gradually go home.

The Mạṅjhi is the head of the village people. All people in the village will have to follow his lead. In ordering and inviting, in calling and restraining, at the namegiving, at the initiating festivals, at marriages, when hunting and chasing, at feasts and festivals, at religious instruction and worship, in connexion with rice and curry, with beer and liquor, with spirits and mountain spirits, in quarrelling and squabbling, in strife and dispute, when there is hunger and thirst, with landlords and money-lenders, when crime and misdeeds occur, in connexion with thefts and stealing, with medicine and witchcraft, with wenches and strumpets, when there is fighting and killing, murder and wickedness, in grief and sorrow, in calamities and dangers, in illness and pain, at dying and falling away, at ceremonies in connexion with death and decease, at cremation and the final funeral ceremonies: in connexion with all this the Mạṅjhi has the responsibility.

The Paranik is the headman's assistant, like a prime minister, and when there is no Mạṅjhi, the Paranik rules the village. If the headman should run away, and there are no sons or male relatives of his, the Paranik becomes Mạṅjhi. Or if the Mạṅjhi dies without having sons, and there also are no male relatives of his in the village, then also the Paranik becomes Mạṅjhi.

---

6 The Siṅ and Man forests seem to have reference to the Singbhum and Manbhum districts to the South-west of the Santal Parganas. Santals have been and are still living in these districts. 7 Hasa is a Ruellia; ḍimbu a creeper.

The Jog Mańjhi is the one in charge of the young men and girls. He has to see to it that no shamelessness shall occur in the village. If anything of this kind occurs and he does not find it out, the village people will tie him with a piece of wood and a halter to a post in the headman's cattle-shed and thrash him, and they will also fine him.

But if the Jog Mańjhi finds out the misbehaviour of any young man and girl, he will seize the young man and give him into the charge of the village council. If the young man agrees in a council meeting to keep the girl as his wife, they will only fine the father of the young man; but if the young man does not assent to marry, the Jog Mańjhi will thrash him in the presence of the village council, so that his skin is torn, and they will fine his father heavily. Some people become utter paupers by again and again paying fines for a son.

During the Sohrae all the young men and girls stay for five days in the house of the Jog Mańjhi, and eat and drink with him, and they also sleep in his house. And if anything should happen, he will have the responsibility.

At the namegiving and social initiating ceremonies and in everything in connexion with marriages the Jog Mańjhi is to the front. And in connexion with the attendance at the worship of the spirits and at religious festivals he is the leader. The Jog Mańjhi gets more beer to drink than all others of the village people.

Formerly the Jog Mańjhis were keeping the young men and girls of the village in very strict order; but nowadays they are very careless. The village girls give them much beer to drink; in this way they treat them with their medicine in order that even if the Jog Mańjhi gets to know something about them he may not reveal it, or, in case they should go astray anyhow, there may not be inflicted too heavy a punishment. The young men also will treat the Jog Mańjhi, when they get an opportunity; and they will also tell him their respective sins. At such a time the Jog Mańjhi will say to them: Walk sensibly here with us; you will have to support them; otherwise I shall flog you white.

The Jog Paranik is the assistant of the Jog Mańjhi, and when there is no Jog Mańjhi there, he will do the Jog Mańjhi's work.

The Godet, by the headman's order, calls the village people together to council meetings. When the spirits are worshipped, he collects the fowls for sacrifice in the village, and if any bundles or the like come to be forwarded, he carries them to the next village. They call the Godet the Big Mańjhi, because his word is more prevalent in the village, he is like the police. The ancestors have said, it is told, that Marań buru was the Godet of Thakur. The Godets are very impetous; they are also very greedy. In many places they have robbed the Mańjhi of his position; they have also become Parganas even. If they become Mańjhi or Pargana, they will not judge righteously; they act covetously. If the Paranik of a village becomes Mańjhi, the Godet by right becomes Paranik.

The Naeke (the village priest) sacrifices to the village bongas, this is his only work.

The Kuḍạm Naeke (the priest of the outskirts) offers his own blood every time the Naeke performs sacrifices, in the name of the Pargana bonga and the bongas along the boundaries. At Janthaṛ (the first fruit offering of the heavy rice) he every year sacrifices a pig to the Pargana bonga, and at that time he also offers his own blood to him and to the bongas along the boundaries. At the hunt he offers to the same, in order that the village people may be fortunate and return well. At this time he makes an invocation: Greetings then, O Pargana, blood offering, pricked out blood is given, is offered to thee for the sake of the hunt, where on the right side or the left side a servant girl or a dog puppy, a lo̱ṭo̱ thorn (a thorny bush), a kaṛke thorn (a pricking bush)[8] may be, in holes and recesses, mayest thou press it down, cover it up. A worn-out winnowing-fan, a ball of cotton thou wilt arrange for us, make security for us, Father my Ṭhạkur, Lord.

e. The division of agricultural land.

When they have appointed the rulers of a new village, then they sit one day and divide the land and homestead fields. They make units. One unit of agricultural land is what is needed for o̱ne plough. Having settled this they fix the rent, and at the same time set aside the land allotted to the offices of Mạńjhi, Paranik, Jo̱g Mạńjhi, Jo̱g Paranik, Goḍet, Naeke, and Kuḍạm Naeke. The Mạńjhi gets four portions, the Paranik gets three portions, the Jo̱g Mạńjhi gets two portions, and the others one portion each as office-land. This they have the use of without paying rent. The Mạńjhi had formerly half a re̱k (unit) following his office. Nowadays some village headmen have very large incomes.

In a new village people plant Horse-radish trees and Pipol trees near their respective houses. They eat the Horse-radish tree vegetables and the Pipol tree they have to get shade, and the Pipol tree, it is said, will be of use also in the next world.

When other people see that they get very good crops in a new village, they also will come and settle down there. The old residents will give them a share, a little of their prepared ricefields and of their highland fields, and the headman will show them fallow land to prepare ricefields. Then the village becomes populous. They work, do their business, they eat and drink, they have dances and games, they enjoy themselves, they live there.

f. Wealthy and poor people.

In the same village it does not go equally well for all there. Some people have both plough-cattle and servants; they are both industrious and also have sense, and they are also very niggardly; such people become wealthy. But some people have, to start with, no plough-cattle; they are also alone; they also suffer a good deal from fever; they have no sense; they are foolish, they are also lazy, they have no children either, and their women-folk waste away all, or they themselves squander all by beer-drinking, or

[8] The lo̱ṭo̱, Randia dumetorum, Lam., and the kaṛke, Briedelia retusa, Sprengel.

they cause themselves to be fined on account of transgressions and thereby become paupers; how should such people become wealthy?

Some people become worn-out by constantly having to pay off the debts of their father; they are unable to raise themselves, they live pressed down under debts; the money-lenders charge an extremely high interest, and they keep accounts unrighteously. If you fall into the hands of a usurer, you will even in three, four generations certainly not be able to pay and free yourself. Your calves and goats, your cows and buffaloes, your kodalis and axes, your paddy and rice they will unjustly take away, and if you forbid them, they will thrash you and strip you.

But if people live along in the Santal country as paupers, while they have the full use of hands and feet, then this is surely mostly due to their own fault. People who have no plough-cattle will easily be able to get hired bullocks at four rupees yearly. And people who have many children are able to exchange service for bullocks. Or they are able to plough by exchange of labour and bullocks. Exchange of labour and bullocks is as follows: A man ploughs two days for the owner and gets breakfast with him, and then he ploughs one day for himself. The exchange of service for bullocks is as follows: A man's son works as servant with the owner of the plough-cattle, and his wages are the hire of a pair of plough-cattle. With the exception of a few landlords they do not take unjust rent. For every unit (rẹk) of land a rent of six or seven rupees has to be paid, and with one unit (rẹk) they earn so much in crops that the landowner gets one seventh part and the farmer six sevenths. And people who have freshly reclaimed land get more. The meaning of freshly reclaimed land is as follows: When they found a village, they will, when four or five years have passed, divide the land into units. So many residents as there are at that time, into so many units they will divide the land, and the landlord will get rent for each (rẹk) unit. At first they have to pay five four-anna bits for each unit. When they have had the use of it for about five years, the landowner will charge more per unit. But it will continue to be the same unit (rẹk), however much fresh ground they break up. When new settlers come, the old settlers will give them about one fourth part of their respective units, and they will divide the rent. Thereupon the old resident and the new resident will, both of them, clear fresh land and make boundaries; this they call khåṛti (freshly reclaiming additional land). However much they may go on reclaiming fresh land, their rent will not be increased thereby; they will only have to pay the rent of the original unit (rẹk). But because they are lazy, some people do not reclaim fresh land; when the landowner raises the rent of people, such ones will feel it heavy, naturally not so those who have reclaimed fresh land.

Lazy people do not work carefully; they plough negligently, as it may go. When such people have just a little, their only interest is to eat and drink and lie down to sleep; they become paupers, what else can happen to them?

One kind of poor people do not become absolute paupers, because when they have no necessary work of their own, they work for wages with wealthy people; thereby they get their subsistence, and people also feel compassion with them. They put their children to work as cattle-herds, or they make them fetch water and leaves, and people give them more than what they have a right to get, and when their children go to glean at harvest time, they leave much for them. People who have no bodily strength they also help in the same way, if they have no relatives who are able to help them. And when orphans have no natural helpers, the village headman and his deputy will take such friendless ones to themselves, and they live in great ease, because no one will be able to snub them calling them orphans. Afterwards when they have grown up, they marry them off. Formerly there were no begging people, and also nowadays only a very few have learnt to beg from the Dekos and walk round in the villages and beg; this they do not call good, and there is no need; because if they have a wish to work, they may easily support themselves in the villages. Halt and lame, blind and not fully developed persons might get gruel, by only watching the houses and doors of people.

Some good people could easily become wealthy; they have plough-cattle, they also have working people; but from fear of people they do not become very wealthy. They earn only just as much as to get food. Some women, it is said, are very envious of wealthy people; they say: These have very fine things to eat and drink; we have nothing. Then they cast an evil spell on them; then these wealthy people become ill, they become utter paupers, and they die. And such women also bury bongas in the house of wealthy people, so that these die thereby.

g. Mutual help in the village.

Formerly people who were not poor also helped each other very much, when there was any need; and nowadays also good people help each other. They ask each other for fire, they give each other lime and tobacco to chew; kodalis and forks, axes and adzes, chisels and mallets, ploughs and clod-crushers, pestles and wooden mortars, winnowing-fans and baskets, and so on, they lend to each other. And if a man has no cart, or he has too few, the village people will without taking any pay let him have cart and bullocks for one day. But if any of the bullock-owner's people go along to drive the cart, the man who has asked for the loan will have to give rice and curry. And also when building a house, when ploughing, planting, making ricefield ridges, and harvesting they help each other, and those who ask for help have only to give rice and curry, and occasionally they also give them beer to make them glad. And in fever and illness they visit each other, they help each other to pass the night, and when there is any necessity, they also help each other fetching water and leaves, plastering the court-yard with cow-dung and pounding, and men who know to give medicine do this without any charge. They get food, and when the patients recover, they entertain the medicine givers. Since the time of the Santal rebellion they are not helping each other so much. However much they may have, some people are so stingy, they will absolutely not give anything, they utterly refuse to help. But no one likes such heartless people, and if they themselves fall into difficulties, no one will look at them; they rather say: Ṭhạkur is punishing this man in retribution.

Paddy and rice, salt and oil, money they also lend each other without any interest, but not for a long time. If they take this for a long time, we call it a debt, and in this case interest has to be paid. For paddy to be used as food 50 pct. interest, for paddy for seed 100 pct. interest, and for money 25 pct. interest has to be paid.

h. Working in company with others.

The Santals, men and women, very much like to work in company with others. When men go to the forest or to some hill to cut wood for a plough, a plough-beam, a yoke, rafters, firewood, posts, roof-beams, cross-beams, and so on, then they go in company. To enter a forest alone is very dangerous, and when you have companions, the work is not so strenuous. Also when going to the landlord or to a money-lender, they help each other, and at harvest time they make their threshing-floors together at the same place, in order that they may not be alone at night, and the work also goes easily in this way. Cattle-herd boys mostly herd in company, three or four of them together; by turns they drive the cattle round about, and when there is any danger, they help each other. The women also, when they go to draw water, or go to pluck vegetables and bring leaves, or when they go to a market or a shop to sell or buy, then they go in company with others.

i. Looking people up for a talk.

When they have no work the village people go and look each other up a good deal. The men go about on the pretext of asking for lime and tobacco; they chew the tobacco, and also talk together about their health and circumstances and so on. In the evening they come together at the Mạṅjhi than; they start some humorous conversation, they jest together and talk together without restraint about a thousand matters, to ease their mind. The women also visit each other on the pretext of asking for fire or something; but they mostly have their deliberations at the place where they draw water. There they tell each other their troubles and joys and anything happening in the village. But some women do not, like the men, talk what is blameless; their words may be aggravating, and therefore very noisy quarrels sometimes arise.

j. Concerning relationship.

The Santals have really two kinds of relationship, relationship by birth and relationship brought about by marriage. But besides these two kinds the Santals arrange village relationship without there being any real relationship. Some people arrange a relationship in accordance with that by birth, and others do the same in accordance with relationship by marriage, without being really related. The village (artificial) relationship is only meant for behaviour and paying respect to one another. Santals address each other in accordance with the relationship they stand in to each other. In certain kinds of relationship you say "thou" to one person, in certain kinds you say "you two" to one person, and in certain kinds you say "you" (plural) to one person.

Husband and wife, parents and children, brothers and sisters, father's elder brother and his wife on one side and nephew and niece on the other side, sons and daughters of brothers, father's sister and her husband on one side and her brother's children or her husband's nephews and nieces on the other side, the sons and daughters of a man and of his sister, father's younger brother and his wife on one side and their nephews and nieces on the other side, maternal uncle and paternal aunt on one side and their nephews and nieces on the other side, brothers of the wives of maternal and paternal uncles, children of sisters, a man's wife and his younger brothers, a man and his wife's younger brother or sister, grandparents and grandchildren, all these address each other using "thou".

Father-in-law and mother-in-law on one side and son-in-law and daughter-in-law on the other side, father-in-law's elder brother and his wife or mother-in-law's elder sister on one side and son-in-law or daughter-in-law on the other side, father-in-law's younger brother and his wife and mother-in-law's younger sister on one side and son-in-law or daughter-in-law on the other side, the brothers and sisters of the mother-in-law, brother's wife on the one side and son-in-law and daughter-in-law on the other side, elder brother of husband or wife on one side and younger sister's husband or younger brother's wife on the other, husband's or wife's elder sister on one side and younger sister's husband or younger brother's wife on the other side: all these address each other saying "you two" when they speak to one person.

The parents of married pairs with their brothers and sisters on both sides, these are all co-parents-in-law, and when they address each other, speaking to only one person they say "you" to him or her.

The relative whom you address saying "thou" will use "I" of himself or herself; the one whom you address saying "you two" will say "we two" (using the exclusive dual) of himself or herself; and the one whom you address saying "you" will speaking of himself or herself say "we" (both you and I and they and I).

When they say "you two" to one person, they include his wife or her husband; and when they say "you" to one person they include the two married children. And when they answer they in the same way also include those mentioned, without these being present. This is a greatly honouring behaviour.

k. Concerning mutual behaviour and respect.

At the time when we were boys, all members of a family living in the same village greeted each other in the morning, as soon as they got up, and the people in the village also greeted each other when they met, and when members of a family go anywhere on a visit or come back, then also they greet each other. And when the young people of a village go to attend a festival, they bow to the Mạṅjhi haṛam and Mạṅjhi buḍhi (the village headman and his wife), when they leave. In the house the master and his wife once daily are sure to kiss their sons and daughters-in-law, big or small. The young men and girls all honour the old men and ladies much. What these say to instruct or exhort them, this they fix in their mind. They are not impudent towards old men and women; in their presence they do not sit down on a bedstead even; young men and girls do not drink beer or liquor; the young men do not go to a place where an ox is eaten either. Women pay much heed to what the men say; they do not let their hair down in the presence of men. The village people honour the village headman and his deputy much, and these two also do not neglect what the village people say.

Nowadays the age has been spoilt. The women do not honour the men; the sons do not respect their old fathers either; daughters are also very impudent towards their mothers; they do not greet each other either; they pass each other like animals; the young men and girls drink an awful amount of beer; when old men come, they do not get up either; when old men or the parents upbraid them, the young men and girls answer back, or they run away in the sulks, and only when coaxed a good deal, will they come back home. The women and the children have become the kings in this age. Some few people are good even at the present time; but most people have become bad. The village headmen also judge covetously (taking bribes), and the village people do not follow the headman's order either. Also co-parents-in-law are quarrelling a good deal in the present age; formerly they never quarrelled, they were very respectful towards each other. The ancestors said: "Rice like flowers, curry like fish, liquor like fire, and a friend like a co-parent-in-law, where will you find such a one?"

l. Concerning friendship.

Living in the same village all are relatives, quite so; but there is not friendship with all there. In a village many people are on friendly terms with each other, and some people also are on good terms with each other, but friendship they have only with one or two others, and intimate friendship they have only one with one other, and this is very rarely found. Intimate friends will give even their life to help each other in calamity and danger. People who are intimate friends tell each other the sorrows and joys of their heart, and in all matters they help each other, when there is any necessity. In the village elderly men also become intimate friends, and also elderly women; but the time for becoming intimate friends is really when men and women are young.

Cattle-herd boys become great comrades, and mostly at this time intimate friendship between them is established. Those among the comrades whose hearts are especially bound together, become intimate friends; they stay together, they blow the flute, they kill birds, hares, and peafowls; they sing, they drive the cattle about by turns, and they help each other when there is any danger. They eat rice from the same leaf-plate, and when they kill birds or anything they divide and eat them. When they kill a hare, they give the killer the hind half. Persons who have become intimate friends in their boyhood, do not forget each other even when they have grown old, they remain friends all life long. When they, after having lost sight of each other, meet again long afterwards, they become very glad; they kiss each other.

Girls also become intimate friends in the same way, and it lasts all life long with them. Instead of the fellowship of the boys girls become what is called karam-branch friends. If the hearts of two girls have been bound fast together, they will at a karam festival[9] take two leaves of a branch and put these upon each other's head and thereupon salute all the people there. Afterwards they give the village people beer and food. These two do not address each other using their names, but address each other saying "karam branch". Young men and girls do not become intimate friends, except in connexion with marriage.

Nowadays the intimacy of former days is being lost; the mind of the people is going to the bad. People mostly look out for their own happiness, let other people have whatever may happen.

m. Sticking together of the village people.

The Santals consider it an honour when their village is honoured, and they feel it a dishonour when their village is dishonoured; therefore if some one in their village gets into a quarrel with people of another village, then the whole village stands up for him. And if they hear any disgraceful statement concerning their own village, they apply to the headman of their village; thereupon they all, the village headman included, seize such people and say to them: Prove to us what you have spoken about us; otherwise we are not letting you off If they are unable to substantiate it, they fine them very heavily. If any village has become famed, then the people of this village, when meeting with the people of the country in connexion with any matter, feel themselves high like hills; they take pride in the reputation of their village, even when they themselves are fools.

---

[9] The karam is a large forest tree, Adina cordifolia H. f. & B.- The karam festivals will be described later on.

n. About pride.

Sensible people do not feel proud. Only stupid people swell up like frogs; all feel disgust for such people. People who were paupers and have become a little well-to-do, or who have acquired a position for themselves by dishonest means, the conceit of such people quickly rises up. People say: "If a servant girl becomes the wife of the village headman, and a servant becomes an overchief, their conceit will not go even on twelve carts". This has been seen from time to time. A few Goḍet men have in the country deprived village headmen or overchiefs of their position; these mostly swell like boils; among them some are utterly covetous, and their women also scoff at poor people.

Thinking they look nice some girls let themselves be praised like a Paradise Flycatcher bird, although they are looking like an owl; they are giving themselves airs.

o. About mocking people.

Santals cannot endure mocking; it pains them very much, and it makes them awfully angry. They will rather stand upbraiding and rebuking words; mocking words they feel itching like the etka[10]. Men do not mock much; women speak vituperatingly to give people pain; they speak very irritatingly, they may make you vexed. Through women's mocking much quarrelling is caused, and thereby people are separated, they are even divorced.

p. About getting angry and sulky.

Santals do not, like the Dekos and the Turks, become quickly angry; still they become angry when they are much hurt. The men especially get angry, and at such times they are quick to strike; the women become sulky; they quickly become cross and sullen. If you ask them anything at such time, they snarl, and when you say anything to them, they snap at you, as if they were burning you with a nettle. Both elderly women and girls are such. The anger of men is easily appeased; but the sulkiness of women is assuaged only when you coax them a good deal; therefore the women break people in, without needing a training yoke.

q. About passionate and irascible speech.

Some men are, when angry, unable to restrain their rage; therefore when people say something to them, they speak passionately to them; but when a woman has become sulky, she will speak irascibly to you, even when you talk friendly to her. The passionate word of a man will glance off like a blunt arrow with a bamboo head; but the rage of a woman is as when your shoulder-blade is shot through with an iron arrowhead.

---

10 Mucuna pruriens, DC., has hairs that cause an unbearable itching.

r. About harbouring suspicion.

Formerly we had it very strict orderly, and the Santals also had a healthy fear of what is right; therefore men did not look at another man's wife. If they seduced the wife of another man, the woman's husband would cut them down; therefore there was no need of being suspicious. But nowadays there is no strict order; to cut people down they have also given up, and the Santals are also becoming very licentious; therefore people have no feeling of security; men and women suspect each other; there is no happiness at home. Nowadays they are also suspicious without cause, mostly so the women. As soon as a man looks at a girl or a married woman, his wife will at once accuse him; in this way much quarrel arises, and on account of this they also beat each other a good deal. Worried by the woman good husbands have also, in anger, got themselves co-wives.

s. About envy, and malice.

From olden times the Santals have been envying each other; but nowadays it is becoming more common. Men do not harbour much envy; mostly when in their youth some girl, being unwilling to agree to them, is married to some other young man, then they feel envy. Women are awfully envious. When they see others better off than themselves, they envy these; they feel envy towards those whom they suspect. They are envious towards those who look nicer than themselves; against men who will not marry them, they feel malice, and because of this malice they learn witchcraft and "eat" them, or if they do not "eat" them, they will "eat" the girl whom they are going to marry, and the envy of the wives of brothers destroys and maimes like leprosy. Half of the mutual complaints and fining that we have, have their origin in envy and malice, because the women do not only feel envy; they "eat", and they also set their husbands and relatives aflame by their talk; and the whole village is reduced to ashes.

t. About hating and taking revenge.

Santals do not much harbour hate; rather they get angry and furious; such anger will not, however, last a long time.

People who hate do not let their inner anger show; rather they speak sweetly to you; still they will not leave you, until they have done for you. Women especially harbour hate; like the fire in a warming-pan their mind is burning smouldering; and only when they get revenge, then only their mind cools down. Like snakes they bite when it is dark; you will never know anything, until the poison has taken effect in you.

u. About buying and selling.

In a former age there was no money, it is told, neither was there any buying and selling. All necessaries they were earning or making. For cooked food they had the millets iṛi, gundli, layo, erba, and janhe̱, further maize, bajṛa, and paddy, and for curry the beans hoṛeć, raheṛ, ghaṅgra, sutri; further alpalua, vegetables, fowls, pigs, goats, hares, peafowls, the Indian Gaur, the Sambar Stag, birds, and the winged creation. And salt they were preparing from saline earth. They scrape off and bring some earth, mix it up in an earthenware pot and strain it with water; they boil the water, and when the water evaporates, the salt comes there. Because it is very pungent, they cover it up in a cloth and bury it in hot ashes; then it becomes tasty salt. They were preparing this during the cold season. Oil they were pressing out of different forest fruits; they were weaving clothes for themselves. People of the Ṭuḍu sept were making all kinds of implements of iron; and they were themselves making winnowing-fans and baskets, earthenware vessels, and so on. Whether we formerly had gold or not, we do not know; but in the old country they called gold samanom. Later on people of the Baske sept were transacting business, buying and selling by barter, and since rupees and pice have appeared, we buy and sell using money. Formerly also the village people were bartering, some bartered buffaloes for goats, some goats for pigs, and so on.

Nowadays people of both sexes have become very lazy; they do not press oil, neither do they prepare salt; they do not much weave cloth either; they buy everything; thereby we Santals are becoming poor, and we are becoming deeply involved in debt to the money-lenders.

v. About debts and loans.

In former times no people were getting into debt or taking loans from the money-lenders; and there were no money-lenders either. In the Sikhar country the money-lenders found us for the first time. There the first money-lender with the Santals lived in Nanduaṛa. From that time up to now we are in their hands, and they are tearing us up like vultures. By constantly paying we become numb; still the debt never comes to an end. They say: "If a seer has come into the house, it will never get out again"; "a Deko usurer, an old hyena, even old bones they crunch". Really it was also due to hardship in connexion with these that we ran away from Sikhar. At first they did not unrighteously charge us interest to such a degree; they were taking only 25 pct., in paddy or money; but gradually they commenced to charge exorbitantly. For a debt of three or four rupees they would without justice or reason drive pair after pair of plough-cattle away, and if you remonstrated with them, they would at once commence to strike.

But there is fault also on our side. Foolishly the Santals run into the hands of the usurers; whether they will be able to pay back or not, this they do not think of, and when they have what is needed to pay with, they will not pay at once; consequently interest upon interest is heaped up; thereupon the money-lender comes and carries all and everything away. And in the present age many Santals also deceitfully cheat the usurers and money-lenders of what is their right.

VII. CONCERNING PLEASURE AND JOY

To forget care and anxiety we have pleasure and joy: Dancing, singing, drumming the dancing-drum and the kettle-drum, blowing the flute and the horn, playing the fiddle, folk-tales, stories and conundrums, hunting in the forest, catching fish, and beer drinking. Also metaphorical speech will bring pleasure; but this is to tutor people, we use it mostly in connexion with serious work.

a. Singing and dancing.

We have very many kinds of dances, and in connexion with the separate dances we also have songs. In connexion with dancing and singing we drum the dancing-drum and the kettle-drum, and we blow the flute. The names of our dances and songs are the following: lagṛẽ, dọṅ, guluạri, ḍahar, baha, riṅjạ, bhinsạr, jhikạ, humṭi, guṅjạr, sọhrae, lọbọe, and duṅgeṛ. Dances without songs: the sword dance, the Dom dance, and lạuṛiạ. And songs without dancing are: forest songs, marriage recitation songs, folk-tale songs, rice-planting songs, and dirges. We blow the horn, for pleasure, at the Flower festival and during the hunt without any dancing. We play the fiddle with all songs. We make the flutes of hollow bamboo, called bar laṅga bamboo. The horn we make of the buffalo-cow's horn and of the horn of the buffalo, and also of the horn of the Black Buck. The fiddle they make of wood or of a pumpkin shell, and on this they put a string of catgut, only one, and having strung horse-tail hair on a bow they fiddle; on the hair of the fiddle bow they apply salga[1] raisin; then only it sounds. The kettle-drum they make of an iron frame which they cover with buffalo skin. The dancing-drum they make with a cylindrical earthenware frame and cover it with skin of goats, etc.

Lagṛẽ, guluạri, and humṭi they dance at any time, the flower dance only at the Flower festival; the sọhrae, matwar, and guṅjạr dances they dance at the Sohrae festival; riṅjạ and bhinsạr they dance at the Karam festival; dọṅ they dance at marriages and at the Chạṭiạr festivals; ḍahar they dance during the hot season, only girls; jhikạ they dance at the Chạṭiạr, the Dom dance at marriages; and pạk dọn (the sword dance) and lạuṛiạ they dance at Sohrae and Sakrat, men only; lọbọe they dance at the Durga festival, and duṅgeṛ they dance when they spend the night at the

[1] Boswellia thurifera, Colebroke.

hunt. The rice-planting songs they sing when planting rice in the rice-fields, without dancing; the folk-tale songs they sing sitting down during the hot season in the evening; and the forest songs young men and girls sing in the forest, and also during the Sohrae, metaphorically. Dirges they sing at the final funeral ceremonies; these they also call "crying songs".

Except in the sword dance, the lạuṛiạ, and ḍahar (road) dances girls and young men dance together in all dances. When dancing the girls take hold of each other's hands and the young men dance in front of and opposite to the girls, without taking hold of each other. Some young men will dance themselves alone while drumming the kettle-drum; some young men will, while drumming the dancing-drum, dance together with those who drum the kettle-drum; some young men blow the flute and dance at the same time and some young men only dance, and they sing together with the girls. Young men and girls enjoy dancing very much; they dance the whole night, and during day-time they work; still because of their joy they do not feel tired. The old men and women do not warn the young people not to dance, rather they go to look at them, and when they feel drowsy and go home, they say to the young people, as they leave: Do stop now, otherwise you will be drowsy when you have to work to-morrow. The young people answer them: Well, we are stopping presently. Still they continue dancing, until they are done for. While they are dancing the Jog Mạṅjhi does not stay there either, the young people are there alone right up to the end. Having danced until cock-crow they lie down just a little.

Elderly men and women do not dance the lagṛẽ much, only now and then for a short while; but during the Chạṭiạr, the Flower and the Karam festivals they dance. Any one who knows the jhikạ, starts this, and they dance slowly and sing.

b. Beer drinking.

The real joy of old men is in the beer. When they have drunk themselves jolly tipsy, they start a thousand things, about the old country, about landlords and usurers, about dancing, singing and whatever it may be; then they laugh, they are rejoicing, they feel exceedingly well. If they become drunk, they lie down and sleep, and there is an end of their joy. Elderly women also drink a good deal. Formerly elderly women did not drink much, and young men and girls not at all. Nowadays all Santals drink very much, a great shame. Formerly no one drank from a brass-cup; they used leaf-cups; nowadays they pour brass-cup after brass-cup down; still they are not satisfied. Formerly they did not drink Suṇḍi[2] beer, only now and then they would drink liquor. Nowadays many Santals are becoming paupers by drinking Suṇḍi beer. If they have no money they take paddy

---

[2] Low-caste Hindus, who brew beer, distill liquor, and sell it.

or rice along with them, so that there is no food at home; in spite of this when they come home and no food has been prepared for them, they scold their wives a good deal and even beat them. The poor wife, where is she to get anything with which to prepare food? If they have no paddy or rice, they will drink, making debts. Then in the month of Magh (middle of January to middle of February) the Suṇḍi comes, harasses and threatens them, and carts their paddy bundles away. The wife and children of such a man pass their time in much suffering, as regards food and clothes. From the forest they bring vegetables and different kinds of tubers, cook and eat these. Formerly they were drinking four, or six, or if it became very much, eight leaf-cups; in this way their strength was not diminished; they were very strong and vigorous like youths. Nowadays, by constantly drinking and by marrying before they are fullgrown, they are becoming puny and stunted in growth; by behaving in such a way, — how should they retain their strength?

c. Stories and folk-tales.

By fairy-stories, folk-tales, and conundrums the Santals feel much enjoyment. In the evening the old men teach them this. The sons and daughters-in-law are occupied in the evening cooking rice and curry, making leaf-cups and leaf-plates, and the old people, husband and wife, tell the children fairy-stories and folk-tales and ask them riddles, to make them happy. If anyone knows a number of fairy-stories and folk-tales, the young people of the village will also gather at his place. And at the threshing-floors, when it is cold and they lie in the huts there, the young men learn much of this. Some people know so many; they tell the others folk-tales the whole night until dawn, still they are not finished, and those who listen do not get tired either; at such times they have no thought at all of dancing; listening they are utterly charmed by joy[3].

Girls and boys mostly learn riddles, and all day long they ask each other such. The young men learn more fairy-stories and folk-tales; even if girls learn the same, they will only get enough courage to let this be known in the presence of people when they have reached the age of old women. The folk-tales are especially about jackals; the fairy-stories are about kings and landlords and about different kinds of people, and the riddles are about a thousand different matters. When they start a riddle, they say: "A riddle, kite, kite", thereupon they give out the riddle[4].

---

[3] The Santals have a very large number of folk-tales and stories. The present writer has collected several hundreds. Ten such tales have been published in the Publications of the Indian Institute of the Royal Frederik University, Kristiania 1924, and 93 other tales by Instituttet for Sammenlignende Kulturforskning (Santal Folk Tales, vol. I to III, Oslo 1925, 1927, and 1929). A few have also been published in a similar way by the Asiatic Society of Bengal, Calcutta. The manuscript of several hundreds, all written down for me by Santal men and women, is now in the University Library, Oslo.

[4] See P. O. Bodding, Santal Riddles. Witchcraft among the Santals. Oslo Etnografiske Museums Skrifter, vol. 3, fasc. 5. Oslo 1940.

d. Mimicking.

We have something to make people in a way enjoy themselves, this is the game of mimicking. Only jocular people can perform this. Seeing this, people laugh awfully. In this game they show the faults of people by mimicking, e. g., how husband and wife act towards each other when in the sulks, how husband and wife go to her father's house, the sham crying of widows, the way of walking, dancing, eating, working, married people's behaviour, and so on. When they mimic women, they put on clothes like a woman, and making their voice sound like theirs they give themselves airs, and the people laugh, holding their stomachs.

e. Catching fish.

Catching fish is also joyful work. They catch fish in ricefield ponds, in dams, and in rivers. The headman of the village inside the boundaries of which the place for catching fish lies, makes a public announcement. About noon on the day fixed, the people of the neighbourhood gather there. If there is any impediment in connexion with the bongas, they make a sacrifice; thereupon they catch fish with nets. Some people also catch with their hands; they start a tremendous noise; they enjoy themselves greatly. When they have done catching, they collect the small fish in the different nets, and if there are big fishes, they cut them into pieces; thereupon they collect half of the big fishes from every net, and all these the people of the village get. They make three portions of these. They give one portion to the owner of the ricefield pond or the dam, and two portions the people of the village divide among themselves. If the catching is in a river, the village headman of the boundary gets one portion, and if it is within the boundaries of two villages, the headmen of the two villages get one portion, divided into equal half-portions, and the remaining two portions the people of the two villages get. We have a special way of killing fish; this they call fish-poisoning. They bring different kinds of roots and stuff from the forest and crush this and throw it into the water. Then the fishes become intoxicated, and some of them die and float up. Then they are easily caught. The names of the poisons are: the root of the stemless Date, the fruit of corco, jīoti grass, the bark of kumbiṛ, the bark of sạkṛi phǫl, the fruit of lǫṭǫ, and others. This we call haṛ (fish-poison)[5].

Concerning our every day catching of fish we act as follows: A couple of men invite each other to come along, and baling out the water in a ravine or the pool of a ricefield they catch the fish. During the rainy season we make weir-baskets and set them during the night in a ricefield or a river. Fishes are caught in this, and in the morning we shake them out and bring them.

---

[5] Of the poisons mentioned, the stemless Date is the Phoenix acaulis, Roxb.; corco is the Casearia tomentosa, Roxb.; jīoti is a grass growing in ricefields and moist places; kumbiṛ is Careya arborea, Roxb.; sạkṛi phǫl is a tree, sometimes planted by the Paharias; lǫṭǫ is Randia dumetorum, Lam.

f. Hunting.

The great joy of us men is the hunt. From olden times we have continually been hunting, and in however great a danger we may fall, still we do not give up hunting. And if a person will not go, we despise such people and call them women. Our ancestors have fought tigers and bears with great courage; sometimes the tigers and bears have gained the upper hand, and sometimes the men, and so it is going on until the present day.

In former times they used to announce the hunt by sènding a branch from village to village, by stages; but since our stay in Sikhar we notify the day at the Pata (the hook-swinging festival)[6]. As there is a village priest and a priest of the outskirts in the village, there is similarly a dihri (hunt-priest) for the hunt. There is one hunt-priest for every single country. He carries the branch round at the Pata; the people of the country then ask him: In connexion with what is your branch, Sir? He then tells them the name of the forest: In such and such a forest, on such and such a day, at such and such a place we shall meet. He also tells them where they will spend the night. When we come home, we men in the village tell each other the news, saying: At such and such a date they are to hunt through such and such a forest or over such and such a hill. The men of the village then get their different hunting implements together, they string their bows, fix the iron arrow-heads and the blunt arrow-heads in the arrows, they grind the iron arrow-heads and make them sharp-pointed, they grind their battle-axes sharp and give them a handle; they put the spear-heads on the shafts, and the swords they polish bright. They tell the women to prepare dough-balls of Mahua for food, and they make them pound rice to have to take along with them. The village headman has to give five half-seers of rice and one small bundle of Mahua as hunt-bounty. This the hunting men eat, or if some poor men have nothing, they let them have a sufficiency of this. The village priest sacrifices five fowls for the sake of the hunt.

When the fixed day is reached, a couple of men go at cock-crow in advance out to an open plain to bring the whole male village population together there; they also take kettle-drums and flutes and horns along with them; and until the village men have all come out, they beat the kettle-drums rat-a-tat, blow the flute harmoniously, and blow the horns tootingly, and they sing any amount of forest songs sweetly. When they have all assembled, they shout with one voice together; thereupon they go to the place where they are to meet. Here they eat their noon meal. One after the other the people of the country come and assemble there; the hunt-priest has been there from cock-crow.

Until the people of the country arrive, the hunt-priest makes a divination about good or bad happenings. If he gets anything bad in any direction, he calls the country people

---

6 The Pata should be held on the last day of Cạt, about the 15th of April; among the people living in the Santal Parganas it may be held any day during Bạisạk (middle of April to middle of May). The dihri has a Sal-branch with as many leaves as there are days remaining before the hunt is to take place.

together and summons the people of that locality. He asks them: From what villages of such and such a locality have you come? They then one after the other mention their villages to him. Thereupon he makes divination in oil for these different villages. If he gets proof for any village that a tiger will eat them, he tells them this. He says to them: Do make your arrangements, or go home. They answer him: Please, Sir, you make arrangements for us.

The hunt-priest then selects the men the tiger will eat. He removes the occult influence in their name by offering a fowl. At this time he makes an invocation: Be greeted then, thou Day-spirit of the heaven, thou art spread like a mat, thou art covered up like a kiạ[7], the four parts, the four worlds thou hast covered; now then a widow, a woman of ill omen has decreed, has ordained a death; she who has destined for destruction, has shut up for dying, may a tiger eat her eldest son. And these men who have been destined for destruction, have been shut up for dying, guide them out, follow them out from my forest, Father my Ṭhạkur.

Thereupon the hunt-priest sacrifices five fowls, one fowl he sacrifices to the hunt-priest bonga and four fowls to the bongas of the forest. After this he pricks himself and lets the blood run down on some rice, and this rice he offers to the bongas of the forest. He then cooks the flesh of the fowls together with rice. As many villages there are from which fowls have come, for all these he divides the hash, that is to say, of the sacrificed five fowls. Of the remaining fowls the hunt-priest sacrifices some in any place, where there may be a hindrance in the forest, making the country people stop and stand there. The hunt-priest will not let the country people pass along until he has made a sacrifice, in a place where there is a hindrance.

After all the men have had food, the hunt-priest tells them where water is to be found. But he himself does not eat until blood has been shed; only when the country people have shot an animal with an arrow and caused blood to drop, then only he may take food. When the hunt-priest performs a sacrifice they hobble him with a rope made of the off-stripped saplings of the Sal-tree, and with a hat of leaves they cover him from the top of his head to his eyes and blindfold him. The country people treat the hunt-priest in this way, in order that the animals may not see and not be able to run away. When the hunt-priest has finished the sacrifice, he rolls himself on the ground, and a couple of men press him down, and some of them pretend to cut him with a battle-axe with leaves. At this time they say: The forequarter, fellows, the forequarter, fellows! A big buffalo has fallen! Then he is loosened. In every place where the hunt-priest performs a sacrifice, they handle him in the same way. If, even after they have sacrificed in this way, tigers or bears eat any of the country-people, they scold him awfully; they brandish battle-axes and

---

7 Pandanus odoratissimus, Willd.

sticks against him and say: Cut him, fellows, kick him, fellows! he has enticed us here to let the people of the country-side be eaten. And the hunt-priest puts his tail between his legs, what can he say, poor fellow?

After he has performed the sacrifices and they have had food, the crowd enters the forest, led by the hunt-priest. Some men go quietly in advance without drumming the kettle-drum, to lie in wait, and some men also hunt quietly along up to the end of the forest; and they lie in wait at the end of the forest, in order that, when the country people host reach there, the animals may not run across to some other forest or to the open plain. Having entered the forest the host spreads itself over the whole, in a line, on both sides; they keep each one kettle-drum, and in the middle they leave some place as they go along. The drummers make a tremendous noise, and the host passes along peeping everywhere.

When they hit upon a hare, a peafowl, or any kind of bird, they shout, mentioning the name of the animal or bird, and when they hit upon a big animal, they shout, mentioning the name of their village. If they kill animals, the people of the country-side cut off for themselves the forequarter and the neck-part. If it is a big animal, they cut off one foreleg with the shoulder, and the neck-part they cut into pieces. The men who are together there divide the meat of the forequarter and neck-part between themselves, and of the neck-part meat they cut off about four fingers' breadth and give to the hunt-priest. Of hares, peafowls, and birds they cut off only one leg of each, that is to say one foreleg of each animal. Of these the hunt-priest gets nothing.

If any one hits a deer with his arrow, they put down a leaf and press it down with a stone there on the foot-mark of the deer, and continuing to shout they follow the tracks assiduously, until the deer falls down. When the deer has fallen, the men who are there cut off the forequarter and the neck-part, after having investigated the case. The forequarter, in which there is the mark of the arrow, they do not cut off. If a man only hits an animal with his arrow, and some other man shoots and kills the animal, then the man who shot and killed the animal gets the forequarter part for killing, and the man who first hit it gets the deer. Also in this case the people of the country-side get a forequarter and a neck-part.

When the men catch sight of tigers or bears, they inform each other loudly, and if they bite anyone in passing, then a drummer who is near by, will drum the alarm three times; then the people of the country-side on the right and left side know that a calamity has happened; therefore they who are near come together running. They apply medicine to the man bitten. Then they hunt along. Now and then when they meet bears, and on account of the multitude of people there are unable to shoot them, they beat them with sticks, so that they fall down. Sometimes they kill them, and sometimes, when a bear is unable to stand any more, he will get up and run away howling right through the people. When they beat bears, these sometimes forcibly take the stick. When a tiger bites people, mostly brothers and intimate friends will, risking their life, try to rescue each other; they will either rescue the man, or they will all let themselves be eaten. Nowadays people have become very cowardly; as soon as they hear the word "a tiger, a tiger", they run away, with their loin-strip hanging down in their hand.

When it becomes evening, they come out from the forest and go to the place where they are to spend the night. When they have come together, the men of every individual village collect in one place the Mahua-dough or the flour, and sharing this among themselves they eat. We have a story about this. Formerly once, it is told, a poor man had brought with him some fig-dough, because he had no food. At the place where they spent the night, the people of his village, seeing this, did not mix what he had in with theirs; they said: What have you brought? eat what you have yourself, as best you can. And so, poor fellow, he stayed on there eating just this. Next day he shot a Nilgae. Then instead of shouting the name of his village, he shouted "Fig". The men of his village came near and said: It is our deer, fellows! So and so has killed it. The people of the country-side asked this poor man: Why did you shout in such a way? He then told his grief before the country people, saying: When yesterday evening the dough was divided they kept me outside. When they heard this, the country people scolded them a good deal, and the men of the village became humble. They fined them severely through the people of the country-side. From that time up to the present day we do not act in such a way.

When they have eaten the dough, they commence to prepare rice and curry. The camp fires look like a burning forest, such hosts have assembled. They who cook the rice do this, and some men singe the hares and peafowls; the stomachs and legs they make into curry. Felled deer remain as they are. When they have had their evening meal, the hunt-priest calls out that they are to have their council meeting. Thereupon five or six men from every village go to the meeting, and others blow the flute and sing forest songs; they are highly lascivious; some lie down to sleep. The young men from the village of the hunt-priest wander from camp to camp, singing and begging (as at the Dasãe festival), and the men of the camp each give them a handful of rice, and they on their side make all kinds of fun, and make people laugh.

The hunt-priest is the headman of the hunt-council, and the people of the country-side are his tenants. Where he sits down to have the council, there the hosts gather, and sitting round there they keep him in the middle, as when there is a halo round the sun. Leading men sit down near him. The hunt-priest now asks the people of the country-side: Do, Sirs, men of the land, if any of you has any distress or grief or any unsettled quarrel, let us hear. Are we all well or not? The men of the land then answer him: So far as mind and body are concerned, we are well by your blessing. The hunt-priest then answers: By the blessing of Ṭhạkur we shall get what is good.

Now, one by one, they tell their grievances before the hunt-priest. One man says: With such and such, and such and such villages we have got into a dispute over a hare. The hunt-priest then asks them: In what way? The man then says: I threw it down with a stick. Another man says: My dog caught it. The hunt-priest then asks both of them: Have you any witnesses? They both answer him: We have, men from such and such, and such and such villages. The hunt-priest then sends for the witnesses; when they come, he questions them, one after the other, on both sides. He who is proved to be the first, he will get it. The men of the land assist the hunt-priest in judging; but the hunt-priest gives the order. If the two have no witnesses, or if, because of cupidity, the witnesses muddle the matter, the hunt-priest will next morning, when the sun is rising, plant an arrow, belonging to each of the two litigants, in the ground. He applies sindur to both arrows, and having a loṭa with water in his hand he stands and says: O Father Ṭhạkur of heaven, by thy grace we judged, the two did not obey; thou art there, filling the heaven, o Ṭhạkur Father, and we also, as is seen, sitting here filling the earth, we have judged; as this judgement did not stand, we so many men of the land, are not to be blamed, now then, thou knowest the matter of these two, judge thou between them! The hunt-priest and the men of the country then say to the two litigants: Do bow to the Day-spirit and take up these arrows of yours, we, so many men, are free from responsibility. Do, each of you, take yours, do not fear us, fear Ṭhạkur. They thereupon make the one who tạkes up his arrow say: Have a care then, O Ṭhạkur, if I am acting unrighteously, may a tiger eat me in this forest of the hunt, and if I am not acting unrighteously, I shall return home safe and sound. If the other man also has the courage, he will do the same, otherwise he will withdraw. The hunt-priest then at once pours the water in the loṭa out where the arrow had been put in the ground. When he has done this, he bows to it and says: Do, O Ṭhạkur, judge thou between them, what is good or bad. Thereupon during the hunt that day they make them, if they have both sworn, both stay together, and in the middle of the forest a tiger will come out roaring, and he will come running straight for these two, and he will first stand with his forelegs on the man who has spoken the truth, but will not do him any harm; thereupon he will leave him and make an utter end of the unrighteous one. This we have many of us seen with our own eyes. If he is saved from a tiger, he will surely die by some other calamity.

At the night-council of the hunt the hunt-priest and the men of the country together dispose of disputes in connexion with killed animals, one after the other, if there are witnesses; and if not, they next morning make the disputing men swear, just as I have told. When they have settled the disputes in connexion with killed animals, the hunt-priest says: Well, Sirs, men of the country, if you have any other disputes, tell it. Then everybody, one after the other, tell their grievances. One man says: As for me, the village headman and council have without any cause fined me; or: The Pargana and the headmen of five villages have passed an unrighteous judgement in connexion with some riceland, or in connexion with a bride and bridegroom; or: Me they have without any cause called a witch[8]; or: I have on account of this or that in the meantime forbidden so and so people to fetch water and touch the drinking vessels; or: As for me, the village people have without any cause or reason shut my door, — they make a thousand complaints, because the hunt-council is our High Court. There the Pargana, Dẹs Mạñjhi, and village headmen have no power to intimidate any one, the men of the country, small and big, judge, and there they utterly subdue the greedy, fat people, if they have in any case acted unjustly. Some greedy people do not go there at all out of shame or fear. If they have not gone there, the men of the country will next day seize them, and if they do not obey, the men of the country will next day go in crowds to their home, and if they find proofs of their injustice, they punish them so as to make them flinch. At the hunt judging they judge very righteously; they do not let any injustice pass at all. In the village the headman or the Pargana scold and intimidate us, as they take us to be of no account; but at the burnt forest they have no power to silence us; then they become slinking like the tail of a cowardly dog; for this reason we poor people have great trust in the judgement of the burnt forest[9].

Continuing to judge, dancing the d u ṅ g e ṛ, singing forest songs, and blowing the flute they continue until dawn. They then prepare their morning meal and eat; thereupon the hunt-priest sacrifices the remaining fowls. Now they enter the other forest and turn back hunting. When, at noon or in the middle of the afternoon, they have finished hunting they disperse. Thereupon they start for their various villages, hunting as they pass along.

Formerly they were hunting up to five days, being continually out so long; but nowadays, what can be done, when there is no such big forest? Formerly when the hunters entered and passed through the street of any village, the girls of the village washed their feet, and the hunters gave these girls c a m p a flowers[10], and they saluted each other. Thereupon the village people gave the hunters Mahua dough and water to eat and drink. Nowadays this custom of ours has been discontinued.

When the hunters come home, the respective household people wash their feet, and they salute each other, because they have come back saved from death; as they say among us: The danger for women is at childbirth; the danger for men is during hunt and chase; if you get through this, you will see ages. When they have washed their feet, they give them food. They eat; thereupon the hunters go to where there is water; here they gather, and when they have come together, they singe and cut up the killed animals. The one

---

[8] i. e., his wife or a daughter or a related woman living in his house; a man is not a witch. [9] The hunt-council is constantly referred to as "the burnt forest". Every year the Santals in the beginning of April set fire to the undergrowth and especially all the dead leaves lying on the ground. [10] Either a small bush, Ochna sqarrosa, Roxb., or a large tree, Michelia champaca, L.

who shot the deer, him they give the hind half; and of the head they give him one split piece, of the spleen one split piece and of the liver one split piece. To the village priest they give the flesh on both sides of the backbone and a part of the liver, to offer to the spirits. For the village headman they take out one thigh as his part of the rump belonging to the killer, the village headman gets the upper part of this; what is below this his deputy gets, and the end of the leg the Goḍet gets. And the kettle-drum drummer gets for himself a separate part of this. The remaining flesh the hunters divide equally among themselves, and for the men who did not go to hunt, they leave a little flesh, and this they apportion to them, house by house; this portion they call an extra share (capo joṛo). Of hares and peafowls the village priest has no right to get anything, neither has the village headman any right, nor have they any right to get an extra portion; of these only the one who shot gets his share, and the remaining flesh the hunters divide in equal portions among themselves. They who carry get the belly, of deer and of hares. This they call the belly for carrying. Of all kinds of birds the carriers get the gizzard.

The village priest wraps the flesh he is to offer up in a dry leaf and roasts it and offers it to The Five the Six, Pargana haṛam, Mạṅjhi haṛam, and Maraṅ buru; having offered it he eats the flesh.

The village headman has, by customary law, to give five half-seers of rice as a hunt bounty; this the hunters cook together with the flesh of the heads into a hash and eat. Thereupon they come to their respective homes with their portions. The shooter's rightful portion and the village headman's portion they carry along; the headman's portion they bring into his house, and the rightful portion of the killer of an animal into his house. They who carry and bring this, get beer and food at both places. In the house of the shooter they separate from his rightful portion the pot-flesh on the underside of the knee. This the sisters and daughters of the shooter get. However far away they may live, the shooter brings this to them and leaves it there, and these treat him to beer and food, and they look upon this as a great honour. His part of the head and the liver the shooter cooks with rice into a hash and offers this to the ancestors of his family.

g. Composing songs and the like.

Parables they have gradually composed, at different occasions. Taking up what has been seen they have composed these. If a person suddenly speaks and reveals this or that, then others, thinking that this is good and fitting, will also speak the same, and thus it is spread about. Folk-tales and fairy-stories are not composed nowadays, only old ones are in vogue, learnt one after the other. Riddles we have also only old ones. To mimic no one is able to learn, only by having a natural ability people are able to mimic, to show the faults of people. The songs are mostly old ones; still they are now and then composing a few new ones. Men have composed riṅjạ, matwar, and marriage songs, and women are mostly composing forest songs, Sohrae songs, lagṛẽ songs, and dọṅ songs. The forest-songs mostly divorced women compose, and they make girls their disciples, when they pluck vegetables and bring leaves. The young men learn these from them. Also among the forest-songs there are a very few ones that are good, otherwise they are only what is shameless; therefore they do not sing these in the villages or at home, and if they sing them here, people scold them. Elderly married women do not sing forest-songs, but foppish half-elderly women sing such in the forest together with the girls. By singing these also good people get their mind spoilt, and they are led astray. Remembering these, girls and young men also neglect their work, that is to say, a few, and when married, such people will not endure living together; they will be divorced.

VIII. CRIME AND ITS PUNISHMENT

a. The councils.

We have three kinds of councils: The village, or headman's council, the outside, or over-chief council, and the hunt, or the council of the people of the country. In the village council the village headman is the president; in the outside-council the Pargana is the president, and in the hunt council the hunt-priest is the president. In the headman's council the 'five men' of the village[1] assist the headman in judging. In the Pargana's council the village headmen under the Pargana and the village people of the neighbourhood assist him in judging. In the hunt-council the people of the whole country assist the hunt-priest in judging. The headman is above the village; the Pargana is above a number of villages. There is nothing fixed; they have not the same number of villages, some have many, others have only a small number under them. We have Dẹs Mạńjhis, these are the assistants of the Parganas. From a village headman's judgement they may appeal to the Pargana, and from the Pargana's judgement they may appeal to the people of the country in the burnt forest. From the judgement of the people of the country there is no appeal.

The customary perquisites of a Pargana are as follows: From every single village under him he is to get year by year one rupee, half-a-seer clarified butter, and eighty cobs of Indian corn. The Dẹs Mạńjhi gets eight annas, a quarter seer clarified butter, and forty cobs of Indian corn every year in the same villages. When the village headmen under the Pargana pay in to him his perquisites, he gives them a feast, and the Dẹs Mạńjhi also does the same. Nowadays some village headmen do not give the Pargana the rupee, neither does the Pargana give any feast to the village headmen who pay: they let all pass into desuetude, since the Europeans have appeared in the Santal country. Since these have appeared, the Parganas and the village headmen have become utterly greedy; anyone who is able to give them most money, in his favour they judge, and people of this kind they help in the public courts, and poor people who have no money, they do not take any notice of; without cause or reason they scold and browbeat them and cause their suit to be dismissed.

The people of the country are not nice either. They do not inform the village headman, neither do they complain to the Pargana, and to the people of the country they do not

[1] See Dictionary s. v. mȭṛẽ hoṛ.

appeal either. Also a quarrel between husband and wife these wretched fools at once bring in before the European magistrates, a crying shame; the deceitful Indian pleaders cheat them of their money a good deal; they get one another into prison; their mutual hatred remains with them smouldering like hot-pan fire; this is what they have gained by transgressing the customary judgements of the ancestors. Let them take the great crimes to the courts; but what we have from olden times disposed of ourselves, why do they take heaps of such matter to the courts?

b. Concerning witnesses.

From ancient times up to near the present day we Santals did not know false statements; we were stating what we had seen with our eyes, both about enemies and about our brothers and sisters. After the Europeans have come, a few Santals have been judged to be hanged, because they have spoken the truth. There were no witnesses of their crime; if they had lied and denied it, they would have been set free. In our councils we did not bring the witnesses in one by one; we put all the witnesses forward at once; still they did not tell falsehoods. Nowadays they have learnt deceit from the Dekos, and like them they sell their soul and honour for one brass-cup of beer; and as the magistrates do not know our language, they cannot distinguish falsehood from truth; they are only led astray by the words of the deceitful Indians; therefore we do not get just judgements. Wo would have any fear of the light swearing in the courts? Let them make them swear like the oaths of our ancestors, then they would tremble, fearing for their life, and they would surely not speak falsely. A few magistrates have let a very short oath in our language be made up by some Dekos; but we only laugh at this oath, because what is said aims at the one who administers the oath. They make them swear like this: "Speak the truth; if I speak what is false a tiger spirit will eat thee". The witness repeats this, following him: "Speak the truth; if I speak what is false, a tiger-spirit will eat thee". Why should witnesses have any fear from this?

c. The different kinds of crime.

Among the great crimes are the following: To kidnap children, to sacrifice them, to kill a person by carelessness, to rob one of his wife, to rape a woman, forcibly to apply sindur to a woman. Our punishment for this was death. The kidnappers steal children, or catch a person on the road, and sacrifice them. If they were caught at the moment, they killed them without any judging, and there was no appeal in this case. When some one inadvertently shot and killed somebody during the hunt, the people passed judgement and let the person be killed in return. At such a time they let the man who shot and killed the other, stand where the man was who was shot and killed, and where the man who shot and killed was, there they let a relative of the shot and killed man stand. If he shoots and kills the man who shot and killed from there with one arrow, well and good; otherwise he is set free. And if a man is killed by an arrow passing through an animal, then, in the same way, they let some animal stand, and let the man who shot and killed stand behind the animal, so far away from the animal as the killed one was. If shooting through the animal placed there he kills him, well and good; otherwise he is free.

A man who has been robbed of his wife may, without any judgement, kill both on the spot, anywhere he may track and find the two, like a deer in the forest. His relatives will help him tracking them, but he himself will do the killing. Nowadays they do not kill them; but the seducer will have to pay five rupees to save his head.

Those who raped women they also treated in the same way. Also these have nowadays to pay five rupees to save their head, and besides this they fine them as heavily as they can. Mostly they make them pay a score of rupees. They cut off the right hand of a man who forcibly had applied sindur to a woman, and with a spindle they poked out one of his eyes. And there was a separate fine. Nowadays these also have to pay five rupees to save hand and eye; they get a beating and also have to pay a fine. We had no murder without a cause.

As to witches, formerly we drove them away after having treated them disgracefully; only now and then have we killed them. Also nowadays they drive them away, and sometimes they also kill them.

But this is not right, because the ancestors of old did not act in this way. If they were accidentally killed when they were beating them in anger, the ancestors of old did not call this murder; therefore they did not punish those who beat them to death.

Our punishment for illicit intercourse between relatives and with a person of another race was outcasting, and so it is now also. Nowadays this is also slackening off with us; some persons quite confidently act in this way; the people do not do them anything.

Formerly the Santals did not steal; but nowadays they have learnt this also from the Dekos. From former times only one kind of theft is remembered, viz., to steal and eat sheep or goats. When such animals had gone astray anywhere, then the whole village population would kill and eat them when they found them, and the village headman they would give a double share. If this was proved, they would then restore the head (give a fresh animal instead), and would fine them five four-anna bits each. Nowadays they take all to the smooth verandah (i. e., the courts).

Abortus provocatus we have had from old times. They were doing this when birth would be improper (on social indications). If it is proved, we fine both the medicine giver and the treated one ten rupees each. Nowadays we take such crimes to the courts. If they defame anybody without cause, they will have to pay five rupees to wipe off the defamation and five four-anna bits to the village council. The crime of sodomy is the act of drunk men only. Formerly we gave such men an awful thrashing and fined them ten rupees. Nowadays who can say whether they take them to the courts or not? Besides this we have a couple of shameful sins that are not publicly mentioned.

When anyone has caused any loss, we make them pay the price or the estimated damage, and we also fine them. We fine both who strike each other, when both are guilty, otherwise one of them. If bullocks or cows butt and kill each other, we take the one who caused the death; and if anyone kills a bullock by ploughing or beating it, we make him pay its price. Anyone who falsely complains or makes a claim, him we punish contrarily. Those who without cause backbite people, we fine heavily.

A girl who commits the fault of mounting a tree in the sacred grove, or of entering the sacred closet in a man's house, will have to give a sacrifice animal.

When there is a dispute in connexion with the boundaries, the Pargana and the village headmen of the neighbourhood come together and settle the matter; and when there is a dispute in connexion with riceland, the village headman and the village council settle the matter. They fine the guilty person. These two kinds of mutual robbing have spread over the whole country through the instigation of the Dekos; otherwise formerly we had no such quarrels. Nowadays the Dekos also rob us of our villages; they both encroach on our boundaries and steal our riceland. People say: The Dekos enter like a needle, and they swell to be as large as a plough-share. They are also making us rob each other and quarrel. Where they are, there is no peace. Causing false evidence to be given in the courts, they rob us of all we have; and the magistrates do not understand our language; therefore we shall probably some day in the future again have to run away somewhere. If Deko cats were not living among Santals, it would be good for us Santals.

IX. RELIGION AND WORSHIP

a. Ṭhạkur.

In the primeval age we had no bongas[1]. During our wanderings we have got them. The Siṅ boṅga (Sun or Day spirit) we also got on our way in Siṅ duạr (the Sun or Day pass). The primeval ancestors were worshipping only Ṭhạkur. Having got the bongas we have gradually forgotten Ṭhạkur; only the name is left. The people of the present age have mostly forgotten also the name; only we who have learnt the story of the ancestors and a few old men are remembering his name. In the present age the Santals say the Siṅ boṅga is presumably Ṭhạkur; therefore, when worshipping, they look towards the sun and call this their Ṭhạkur; but our ancestors of old have handed over to us, viz., to us gurus, that Ṭhạkur is different; he is not seen by human eyes; but he himself sees all. He himself has created earth and heaven, the human beings, the animals, the birds and winged beings, the insects, the snakes and reptiles, the fishes and crabs, the trees and plants, the paddy and rice, the bajṛa and Indian corn, all and everything, and he supports all, small and big, he feeds us all. He is the one who brings us here, he is the one who takes us away. By the word of the bongas and the mountain spirits or of a human being we are not born, nor do we go away; Ṭhạkur has measured out to us our seer, and until this is finished, no one is able to take us away. As we are living here, in the same way we shall, when we have gone to the other world, get good or bad by his order.

The Sun bonga we call a good bonga: he brings the dawn, he brings the evening; he gives us warm sunshine, he gives us rain; therefore at the time of religious observances we appeal to him. He is the man, and the moon is his wife, and the stars are their children. The ancestors have told, it is reported, that these two, husband and wife, had very many children. The sons stayed with their father, and the daughters with their mother. Due to the heat of the sun and the day-stars it was felt like being burnt on the earth. The moon then said to the sun: We shall eat our children; otherwise humanity will be destroyed. The husband then said: Do you eat your daughters first; if the human beings do not get any relief thereby, I shall eat mine also.

---

[1] See Dictionary s. v.

Then the moon (woman-kind, we know their craftiness) covered all her daughters up in a huge basket; thereupon she went to the old man and said to him: I have eaten and made an end of all my ones; how is it, the hot rays are not abating. Only if you also eat your sons, then only will the human beings be saved. In this way the old wife outwitted the old man; the foolish old man complied with what the woman said and really ate all his sons. It became night, O great mother, he saw them, all her ones are there. Then he became furiously angry, and taking his sword he pursued and reached the old woman and cut her; he might have made an utter end of her; but as the old woman gave him two daughters, she cooled him down a little.

Even now he continues to pursue her; and when he remembers her craftiness, he cuts her, month after month; only when the old man's soul cools down, the moon gets a little relief for a couple of days. The names of the two daughters, that the old man got, are Bhurkạ[2] and the evening star.

As most of the people of the present age erroneously call Siṅ boṅga Ṭhạkur, in the same way they call all bongas their Ṭhạkur when they make an invocation. They invoke them saying: Be greeted, Lord, Father my Ṭhạkur. In this way they are honouring them, in order that they may help them with pleasure; otherwise they are not Ṭhạkur; they are only bongas.

b. The bongas.

Among the bongas the Sun bonga is our great bonga. After him comes the Jọm sim bonga; after him Maraṅ buru (his real name is Liṭạ), after him Jahẽr era, the Lady of the sacred grove (her real name is Ram Sạlgi), after her Mõṛẽko Turniko, The Five (we certainly praise The Six, but we do not sacrifice to them), after these Gosãe era (her Ladyship), after her Pargana haṛam, after him Mạṅjhi haṛam bonga, after him the (Oṛak̇) House bonga, and after him the Abge bonga. Besides these the ojhas have separate bongas[3]; persons who wish to become rich worship Wealth-bongas[4]. There are boundary bongas, bongas of the hollowed-out water-holes in rivers, bongas of the water-pools, bongas of tree-roots and stumps, forest bongas, mountain bongas, and so on.

The Abge[5] bongas are numerous; the different septs have different ones; the same is the case with the House bongas[6] also. Those of the same sept are not the same either, while those of different septs also may be the same. The name of the Abge bonga and of the House bonga they do not make known to other people, neither do they tell their women-folk.

---

[2] The morning star, Venus. The word is borrowed from Hindi. [3] The names of the numerous bongas invoked by the ojhas will be found in the writer's paper Studies in Santal Medicine and Connected Folklore, Part I, p. 64 ff. Memoirs of the Asiatic Society of Bengal, Vol. X. [4] See Dictionary s. v. kisạ̃ṛ boṅ ga. [5] See Dictionary s. v. [6] See Dictionary s. v. Oṛak̇ boṅga.

When an old man is dying, he tells the name in a whisper to his eldest son, before he departs. From primeval times we gurus know the names of the Abge bongas and House bongas of all septs. The Abge of some of the Hãsdak' sept is Dhara Sõṛẽ or Dhara Saṇḍa (of the Nij Hãsdak' sept), and Kaṭkọm Kudrạ, and their House bonga is Bãspahaṛ and Desoali. The Abge of the Kisku sept is Campa dana gaṛ, and their House bonga is Sõs; the Abge of the Hembrom sept is Gaṛsiṅkạ and Lilạ cạndi, and their House bonga is Gurạiạ. The Abge bonga of the Mạrṇḍi sept is Dhanghara and their House bonga Gurạiạ. The Abge bongas of the Murmu sept are Kudrạ Cạṇḍi, Bahaṭa, Duạr Sẽṛẽ, Kudraj, and Gosãe Rae, and their House bonga is Baṭpahaṛ; the Abge bonga of the Soren sept is Acrạli, and their House bongas are Gurạiạ and Sar Cạṇḍi; the Abge bonga of the Ṭuḍu sept is Dhanghara, and their House bonga Ṭhuṇṭạ tursạ; the Abge bonga of the Baske sept is Desoali, and their House bonga is Baṭpahaṛ; and the Abge bonga of the Besra sept is Campa dana gaṛ, and their House bonga is Sõs. The names of the Abge bongas of the Pãuriạ sept and of the Cõṛẽ sept I have forgotten.

The Jọm sim[7] bonga is also different with them. Some call their Jọm sim bonga Panhar, others Anhaṛ, others Boerạṅgi, others Seowani, others Baraṅ baraṅ, and again others Baḍha Ahaṅ. The bongas of the ojhas are Siṅbạhni, Maraṅ buru, Kạmru guru, Sidhạ guru, Gaṇḍo guru, Lọhbọr guru, Buạṅ guru, Jitu guru, and others, and the guru from whom the ojha has learnt. The name of one wealth-bonga is Kal Cãora. The wealth-bongas, people tell, steal from other people and bring it to their own master. Now and then wealth-bongas rob each other, it is told, and the master of the one among them who gains, he gets much wealth. Now and then, people tell, the wealth-bongas have been driven away by people. One day a wealth-bonga was carrying paddy in a sling away from a man's threshing-floor; just then the owner of the paddy happened to come, and taking him to be a thief, he threw something at him making a great deal of rattling noise; he chased him right up to the house of his master. The bonga got quickly inside and was running about all over and in the sacred closet, making a rumbling sound; he broke all the earthenware pots and vessels into pieces. The man who was chasing him called out to the master of the house and made him get up and reviled him to his heart's content; he said to him: This is your stealing bonga; I have chased him and driven him inside your house; who knows for how long a time he has been bringing my things here; therefore nothing matures for me. From that time on, whenever this man came to the house of these people, the bonga ran in fear about all over and in the sacred closet, making a rumbling sound; therefore the master of the house implored that man, saying: Don't come to us; in fear of you the bonga is breaking all we have into pieces.

7 See Dictionary s. v.

The Jọm sim bonga was not from the beginning; at the Jọm sim festival they were offering only to the Sun bonga. They had, it is told, had a sacrifice to their Abge. When they had eaten and were going home, they forgot a battle-axe and left it there. When they remembered this on their way, one of them ran back to fetch it. To this man the Jọm sim bonga revealed himself; he was picking up and eating what was lying scattered there. While he was eating the bonga was talking to himself: Oh, now I have felt pleased for the first time. Then seeing the man, he disappeared. The man brought the battle-axe but he did not tell them of the bonga that had revealed himself. After this they got a good deal of fever, so that they were near dying. Then they had some divination made for them. The ojhas told them: Some bonga or other is revealing himself to you. Then the man who had fetched the battle-axe remembered what had happened to him, saying: Really I saw him when I was fetching the forgotten battle-axe. I heard him say: Now I have felt pleased for the first time. Therefore they called this bonga Ahaṅ. The ojhas said to them: This bonga says: Offer to me at the Jọm sim festival. From that time the Santals worship him.

c. Worship and festivals.

The Sowing fowl is the first offering of the year[8]. In the month of Asaṛ (middle of June to middle of July) we eat the sowing fowls, in the name of sowing and scattering the seed. Every house has to give one fowl. The village priest offers these in the sacred grove. He offers one fowl to each, to Maraṅ buru, Jaher era, Mõṛẽko, Gosãe era, Pargana, and Mạṅjhi haṛam. He offers one black fowl to the bonga of the surrounding boundary. The remaining fowls he offers to the bongas along the boundaries; and if there are fowls left, they kill them wringing their necks. They do not offer them in a lump, but each separately. They make an invocation, as follows: Be greeted then, Father my Ṭhạkur, Jaher era (or Maraṅ buru, and so on), here then in the name of the Sowing fowl this is given to thee, handed to thee; we shall sow in one place, in twelve places may it shoot up in tufts, may they blow and bring, flood and bring rainy season rain, burning rain; into this village, this hamlet do ye not let suffering and sin, disease and illness, stomach-ache or headache enter, penetrate; with golden slings, with golden shoulder-yokes ye will carry it away on your shoulders, ye will carry it away with shoulder-yokes to another side, another boundary, Father my Ṭhạkur. Widows, women of ill omen, a torn leaf, a folded leaf they will select for destruction, will doom; so then do not ye let them get good omens, favourable signs; then one day, half-a-day they will pry, stand on tiptoe, do not let any spell be thrown, any hurt be done, the calf-mothers, the goat-mothers may they wander about, walk about satisfactorily, the Siṅ forest, the Man forest, the half-grown dogs may ye press down, cover up, Lord, Father, my Ṭhạkur.

---

[8] The Sowing fowl, the fowls sacrificed in connexion with the sowing of paddy.

When the village priest has sacrificed the fowls they cook them with rice into a hash, and all the men of the village eat this. The fowl for Jaher era and the fowl for Mõṛẽko the village priest alone eats. The next day or the day after this they have offerings in every house; they make sacrifices to the Abge bonga, the House bonga, and the ancestors, and Maraṅ buru.

When they have finished planting the rice they offer in the month of San (middle of July to middle of August) the "Green" fowls[9], that the paddy may grow green. On this occasion they sacrifice only to the village bongas. Then also they make the same invocation, they only insert the words "for the sake of the Green fowl" instead of "for the sake of the Sowing fowl".

The offering of the first fruits of iṛi and gundli takes place in the month of Bhador (middle of August to middle of September). Then the village priest bathes and goes to the highland field of such a one where the crops have first ripened, and whatever he, standing in one place, is able to cut, this he takes to the Sacred grove, and after having cleaned the places with cow-dung, he offers it to the bongas of the Sacred grove in succession, first to Jaher era, thereupon to Mõṛẽko, thereupon to Maraṅ hoṛ[10], then to Gosãe era, and finally to Pargana. Thereupon he pours out milk as a libation, and he makes an invocation: Be greeted then, Father my Ṭhạkur, Jaher era, here as ye see, new crops, new ears I am giving ye, handing ye; consequently we shall eat, take it into our mouth; do not let stomach-ache, head-ache be created, be formed, Lord, Father, my Ṭhạkur. After this he goes to the village, and in the same way in the Mạṅjhi than, making an invocation to Mạṅjhi haṛam, he makes an offering to him. What is left, the village priest takes with him.

Janthaṛ (the offering of first-fruits of low-land paddy) they offer in the month of Aghãṛ (middle of November to middle of December). At this time the village people buy a pig or a ram. This they call the sacrificial animal for Janthaṛ. This sacrifice the priest of the outskirts offers at the place of the Pargana in the Sacred grove. What is needed for the sacrifice the priest of the outskirts has to provide, and also the rice for cooking the hash of and eating the sacrificed animal he has to give. When the sacrifice is performed, the men alone eat it. The invocation is as follows: Be greeted then, Father my Ṭhạkur, Pargana, in the name of the Janthaṛ we are giving thee, handing thee sacrifices, offerings; consequently we shall eat, take it into our mouth, do not let stomach-ache, headache be created, be formed; in the ricefields, on the threshing-floors we shall reap, we shall thresh; mayest thou make it fertile, make it rich; mayest thou add to it, multiply it; rat and field-mouse will attack it; these also thou wilt restrain, keep back, Father, my Ṭhạkur. — The village priest offers the first-fruits of the paddy, as he did of the iṛi and gundli. The village people also offer the first-fruits of paddy in every house.

---

9 "Green" naturally refers not to the colour of the fowls, but to the growing crops. 10 Maraṅ hoṛ is here used instead of Maraṅ buru.

Sọhrae[11] is our great festival. We have this in the month of Pus (middle of December to middle of January), when we have reaped and threshed the paddy. As we have got fresh crops, we also fill our bongas; and our relatives we also entertain, as we have food and drink. Small and big, poor widows included, all of us then feast.

The village headman gathers the village people to have a council. Then they fix the time for the Sohrae. The village headman now gives the Goḍet an order: Do collect the beer-contributions and tell them in every house that they are to brew beer; after so and so many days we shall bathe for the Sohrae. In every house they now brew beer, and they invite their respective relatives to come. On the fixed day sisters and daughters, sisters' children and male relatives, all come together. In the evening of the day before they bathe the Goḍet takes three fowls and brings them to the village priest, two white ones and one speckled. The village priest binds them, and this night he himself observes religious abstinence, that is to say, he lies on the ground on a mat. When it becomes dawn, the Goḍet takes one fowl and half-a-seer rice together with salt and turmeric in every house. Having had her bath the wife of the village priest comes and pounds meal for the priest. About the middle of the forenoon (ca. 9 o'clock) the village priest goes out to the water's edge to sacrifice. The Goḍet goes along with the priest, taking the fowls collected in the village with him; a couple of the men of the village also go along.

After having bathed and come up from the water the village priest makes a magic square, plastering a long spot with cow-dung, in the direction of North and South. Along the magic square he puts small handfuls of rice in many places; thereupon he makes marks of sindur near the small heaps of rice, three marks at each heap. Thereupon he sprinkles water on the speckled one of the fowls that were taken the first day, and applies sindur to its head, and thereupon sindur to its wings and legs. Next he puts an egg down on the small heaps of rice, marking it with sindur; and letting the fowl eat from the rice, he makes an invocation: Be greeted then, Jaher era, Father my Ṭhạkur, in the name of the Sohrae this is given to thee, handed to thee; with pleasure and delight mayest thou receive, mayest thou accept this; this mayest thou be pleased with, mayest thou be agreeable to; we are inexperienced girls, inexperienced boys, we do not know and recognize; in the plastering, in the cleaning with cow-dung, in the observances, in the religious abstinence, where anything may have been forgotten, been indifferently done, we do not know, do not recognize it; may ye bear it, suffer it. In former times, in some manner or other, our ancestors of old, in silk clothes, in women's sindur-red attire, received ye, met ye, Father my Ṭhạkur. In the village, in the settlement do not let stomach-ache, headache enter, do not let it intrude; relatives, persons of our sept, from the other side of the big river, from the other side of the stream we have invited, we have notified sister's sons and daughters, grandchildren and great-grandchildren, they will dance and enjoy themselves, may there

[11] See Dictionary s. v.

be no spells, no enchantments, no loss, no waste, no quarrel, no dispute, may they dance with joy, enjoy themselves, Lord Father, my Ṭhạkur.

Thereupon he sacrifices the speckled fowl. In the same way he sacrifices to all the bongas. Having cooked the fowls with rice into a hash, all the men of the village eat them. And the collected beer they drink there. All the people of the village, poor and others, then ask each other: Well, how is it? Perhaps some among us have a fever or are ill? If this is the case, we must let each other know. The village men then answer: We are well, Father headman, by your grace. The village headman then says: By the grace of Ṭhạkur we shall all get what is good. As we see, we have brought the Sohrae festival, the great Elder Sister has arrived. For five days and five nights dance and enjoy yourselves, brothers and sisters; let there be no disputes, no quarrels, no covetousness, no greed; if there is any covetousness and greed, look out well, also the fenced vegetables you may pluck, but not what is climbing on poles, nor what is shrivelled up, pluck what is unripe; and the flowers that they have fixed with laths, have tied with thread, do not commit the sin of plucking these flowers for us, Sirs. The village men then answer: With twelve balls of cotton we are shutting our ears up; then whatever there may be, small or big, we shall not see or listen to it[12]. Thereupon they sing[13]:

Who created	Ṭhạkur created	Ṭirmuṭi created
The wide earth?	The wide world.	Kanu the Goala.
Who created	Ṭhạkur created	Towards the East he drove
The cattle, you there?	The cattle, you there.	The cattle, you there.
Who created	Ṭhạkur created	Towards the East he drove
The cattle?	The cattle.	The cattle.

Where, young man, did you lose	On the road I lost
The flute at your waist?	The flute at my waist.
Where, young man, did you lose	At the place of worship I lost
The cattle, you there?	The cattle, you there.
Where, young man, did you lose	At the place of worship I lost
The cattle?	The cattle.

Thereupon they call the cattle-herd boys: Come with them, fellows, bring the cattle, we shall let them trample on the magic square and blot it out. They then drive the cattle near to the magic square. The village priest now asks for all the sticks of the cattle-herds;

---

12 The expressions used all refer to women; they must not touch those who are too young or too old, and not married ones. It is shameless. 13 In a kind of Bihari.

he puts them down at the magic square; he applies sindur to every single stick of theirs. Thereupon they drive the cattle near to the magic square.

Any cow[14], who treads on or smells at the egg put down there, this cow they catch and, washing her legs, they anoint her horns with oil, and apply sindur to her horns. The herd of this cow they lift up and place him on some one's shoulder, and bring him to the village headman and put him down there. The boy bows to the headman and after him to all the elderly men there.

Now they go home, drumming the dancing-drum as they go along. They enter the house of the village priest, who gives them beer. After they have drunk this, they proceed to the house of the village headman, who also gives them beer. At this time the village headman says to the Jọg Mạṅjhi and the Jọg Paranik: So long as the festival lasts, the young men and girls are in your charge, and the festival is also in your charge. If you let the village street become deserted, we shall fine both of you. Thereupon they separate. They take food and drink beer in their respective houses.

It is evening. The elderly men and women go to bed, and the young men bless[15] the cattle. Standing at the door of the cow-shed they drum the dancing drum and sing[16]:

The cows have gone to the Siribandha forest,
The buffalo-cows are grazing on the other side of the Ganges.

The cows come home when the sun sets,
The buffalo-cows come home, after having grazed, at midnight.

On what horn is it to get oil and sindur?
Where on its back is grass and paddy to be strewed on it?

In this way they sing, drum, and blow the flute at every house exceedingly, and all along the village street they shout indecently. Although they hear this in every house, they do not listen to it.

After these the girls perform the waving ceremony over the cattle. They also commence at the house of the village headman. They bring with them sun-dried rice, and sun-dried paddy, mixed together, d h u b i grass and a lighted lamp. They make an invocation: Take it, you reddish one, through you, reddish one, may there become one hundred reddish ones, by your guiding them, following them, fill this cattle shed, this place of omen, fill it to overflow; may you earn, may you produce, to the backside of the house, to its eaves;

---

14 The word used may also mean any piece of cattle, not necessarily a cow. 15 The word translated "bless" is ordinarily used about "awaken"; the object of the proceedings is to cause the cattle to become fruitful and effective. 16 In a kind of Bihari.

may water from the eaves fall down on it, may mushrooms spring up, your owner, your watchman, on the other side of the big river, on the other side of the stream, co-parents-in-law, their near relatives, may they eat, may they drink; hear it you, listen you, the Turks' measure of capacity[17], awfully large, your owner, your watchman with his arrow, his battle-axe may he dig and smite, pierce and smite.

Take it, you Sugi, through you, Sugi, may there become one hundred Sugis, by carrying them on your hip, by bearing them, guiding them, following them up here, may you fill this cow-shed, this place of omen, fill it to overflow, your owner, your watchman on the other side of the big river, on the other side of the stream, co-parents-in-law, their near relatives, may they eat, may they drink, hear it you, listen you, the Turks' measure of capacity, awfully large, your owner, your watchman with his arrow, his battle-axe may he dig and smite, may he pierce and smite.

At the same time when they make this invocation they strew out the dhubi grass and the sun-dried paddy and rice towards the cattle-shed and the cows. Then they sing[18]:

Having taken sun-dried rice in the hand,
Having arranged the betel nut, a bunch,
Come along, so and so goddess, at the proper time
To bless waving over the cows.

More than once waving and blessing
To wave and bless twice is great.
This happened on the big bullock
Alone.

Wherefore are you crying, bullock?
Wherefore are you worrying, bullock?
I shall give you, my son,
Excellent betelnut.

Slowly he will go, slowly he will go,
The young bullock;
Afterwards I shall apply sindur.

In this way the girls perform the waving ceremony in house after house and continue singing at every cattle-shed. In the village street they sing in another way:

---

17 The translation is literal; no Santal has been able to explain to the writer what is really meant.

18 In corrupt Bihari.

The dove is always on the move,
The crow is eating with legs spread out,
The young servant of the headman's family
To-morrow he will go out;
The servant girl of the deputy headman's family,
Later in the day she will come out.

At the cow-shed of people who have buffalo cows they sing the praise of these differently, when they perform the waving ceremony:

Whose cows are these? the cows are shining white.
Whose buffalo cows are these? the buffalo cow is black and bulky.

The cows of so and so, the cows are shining white.
The buffalo cows of so and so, the buffalo cow is black and bulky.

The leg of the buffalo cow is thick and fat,
The leg of the green dove is covered with feather low down.

These ones went to the Sińegọr forest,
These ones went to the Manegọr forest.

Do, you so and so, turn them round,
Do, you so and so, turn them round back.

In the Sińegọr forest, mother, is the tiger,
In the Manegọr forest is the young leopard.

These will graze making scratching sounds in the straw pins,
The saline soil you will clear quickly.

The young men finish blessing the cattle, and the girls also bring the waving ceremony to an end; thereupon they all wander in the village street and sing; they drum the dancing-drum and the kettle-drum, and blow the flute, that is to say, the young men do this and the girls beat the cymbals and dance, they make a tremendous din and noise.

At cockcrow the young men again bless the cattle once, and following after them the girls perform the waving ceremony. The young men sing[19]:

The cock has crowed,
It has dawned.
Get up, my son, to let the cattle out to graze.
Get up, my son, to let the cattle out to graze.

[19] In corrupt Bihari.

Don't, father, make me stand up,
Don't, father, awaken me;
The sleepiness is calling out to me,
The sleepiness is calling out to me.

In his hand he took the stick,
On his feet he took the wooden sandals;
He went along, so and so man,
To let the cattle out to graze.

The girls sing, when they perform the waving ceremony over the cattle in the morning[20]:

The cock has crowed,
It has become morning;
Get up, my son, you so and so,
To let the cattle out to graze.

Don't, mother, make me stand up,
Don't, mother, awaken me;
The sleepiness is calling out to me.

In his hand he took the stick,
On his feet he took the wooden sandals;
He went along, so and so man,
To turn the cattle round.

The stick of gold, mother,
Will turn the cattle round.
The silver-flute, mother,
The flute he will blow.

When they have finished the waving ceremony, the cattle-herds let the cattle out. The girls stop dancing and begin to do their separate work. And the young men dance the ḍaṇṭa[21] in the street outside the village headman's house. They sing:

Come along, children,
We shall go to catch fish.
The fish was pierced by a thorn,
The fish was pierced by a thorn;
We shall go along leaving the marsh,
We shall go along leaving the marsh.

---

20 In corrupt Bihari. 21 See Dictionary s. v.

Some say the old man is dead;
Some say he is alive.
Exorcize him slowly, sitting,
Smearing red earth on him.
The old man is fidgeting,
The old man is fidgeting.

The women do their separate work, clean the ground with cow-dung, make flour, and so on; and after having finished dancing the young men go about and beg for fun's sake. Once they beat the brushwood fences from one end of the village street to the other end, and when they reach the house of the Goḍet, they shut the Goḍet in, closing the door to the village street. The Goḍet then gives them one earthenware pot with beer. Then they open (the door) for him. Thereupon they continue beating right up to the end of the village street. There at the end they make different "dancers" of straw; when they have made these ready, they take them to the house of the village headman. Here they make them dance, and the headman gives them rice. In this way they beg from house to house. When they have done begging, they give what they have begged together in charge in the house of the Jog Maṅjhi. Now all the men go to bathe, taking yokes, battle-axes, and knives along with them. They have their bath and come back.

Thereupon they sacrifice fowls and pigs in every house. They sacrifice them to Maraṅ buru and to the house-bongas; to the ancestors they fell them. With flour they make the magic squares, two; in the middle of each they put down a small heap of rice and they make five marks of sindur, and on the animal to be sacrificed they sprinkle water and smear sindur on it, on its head, shoulder, and hoofs. Thereupon they let it feed on the rice in the magic square, and they make an invocation: Be greeted then, Maraṅ buru, Father my Ṭhakur, now then, in the name of the Sohrae, I am giving thee, handing to thee offerings, sacrifices; with this mayest thou be pleased, be agreeable; with pleasure, with delight thou wilt receive it, accept it, thou wilt fondle it, consider it great; formerly the ancestors of old received ye, met ye in silk clothes, in sindur-red women's attire; we are inexperienced girls, inexperienced boys, we do not know, do not recognize; in the plastering, in the cleaning with cow-dung, in the observances, in the religious abstinences, some may have been forgotten, been indifferently done; may ye bear it, may ye suffer it all, Father my Ṭhakur. Thereupon they make further invocations; but these I have quoted formerly. They make the same kind of invocation to the house-bonga. And letting the fowls feed on rice on a small leaf-plate they fell them, offering them to the ancestors, and they pour beer on the ground as a libation to Maraṅ buru and the ancestors.

Having finished the sacrifices they prepare rice and curry. They cook separately the flesh of the animals offered to the ancestors. This they throw down to them together with the rice. At that time they make the following invocation: Be greeted then, white-haired one, Father my Ṭhạkur, in the name of the Sohrae I am giving ye, handing to ye rotten food, rotten cooked rice, with this may ye be pleased, be agreeable. On the other side of the big river, on the other side of the stream, relatives, people of our own sept, daughters, sisters we have invited, we have notified; what remains, what is left by ye, they will eat, take into their mouth; do not let stomach-ache, headache be created, be formed, Father my Ṭhạkur. They make some further long invocations. Thereupon they all eat and drink. They sing:

Small, small fowls and pigs,
Numerous are your relatives;
I shall prepare the rice, the curry,
As for me, Father, I will certainly not serve it out.

When they have eaten, they paint atnak leaves with wetted flour in the door of the cattle-shed, that it may look nice, and on the posts of the cattle-shed they splash flour-water and smear sindur; the yokes and the bar-posts they also treat in the same way. The married men and women go from house to house and drink beer and sing, and the young men and girls dance the whole night along in the village street.

When married men and women go to an other house to drink beer, they sing, as they go:

This year, Father, make my cloth bordered,
Next year, Father, make my cloth with white and red stripes.
The village headmen of the Jhạriạ pạṭi country
Are coming on a visit.

In the house where they go in, the people of this house meet them singing:

Please, sit down,
Please, stand;
Food and drink, my companion, we have none,
To meet and see each other, my companion, is a bewitching courtesy.

He made bad seasons, my companion,
He made good seasons;
Seed and seed-grain, my companion, we did not get;
All my children have become utter paupers.

Next day dawns. Then they drum the kettle-drum at the village headman's house, in order that the people may come together. The leading men of the village assemble. When they have gathered, the village headman asks them: How is it, are we, poor people, all of us well or not? They answer him: Father headman, we are well; when it is well, why should we say it is bad? The headman gives them beer without restriction; while they are drinking, the headman asks them: Well, shall we tie the bullocks to posts or not? They anwer him: Yes, Father, if you order it, we shall tie them to posts. The headman then says to the Jo̤g Ma̤ṅjhi and the Jo̤g Paranik: The people of the country will come, you two be on the watch and receive them for us. They get up and away from there. Thereupon the Jo̤g Ma̤ṅjhi says tó the young men of the village: Do dig holes for the posts.

To dig holes for posts is really a customary duty, in the village street outside the houses of the headman and of his deputy, of the Jo̤g Ma̤ṅjhi and the Jo̤g Paranik and the Go̤ḍet; outside these five houses the Jo̤g Ma̤ṅjhi makes them dig. The other village people themselves dig holes for the posts in the village street outside their respective houses and fix the posts in the ground, to tie the bullocks to these posts. The young men, who set to work, by the Jo̤g Ma̤ṅjhi's order dig holes and fix posts in the ground in the village street outside the five houses mentioned. They arrange ropes to tie the bullocks. The Jo̤g Ma̤ṅjhi gives the young men food and beer. The Jo̤g Ma̤ṅjhi orders them to pour out and to squeeze out beer. They do this; thereupon they are set free for the time.

When it becomes the early middle of the afternoon, the cattle-herds bring the cattle; they take them into their respective cow-sheds. In the cattle-shed they smear oil on them. A woman of the house, the master's wife or any other woman, washes the herd-boy at the door of the cattle-shed and anoints him with oil. She takes him inside the house and gives him cakes and parched rice. They do this in every house.

Thereupon the Jo̤g Ma̤ṅjhi says to the young men of the village: Do bless the cattle and plait the straw bundles[22], commencing from the headman's house. And they bless the cattle in house after house, and one man goes along with them and plaits straw bundles. Thereupon they collect squeezed-out beer, one small pot from every house, to treat friends from the country. Thereupon they take the bullocks out to tie them to the posts. Country people also come together. The young men first tie the bullocks to the posts at the house of the village headman. When they have tied the bullocks to the posts, they lash them to make them butt. They drum the kettle-drum for them, blow flutes for them, three times they move up and down the whole village street, lashing them. Thereupon they stop and gather at the headman's house, and there also the country people come together. They all loose their own bullocks.

In the village headman's house they thereupon place bedsteads, wooden slabs to sit on, and stools before the country visitors. The Jo̤g Ma̤ṅjhi then says to the young men of the village: Please, give the visitors from the country beer, each two leaf-cups of poured-out beer and two leaf-cups squeezed-out beer, and give all the people each one handful of flattened and parched rice. They do this. Then they sing[23]:

---

22 See Dictionary s. v. d h ã o a. 23 In corrupt Bihari.

Hearing the sound of the kettle-drum
You came, brothers-in-law;
Sit down on the gold-strapped bed.
We did nothing at all,
Brothers-in-law, as we are filled with joy.

One bowl tobacco,
Smoke this first, brothers-in-law,
It is a fine custom.
Drink at once one brass-cup water,
Brothers-in-law, a great enjoyment.

The country people answer[24]:

Cup after cup of beer, know this,
We have drunk, brothers-in-law,
Leaf-cup after leaf-cup of soup with the castrated goat.
We have not done or arranged anything for you,
Brothers-in-law, as we are filled with joy.

Thereupon the young men of the village and the young men among the visitors dance the sword-dance in the village street outside the headman's house, and the people look on. When they have finished dancing, the visitors go away to their various villages, and the young people of the village wander about in the village street the whole night. Some of the young men and girls appropriate things; from house after house they take Taro[25], egg-plant fruits, beans, and tubers; with straw-rope they make two tiny bundles, and some of it they keep aside for themselves to eat. One bundle they hang up in the headman's door and one bundle in the Paranik's door. Then they sing:

Be careful coming out, Sir headman,
You might knock against the tubers and Taro and hurt yourself.

Give us, Sir headman, our ash-pot,
We shall cook and eat tubers and Taro.

The headman then brings one earthenware pot with beer out to the young men. Also in the house of the Paranik they get, by singing in the same way, one earthenware pot with beer. Both these pots of beer the young men and girls pour out and drink in the village street outside the headman's house, and they dance the whole night until dawn. When day dawns, the Jọg Mạṅjhi and the Jọg Paranik make the young men take up the

24 In corrupt Bihari. 25 Arum Colocasia, Willd.

posts fixed in the street. On this occasion the young men collect one egg from every house, making fun. One of them "dies", and carrying him into the house, they exorcize him and sing chants:

Above it sounds like scraping,
Below it is stiff:
If you exorcize, let the exorcizing take effect,
Otherwise I shall go and plough the sun-grass thicket.

They get one egg and one handful of rice; thereupon the "dead" person quickly comes alive. They act in this way in every house.

When they have finished this, the young men and girls and women do the final functions (dancing and begging) at every house, commencing at the headman's house. Entering the courtyard they sing[26]:

The Jugis beg
For twelve years;
The young men beg
Just this day;
The young men beg
Just this day.

He does not ask for much,
He does not ask for a little,
He asks for one winnowing-fan of paddy
And one small pot of poured-out beer.

In this way they get paddy, split peas, salt, and beer in house after house. When dancing they sing songs, mutually blaming each other. The young men sing, blaming the girls for having maimed hands, and the girls sing, blaming the young men for having swollen legs; they sing, blaming each other in many ways. When they have finished begging at every house, they give all in charge in the house of the Jọg Mạṅjhi during the night. They then dance at the last house and sing ḍahar and other songs.

In the mustard, in the mustard they make their nest;
In the middle-sized earthenware pot they make the juice.
In the large basket are rustlingly the straw bundles,
Witness the strong buzzing sound.

The people of this house give them one earthenware pot of beer, twenty cakes, and five seers of flattened and parched rice. This they eat and drink. They call this dew beer.

26 In corrupt Bihari.

When the young men and girls have finished dancing, they again go to the house of the Jọg Mạṅjhi, to pass the night there. When it becomes dawn next day, the girls plaster the courtyard in the house of the Jọg Mạṅjhi with cow-dung, they draw and bring water, and the young men collect and bring together the straw bundles put on the heads of the bullocks. This they thresh, and this and the paddy that they gathered at the final dancing and begging the Jọg Mạṅjhi measures out to the girls, dividing it between them, to make rice. Thereupon the Jọg Mạṅjhi gives the young men and girls their noon meal. When they have eaten, he gives them in charge in their respective homes. Now the Sohrae is at an end.

When the girls have made the paddy that the Jọg Mạṅjhi measured out to them in rice, they bring it to him. Of this he brews beer. After some ten days he gathers all the people of the village in his house. He gives them this beer, and he gives food to the young men and girls. This beer they call the chạṭiạr (social cleansing) beer of the young men and girls. By this beer the young men and girls are "eaten" back into society again; their exemption is ended, and the closed ears of the village people are also opened.

The Sakrat[27] is the last day of the month of Pus. On the day two days before this day they have a village council and talk together, saying: To-morrow we shall catch fish and crabs, the day after we shall have the Sakrat. Consequently next day they catch fish and crabs. On the day of the Sakrat they at cockcrow kill a fowl in every house. When they have prepared rice and curry and have returned from bathing, they eat the rice and flesh curry, curry of fish, and crabs or any other stuff. When the sun is up, the men go to hunt. They hunt in a near forest. They bring Sal-leaves home with them; they go to bathe and return. In the meantime the women have prepared flattened rice and cakes. This the men offer to the bongas in every house, they offer it to the ancestors, and they pour out beer as a libation to these and to Maraṅ buru. Thereupon they make invocations in the name of the Sakrat, like the invocations at other times. They eat the cakes and the flattened rice. When they have eaten, the Jọg Mạṅjhi invites them to come along and shoot at a target. He cuts down a plantain tree or a ricinus tree and takes this along. In the open place at the end of the village street he fixes it in the ground. Now the village priest first shoots at the target post. After him all the village men shoot, until it is hit. Then when some one has hit it, the Jọg Mạṅjhi goes and cuts the target post down with a battle-axe, and the Jọg Mạṅjhi carries the one who hit it on his shoulder from there to the assembled people. And they both salute all the people, commencing from the village headman.

Now the young men dance the sword-dance and make many kinds of show. When they have finished acting in this way, they return to the village. The target post that the Jọg Mạṅjhi cut down two men carry along on their shoulders like an animal. All enter the

27 Hindi saṅkrānt, the passage of the sun into a new sign.

house of the village headman. This target post they call the headman's piece of hunt-meat. The village headman gives them beer and flattened and parched rice. At this time the headman speaks, saying: As you were so many tenants, you felled the hateful enemy and saved me, otherwise he might have eaten me.

When they have drunk there, they move away to the house of the Paranik. Here they also get flattened and parched rice and beer. From there, urging each other, they go here and there to hospitable people and drink beer. The young men and girls dance lagṛẽ in the village street outside the house of the village headman. When they have done dancing, they go to their respective houses to lie down and sleep.

The Magh fowl they sacrifice in the month of Magh (middle of January to middle of February) for the sake of reaping the thatching grass. From every house they collect one half-seer of rice or bajṛa to brew beer. The Goḍet brews beer of this. The owner of the cow that trampled on the magic square in the Sohrae also brews one separate pot of beer. They brew beer in every house. On the day fixed the Goḍet collects one fowl and one half-seer of rice and salt and turmeric from every house. The Goḍet takes it all to the place at the water's edge where the village priest is to make the offering. The beer that the Goḍet has brewed, and the feast-beer of the owner of the cow that trampled on the magic square, this also the Goḍet takes to the place where the village priest is to offer. After having bathed in the water there the village priest comes up to the magic square and offers the fowls. He offers them to Mōṛẽko, Jaher era, Maraṅ buru, Pargana, Gosãe era, and Mạñjhi haṛam and to the bongas that have come up and have been met with along the boundary. He makes an invocation as on other occasions. When he has performed the sacrifices, they make a hash with rice of them and eat them; the beer they also drink. Some of the hash goes by customary right to certain people. The following get: the village headman and his deputy and the Goḍet, the Jọg Mạñjhi, the Jọg Paranik, the village priest, and the priest of the outskirts, the reapers of the thatching grass, the carters, the thatchers, the water drawers, the bringers of firewood and leaves, the cook, and the beer brewer, they all get one portion each; only the village priest and the priest of the outskirts get two portions each.

At this time they talk together; the village headman says: Well, Sirs, as is seen here at the end of the month of Magh, the thieves have a month of Magh, the farmers also have a month of Mạgh, the village headman and his deputy also have a month of Magh, servants and servant girls also have a month of Magh, consequently we have all got the month of Magh. Well, if any of you will become our village headman, I also give up my position in the month of Magh. The Paranik, Jọg Mạñjhi, Jọg Paranik, Goḍet, the village priest, and the priest of the outskirts also speak in the same way, saying: We also, Sir, have reached the end of managing. Then the village tenants say: Also we, Sir, have reached the end, we give our riceland and grounds into your charge, Father headman, so long as the hot season lasts; only our old sites[28] we shall continue to occupy; these we do not give into your charge, and our huts we shall also keep. The headman answers: Then since you have given it up, what will become of me? I am here. So those who go we shall take away and leave them; they who come, we shall bring here[29]. Thereupon they return to the village, each with one bundle thatching grass and five or six laths.

Arrived in the village they pretend to thatch the house of the village priest, and they drink beer at his place. In a similar way they pretend to thatch the houses of the village headman, the Paranik, the Jọg Mạṅjhi, the Jọg Paranik, the Goḍet, and the priest of the outskirts, and drink beer at each place. Thereupon they drink beer in their respective houses together with a couple of friends, and the young people dance lagṛẽ until they get enough of it.

Five, six, or ten days later the village headman calls the village people together in his house. He has brewed beer; first he gives them two leaf-cups each. Then they ask him: Look here, Sir, what beer is this? He answers: This is the broken rice that they collected; it is beer brewed on this. They reply: Yes, Sir, it is broken rice, quite so; but listen, do they not say: When you prepare rice and curry, it is the salt that makes it tasty; when you give beer or liquor, it is the words that make it tasty; we are not getting the meaning of it. Then the village headman answers them: This is nothing, honourable village people; as you remember, I gave up my position in the month of Magh; now then, I am staying on again, if you village people are pleased with me. They reply to him: Yes, Sir, so many days we also have been waiting for you; therefore we have not tried to speak to anybody; we said: Perhaps his mind will be turned, our Father headman's; an old king, an old bonga, that is good; we have known you as our headman; where shall we find the shade of such a luxuriously foliaged tree? Thereupon he gives them plenty of beer.

In the same way a day later the Paranik calls the village people together, and, giving them beer, he asks them to get his work again. After this the Jọg Mạṅjhi, the Jọg Paranik, the Goḍet, the village priest, and the priest of the outskirts each separately give them beer, and each pretends to get his work back; and after them every single tenant gives the village headman and his deputy and the village people beer and pretends to ask to get his lands back. This is a pretext for drinking beer to make the unoccupied time pass.

Baha (the Flower festival) is our other great festival. This comes in the month of Phalgun (middle of February to middle of March) at the third quarter of the moon. This is a festival in connexion with the turning of the year. The Sal trees blossom at this time, the icạk̔ and the murup̔ also blossom, and the Mahua gets flowers. Before we have the Flower festival, we do not suck the icạk̔ flowers or the murup̔ flowers, and we do not deck ourselves with Sal flowers, and we do not eat the Mahua either. If any one sucks

---

28 The "old sites" are understood to be the wives.

29 The two sentences refer to death and birth.

or eats these before this festival, to their houses the village priest will not go, and he will not eat or drink anything of theirs until the Flower festival is held. The Flower festival is our righteous festival, not licentious like the Sohrae.

When the fixed day comes, on the day of bathing, the young men of the village put up two roofs in the sacred grove, one for Jaher era, Mõṛẽko, and Maraṅ buru, and one for Gosãe era. The village priest plasters all the bonga-places with cow-dung and goes away; thereupon they go to bathe. When they have bathed, the young thatchers come to the house of the village priest, who gives them beer and food. When they have eaten, they call on each other to come along to the village forest to hunt. When the village priest has eaten, he washes a winnowing-fan, a flat basket, bow and arrows, a battle axe, a broom, a bonga wristlet, a neck-chain, a small bell, and a horn, and brings these things up from the water. Thereupon he smears ground spices and oil on the implements mentioned, and on a new earthenware thin-necked vessel, and a skein of thread he also smears with the same. The young men return from the hunt, and evening sets in.

Thereupon the Goḍet takes three fowls to the village priest. These they call the priest-fowls. As soon as the evening sets in, they drum the kettle-drum and blow the horn in the house of the village priest; when they hear this, the bonga-possessed persons come, and the village people also assemble. They all assemble in the house of the village priest. The priest brings their sacrificial implements out. The possessed ones are three persons: the Jaher era comes possessing one, one is the Mõṛẽko, and one is Maraṅ buru. The Jaher era gropes about and puts on the neck-chain, takes the flat basket on the head, and takes the broom; the Mõṛẽko takes the bow and arrows, and Maraṅ buru carries the battle-axe on his shoulder. After this they run off to the sacred grove, and the young men of the village follow after them and pursue them. When they arrive in the sacred grove, the Jaher era sweeps the bonga-places clean, and the two others look on. When they have done this, they return to their homes.

Thereupon the village priest asks the bongas for their implements, holding his hands up imploringly. When they have given them to him, he makes them sit down on a mat. When they have sat down, he gives each of them one handful of rice, to make them understand how matters are. Like the invocations they make at the time when they bring the bongas up at the foundation of a new village, they now also make the same invocations. Having asked how matters are, the village priest asks them to give the rice back, and he puts this in a winnowing-fan. Thereupon he asks the bongas: Please, my Lords, will ye, as ye pass along, see the rainy season rain, the burning rain, or not? Then the bongas answer: As we pass along we shall see, we shall listen, for what purpose should we turn to the right or to the left?

Thereupon the village priest washes their feet, first of the Jaher era, thereupon of the Mõṛẽko, and finally of Maraṅ buru. When he has done this, he pours out the remaining water on the three bongas and rinses them with this. Just as he has done this, they at once jump up screaming. Now the Jaher era commences to wash. He washes the feet first of the Mọ̃ṛẽko, thereupon of Maraṅ buru, thereupon of the two, the village priest and his wife, thereupon of the village headman and of his deputy, of the kettle-drum drummer, of the horn blower and of the singer, and what is left of the water after washing he pours out on their heads. They also call out screaming. The village priest asks the Jaher era to get back the vessel in which the washing water was, and he makes them sit down on the mat like at first. Thereupon the village priest, in order to induce the spirits to leave, says to them: Please, my Lords, now time has passed, it is late, the horses, the umbrellas have become tired, depart ye. They drum the kettle-drum for them and blow the horn. They come to, and the village priest gives to each of them a brass-cup of beer, and also to the village people, that is, to all the men who have gone there, he gives beer and food. To the singer they give beer and food separately, somewhat more, and they do not let him go home either.

Now they commence to dance, and the singer sings in advance for them:

High up in the Pipal tree,
There, Lord, the Crimson-breasted Barbet is singing;
In the hanging branches of the Banyan tree
There, Lord, the Woodpecker breathes.

The country has turned round,
Lord, the Crimson-breasted Barbet is singing;
The country has turned back again,
The Woodpecker, Lord, breathes.

It has certainly turned round,
Lord, the Crimson-breasted Barbet is singing;
It has certainly turned back again,
Lord, the Woodpecker breathes.

Who of you cared for him?
Lord, the Crimson-breasted Barbet is singing;
Who of you was anxious for him?
Lord, the Woodpecker breathes.

The Five cared for him,
Lord, the Crimson-breasted Barbet is singing;
The Six were anxious for him,
Lord, the Woodpecker breathes.

He did certainly care for him;
Lord, the Crimson-breasted Barbet is singing;
He was certainly anxious for him;
Lord, the Woodpecker breathes.

*

In accordance with custom I have put
On my hand a ring;
In accordance with custom I have put
On my leg an anklet.

Where have you, my elder sister,
On your hand the ring?
Where have you, my elder sister,
On your leg the anklet?

In the water of the hollowed-out hole I let it fall,
O mother, the ring on my hand.
In the water of the pool I let it slip down
The anklet on my leg.

Why, my friend picked up
The ring on my hand;
Why, my companion took up
The anklet on my leg.

Tell him to give
The ring on my hand;
Tell him to hand over
The anklet on my leg.

With your friend is not
The ring on my hand;
Nor with your companion is
The anklet on your leg.

They dance the whole night until dawn, and they sing some very beautiful songs. In the Flower festival there are only beautiful songs; there is nothing indecent. The village priest and his wife both pass the night lying on the ground, to observe religious abstinence.

When the day dawns, the wife of the village priest, after having come back from bathing, pounds flour. And the Goḍet catches fowls in the village, one fowl from each house, further a pinch of rice, salt, and turmeric. The village priest arranges his requisites for sacrificing, a new large flat basket, a small flat basket, in which he puts sun-dried rice. The oil, the sindur, and the spices he also arranges in this, and in a winnowing-fan he puts the flour and a battle-axe. In the large flat basket he arranges a chain, an armlet and a broom, just these things; and the bow and arrows, the horn and one narrow-necked earthenware vessel an unmarried young man carries along. The narrow-necked earthenware vessel they call the good omen vessel. Now they go to the sacred grove. Following immediately after the village priest the young men and girls dance and sing, as they pass along:

The hard verandah, the verandah of abstinence,
To-day the village priest spent the night on a bamboo mat,
To-day the village priest lay abstinent on the floor on a bamboo mat.

*

Of the house, of the house,
Of the stately house,
Of the homestead, of the homestead
In the leaf-cup mustard.

Who of you will put it down
In the stately house?
Who of you will receive
In the leaf-cup mustard?

The Mǫṛẹ̄ko will put it down
In the stately house;
The Jaher era will receive
In the leaf-cup the mustard.

They first take omens
For the forest country;
They wander round about
In the villages, the hamlets.

It is there, it is there,
The cow with the black female calf.
It is there, it is there
The speckled pullet.

The village priest goes to bathe; when he has come back from bathing, he applies cow-dung to the bonga-places. At this moment the men again become possessed by the bongas. The bongas get their separate implements, like yesterday night; when they have got them, they run off to the forest. The young men run after them. Any Sal tree that has got very fine flowers, this the Mǫṛẹ̄ko bonga shoots at with an arrow, and the Maraṅ buru bonga climbs this tree and snips the flowers off and lets them fall down. The Jaher era receives the flowers in her flat basket. When Maraṅ buru comes down from the tree, they pick Mahua flowers up and take them along to the sacred grove. Thereupon the village priest, with a cloth round his neck, receives the bongas, the flowers, and the implements, all of it.

Now the village priest makes the bongas sit down on a mat under the shed, and he himself sits down in front of the bongas and sacrifices fowls. The invocation is the same, only that the priest inserts the words "in the name of the Flower festival". At each of the bongas of the sacred grove the priest puts down one flower bud and one Mahua, at each bonga-place. Thereupon they sing:

The Mǭṛẹ̄ko are five brothers,
The Turuiko are six brothers.

The rainy season rain comes peltingly,
The rain of Sita's valley comes drizzlingly.

What will they use for plastering?
What will they use for levelling?

Milk they will use for plastering,
Cream they will use for levelling.

Here, please, is your oil, your sindur;
Here, please, is your eye-paint, your roṛa bark[30].

Receive your oil, your sindur,
Accept your eye-paint, your roṛa bark.

Thereupon the village priest says to the bonga-possessed ones: Please, Lords, look out for what is yours, listen to what is yours. The priest then goes aside; the bongas sip the blood of the fowls that has trickled down. The priest washes the feet of the bongas. The Jaher era washes the feet of the priest in return; thereupon they splash water on each other. And the priest makes them come to. The dancing girls ask the priest for flowers. They sing:

We two shall ask, my elder sister, we two shall ask
The Mǭṛẹ̄ko for Sal flowers.

The girls and the young men each separately receive flowers from the priest and bow to him. Thereupon they sing dancing:

The wild cow, the wild cow
Runs out, runs in;
Very nice is the wild cow.

The Bison cow, the Bison cow
Runs out, runs in;
Very nice is the Bison cow.

30 Mallotus philippensis, Müll. Arg.

The young men and girls then return to the village, dancing the whole way. They sing:

The blind buffalo wallowed
In the Siṅjo river,
In the Siṅjo river, girls, the two girls
In the big river.

The priest cooks the speckled fowl into a hash in the sacred grove, and some of the villagers cook the other fowls into a hash. When it is cooked, they call the wife of the village priest to the sacred grove. The priest and his wife eat the speckled fowl, and the villagers who are there, eat the other fowls. All of them go home, only the village priest remains in the sacred grove.

The village people offer fowls and pigs in their own houses. When they have cooked them, they eat and drink. When it becomes the middle of the afternoon, a few men go to the sacred grove. There they drum the kettle-drum and blow the horn. Now the village people know that the priest is coming, and they say: Come along, we shall go and meet the priest. Then they go to the sacred grove. When they have reached there, the priest arranges flowers in the flat basket; this he lets a young man carry on his head, while he himself takes two or three flowers and the winnowing-fan in his armpit and carries a loṭa with water suspended from his hand. The narrow-necked omen vessel he lets the unmarried young man who is with him carry on his shoulder. In the vessel there is water. The rest of the implements some others take along. They reach the village. The village girls have in the meantime taken water in narrow-necked earthenware vessels, wooden slabs to sit on, and oil in small earthenware cups, out into the village street outside their respective houses. When the priest reaches the village, a girl washes his feet in the village street outside the first house he passes, and he gives her a flower. When she gets this, the girl bows to the priest, and he pours water on her. In the village street they do the same outside every house. Having finished this the priest goes home to his own. There they also wash him in the same way. When the priest is entering his house, he pours the water of one loṭa out on the roof, and then he goes inside. The people who follow him also go in. The priest gives each of them two leaf-cups of beer.

The girls and young men of the village have made a noise; they splash water on each other, and elderly men and women also splash water on each other, that is, people for whom this is permissible. Thereupon they dance in the court-yard of the priest. They sing:

Who is it, girls, in the court-yard,
The reddish white horse?
Who is it, girls, in the place outside
The reddish companion mare?

The priest is in the court-yard, girls,
The reddish white horse;
The priest is in the place outside, girls,
The reddish companion mare.

Moving up and down, moving up and down, girls,
Is the reddish white horse;
Swaying, swaying, girls,
Is the reddish companion mare.

Bind on him the bells, girls,
On the reddish white horse;
Tie on to her the jingle-belt, girls,
On the reddish companion mare.

The dancing ones dance, and the beer-drinkers drink beer. Until sunset they dance in the house of the priest singing Flower-festival songs; and when the sun has set, they go to outside the house of the village headman and dance lagṛẽ in the village street. When they have finished dancing, they go to their respective homes to lie down and sleep.

The next day the priest of the outskirts takes the Goḍet along with him and goes to the forest. Here he pricks himself and offers the blood to the Pargana bonga and the others. At all offerings he acts in the same way.

Offering to the Abge we have every year, sometimes in Aghãṛ (middle of November to middle of December), sometimes in Asaṛ (middle of June to middle of July), there is nothing fixed. To the Abge bonga we sometimes give fowls, sometimes pigs, and sometimes rams. Maraṅ buru and the others with him are bongas common for all, but the Abge bonga belongs to each one separately. The Abge bongas watch over their respective families, in order that no fever or pain, no epidemics, no witchcraft, and no deaths or calamities shall befall them. Santals say, it is told, that if witch women get hold of the Abge bongas, then the members of the family have no possibility of being saved; they will die; therefore they exert themselves to keep their Abge bonga satisfied. And if they make vows to them at times of danger, they will stand up and save them. When they sacrifice to the Abge, only brothers invite each other and eat, the men only; they do not give the women anything. In the open field, near a white-ant hill they perform the sacrifice to the Abge bonga; the invocation is not different, it is the same at all sacrifices.

Also to the boundary bongas they make sacrifices every year, that is, those who plough in the places where the bongas are. The boundary bongas are very jealous; if they are not kept satisfied, they kill awfully; in a moment they make snakes appear; they make tigers eat you, or they cause disease to come suddenly; therefore we fear them very much, and we are quick to sacrifice to them. We give them fowls twice every year, at rice planting and harvesting. When we sacrifice to them, there is no magic square, there is no sindur either, nor is there any religious abstinence, and the invocation is only a few words; we say to them: Beware then, so and so's Boundary bonga, look here, I am giving thee, handing thee in the name of harvesting (or planting); may there be no sudden fear, no sudden alarm. Except women all eat the sacrifice. People say, it is told, that if only you of the family eat, or if you take anything home, then the boundary bongas will enter the house and exterminate the whole family of that house.

These are our real annual festivals and offerings. On the last day of the month of Aghāṛ we have a kind of festival, called sahar luṇḍạl[31]: we press cakes and eat them; but we make no sacrifices. From the Dekos we have from time to time taken over many festivals; but among these there is only one festival that we, the whole village celebrate, viz., the Karam[32]. At that time we offer belaońja flowers[33], sun-dried paddy, dhubi grass, oil, and sindur to Kạrmu and Dhạrmu, and on the karam branch we put, as a screen, a piece of cloth two cubits long. At other festivals taken from the Dekos only the man who celebrates it, worships, and we go to look at it; we do not worship. At the Durga festival such people offer to Durga, at the Kali festival they offer to Kali, at the Monsa festival they offer to Monsa, at the Chata festival they offer to the Chata bonga, at the Pata festival they offer to Mahadeb, and at the Jatra festival they offer to Bạnsiṅ, the Jatra bonga. But as these festivals do not belong to us, Santals do not act rightly offering to the bongas of other races. On account of this our bongas are angry with us; it becomes like the state of having a wife and a co-wife, we are not making anybody satisfied. We have got much confusion in connexion with the bongas. You Europeans have only one bonga; you are very fortunate, because you worship the Ṭhạkur, who has made us.

To the Jọm sim we do not sacrifice every year, only now and then. To the Siń (sun or day) bonga we offer one goat, and to the Jọm sim bonga we offer one goat or a ram on that occasion. The invocation is not different; only at the end we say to the Siń bonga: We are not able to do this every year, do not therefore take offence, be displeased.

Our ancestors of old have left us a word, viz.: Once in your life, somehow or other, do sacrifice to the Siń bonga, even when you are poor, and when you have the means, do sacrifice to him every fifth or sixth year, otherwise he will not call you good in the next world. In the primeval age they were offering only to the Siń bonga; the Jọm sim bonga they have added afterwards. Since we have got venereal disease from the Dekos, we make vows to the Siń bonga to be cured from it; this they call "pair offering". They say, it

---

[31] The meaning of this expression is uncertain; sahar is regularly used about dung, especially cow-dung, and luṇḍạ (or luṇḍạl) about rubbing, plastering with cow-dung. One might therefore be tempted to take it as meaning renovation after the ravages of the rainy season. [32] See Dictionary s. v. [33] Cæsulia axillaris, Roxb.

is told, that Sita made a vow to get a venereal disease when Rabon carried her away to the Lonka (Ceylon) fortress. At that time, it is told, the Siń bonga caused Sita to get a venereal disease, because she made a vow to him; thereby Sita's honour remained unviolated.

The Mak̕ Mọ̃ṛẽ sacrifice occurs only now and then, when all the people of a village make a vow on account of some great calamity. And when a rumour comes from the country that the Mọ̃ṛẽko Turuiko have become sulky, then also they have a Mak̕ Mọ̃ṛẽ sacrifice. They sacrifice goats and fowls to all the bongas of the village. Except the wife of the village priest no woman gets cooked rice with curry of the flesh of the sacrificed animals and birds; all the men get it. They perform the Mak̕ Mọ̃ṛẽ sacrifice in the sacred grove. The young men and girls dance the whole night, singing Flower-festival songs.

The Kuṭạm ḍaṅgra (ox felling) sacrifice is only one man's business; but all the village people eat the flesh and cooked rice. The man who celebrates this fells one ox in the name of the ancestors; he beheads one ox in the name of the house bonga, and also in the name of Maraṅ buru he beheads one ox. The ox that is felled he fells at the foot of an atnak̕ tree, after first having made it eat from rice on a leaf-plate; and the two other bullocks he makes eat from small heaps of rice, after having made a magic square with flour at the foot of a Sal tree; thereupon he beheads them.

The Kuṭạm ḍaṅgra sacrifice is performed when they have the Jọm sim, or some vow has been made. Since we have come under the feet of the Dekos, we have the Kuṭạm ḍaṅgra sacrifice at night, because the Deko landowners impose heavy fines if they get to know of it[34]. The meat of the ox that is sacrificed in the name of the house bonga, that is to say, the meat of the side on which it falls down, and the head, only the people of the family eat, otherwise the people of the whole village all eat. The village headman and his deputy and the Goḍet get one thigh, viz., of the felled ox as their share. The Paranik gets the part of the thigh highest up, the headman gets the middle and the Goḍet the lower part. They take out a neck part for the village council. This they call the neck part of the girls. Outside in the field they eat a hash made only of the head and the liver and lungs. The meat the people of the different houses make into equal portions and take home; the whole family eat it.

---

34 The landlords being Hindus object to bullocks and especially cows being killed.

X. BELIEFS CONNECTED WITH THE BONGAS

a. The witches.

Witchcraft[1] is the great trouble with us Santals. Because of witchcraft people in the village become enemies, the door of relatives is shut, father and sons quarrel, brothers are separated, husband and wife are divorced, and in the country people kill each other. If there were no witches, we should have constant great happiness. The Europeans judge well in all matters, so far as their knowledge goes; but in connexion with witchcraft they are somehow or other blinded; we cannot understand it. The witches eat us; and when we catch them and worry them just a little, the magistrates again turn the matter round and resort to imprisonment; we feel great distress; what can we possibly do, so that it might go well with us; we are utterly bewildered. Also when we explain it to the magistrates, they do not believe it; they say: Well then, let her eat my finger; then only shall I believe that she is a witch, — and then they jail you. The witches do not eat using a vessel and a knife, quite so; by sorcery they send people off to the other world, straight away. Formerly the village headman and his deputy were subduing them, and if they would not be peaceful, they would, together with the village people, drive them away from the village after having disgraced them; but nowadays the magistrates have made them utterly audacious, so that we men have become absolutely disheartened.

The word of a man does not go any more; the women have become the absolute rulers in this age. If you say just a little to her, she will at once throw it into your mouth; fearing this you keep quiet, what can you do else.

The witches have their councils at night, in a forest or an open plain somewhere. When they go out, they put a worn broom or the like down on the bedstead with the husband, and he thinks: my wife is here, because on account of the magic he sees this broom like his wife; but the wives have gone to the bongas to be married to them. It is told they do not go on foot; they climb up into some tree or other and go by magic like the wind. They come down at the playing ground of the bongas and dance with the bongas; they call tigers to themselves; they comb them, kiss them; then they subdue the bongas and make them swear that they shall not appear when divination is made. Having acted in this way they return home at cockcrow.

---

[1] Cf. Bodding: Witchcraft among the Santals. Oslo Etnografiske Museums Skrifter, vol. 3, p. 5, Oslo 1940.

The witches are eager to make disciples; even small girls they entice, in order that the seed may live on when they themselves die. They wander about at night with a lamp; they enter the houses of other people and make the girls get up, to make them their disciples; and if they are not willing, they say to them: If you do not learn, you will die, or: A tiger will eat you. Therefore these are, from fear, eager to learn. When the disciples have got up, the witches put a broom round their loin, and, taking a worn-out winnowing-fan in the armpit, they go with lamps to the sacred grove. There they offer fowls and eat them after having cooked them with rice and made cakes of them. They make the disciples comb tigers, and if they are afraid of these and therefore are unwilling, they say to them: They don't do you anything, girls, don't be afraid. And they teach them incantations and charm-songs; thereupon they say to them, in order to give them initiation: Now, girl, eat your father, or your eldest brother. If they are unwilling, they cause them to become ill or to become mad. With a crab-straw[2] plant they scrape out their liver and lungs, and when they have cooked this, they make the disciples eat this first. From this day all mercy of the disciples ends; if they become angry, they will even eat their own child or father or brother, and they have no mercy on their own husband either; they eat them.

They say, as the story goes, that some time long ago the witches were daily making two young men get up and were taking them along with them to drum the dancing drum for them. One day the witches took out the liver and lungs of a young man and brought it with them, and from the house of these people they brought along to the sacred grove one earthenware vessel of beer, rice, salt, turmeric, big and small earthenware vessels. Having brought it there, they cooked the liver and lungs; they also gave the two young men a portion to eat. But these two did not eat it; they hid it in a fold of their clothes; the beer only they drank. When they had finished dancing with the bongas, they returned home. The next day the young man whose liver and lungs they had taken out got convulsions. Seeing this people became helpless and said: What has happened to him? What has happened to him? The two young men felt pity; therefore they said: Do seize such and such women; then the man will get well. Then they seized and brought the wives of the village headman and of his deputy and of several other well-to-do people in accordance with what the two young men had told. When they came, they were quite unwilling to confess; they began to scold; their husbands were also furious; they said: Prove it against us, you two, otherwise we shall certainly not call you good. Then the two young men before the village council took out of their clothes the portions given to them and said to them: Look here, Sirs, here is the proof of guilt. Seeing this the witches and their husbands were silenced.

---

[2] Rottboellia perforata, Roxb.

11 Oslo Etn. Mus. — Bodding.

Thereupon they brought the Pargana. He gave this order: Do bring a battle-axe. They brought one. Then the Pargana said to the witches: Do make him well; otherwise we shall cut off your heads; you are the firewood, he is the dead body. Then out of fear they made the man well. Witches who have not made ill people well, have in many places been pruned (got their head cut off).

If the wives of the village headman and of his deputy are witches, it is very difficult to get it proved against them, because their husbands will not let it be admitted. Formerly, it is told, an ojha once became angry and called the wives of the village headman and of his deputy witches. The headman and the others said to him: If you do not prove this, we shall make your head fall down. He answered them: Some day I shall show it to you, so that you see it with your own eyes. Then they became quiet. One evening when he had had his food, the ojha went to the sacred grove taking bow and arrow with him. Climbing a tree there he was waiting and watching.

At the time after supper the women whom he had slandered as being witches went to the sacred grove. Just as they had reached there, they danced round once. Thereupon one of them became spirit-possessed. Then they called a tiger to come, naming his name Lukhu. They whistled twice for the tiger; then two came quickly. They combed both of them; they were kissing them; at that time the man in wait suddenly shot the big tiger. Then the tiger thought: these have apparently done something to me. Being angry for this he bit and killed the witches, every one of them, in a mash; also the other tiger he shot with an arrow and killed; thereupon he went home.

When it dawned next morning, they saw: their (wives) were not there; they were asking each other in their different houses, saying: what has become of our (wives)? Then the ojha said to them: Go towards the sacred grove and look for your (wives); I saw them go in that direction. Then they went there; they saw them, the two tigers had bitten and killed them in a mash, and the two tigers were also lying there. Then as they spread the report of this, the people of the neighbourhood assembled and saw them. At that time the ojha told them the whole story. From that time we have been believing in witches.

The ancestors of old tell, they say, that Marań buru was teaching the men witchcraft; but by a trick the women got the magic power first. One day, it is told, the men had sat down in council to consult each other, what they should do with their scolding women. They said: We are men, how is it that our word does not count? When we say a couple of words to the women, they commence to scold shamelessly; we will not stand such behaviour. Then they said: Come along, let us go to Marań buru; from him we shall learn some kind of secret skill, that we may subdue these women. They then fixed a time, viz.: At midnight we shall meet in such and such forest. They went; they called on Marań buru to come; they called loudly: O grandfather, do come here, we a large number of men, have come to thee in distress. Marañ buru came quickly and asked them: What trouble is it that you have, grandchildren? They told their grief, and they implored him that he should teach them some secret skill to subdue their women.

Marañ buru said to them: Well, I shall teach you, but only if you make marks with your blood on these leaves. When they heard this, they became very much afraid and said to him: To-morrow we shall come again and, giving the marks, receive the secret skill. Thereupon they went away; but their women had come there secretly, and had from a hidden place heard exactly all that was said. Then they said: This, as we have heard, is the justice of these men; before they married us, they were continually following after us like dogs; now when we have become wives, they deem us bad; they are thinking of killing us. Well, we shall have a look at them, who of us are able to kill. When they had said this, they quickly went in advance of the men, following a path. On the way they decided what they should do. The men also came afterwards. As soon as the men came, the women met their husbands with caresses; therefore the men thought; they have become good by themselves; what shall we go there for?

Next day the women prepared excellent rice and curry for their husbands, and in the evening they poured out any amount of beer for them. The men drank themselves drunk and tumbled down on the ground. Then the women called on each other and assembled, they dressed themselves in male loin-clothes and turbans, and fixed goat hair on their lips and started to go to the forest to Marañ buru. They called out to him: O grandfather, please come quickly, our women have been plaguing us day and night.

Marañ buru came at once. Then they said to him: Do bring your leaves out quickly; we shall make our different marks; we are not able to stand the worrying of the women. Marañ buru brought out his Sal-leaves, and they pricked themselves, and with the blood they made the marks of their respective husbands. Thereupon Marañ buru taught them incantations and charms and initiated them in the eating of people. Smiling and laughing they returned home.

As the men were not getting up quickly next morning, the women abused and cowed them in every possible way. The men got up half-blinded and were rubbing their eyes with their hands; they awoke from their sleep, and that the women had not become gentle-minded, this they also got to understand. Feeling sick they came together to take counsel together. There they said: Come, let us go! Whatever Marañ buru may say to us, we must learn the secret skill. Consequently at night they went to the forest, and they earnestly implored Marañ buru: Do, father, please teach us, the women are tormenting us awfully.

When Marañ buru heard this, he was astonished and said to them: Why, I have given you the secret skill; what is it you wish to get again and again? Then the men unanimously said: How is that, when have you given it to us? Why, since that day we have never come here, as you know. Hearing this Maraṅ buru became dumbfounded and said to them: I have given it to you, what else have I done. Look here, look at your own marks! Seeing their different marks the men said: The marks are ours; but we have never made the marks; somebody, who knows who, have made our marks.

Then Maraṅ buru put his hand to his cheek and was thinking it over in his mind; then it suddenly dawned upon him: The women have made a mere child even of me. And becoming angry he said to the men: Do make marks here at once, we shall see these deceitful women. They made their marks, and he initiated them as ojhas and witchfinders, in order that they might be able to find out the witches and punish them. From that time the witches and the ojhas and witchfinders are enemies. But the ojhas and the witchfinders are unable to do anything, because the witches easily subdue their bongas, so that they are unable to catch them quickly; other people emerge in the divination, and being hoodwinked the witchfinders name other people.

Some people say that the witches, ojhas, and witchfinders have all learnt from Kạmru guru. It is reported that very long ago our ancestors were disciples with him. With regard to becoming ojhas that is quite so, because ojhas mention him first; but as regards witches and witchfinders, I don't know whether they have learnt from Kạmru guru or not; so far as invoking is concerned, they do not invoke him; therefore my opinion is, that they have not learnt from him.

b. The ojhas.

To become ojhas[3] we have really learnt from Kạmru guru[4]. Very long ago his country and our country were near to each other; our ancestors have told us this. The work of the ojhas is of six kinds: 1) they make divination; 2) they sow rice; 3) they bite people or rub them with a ball of rice flour; 4) they dig up bongas; 5) they exorcize bongas; and 6) they give medicine to people. If ill people do not recover by the medicine, the village people get an ojha to make divination. They bring oil and Sal-leaves to him, and, sitting down, he smears oil on two leaves, and with an incantation he rubs the leaves: Oil oil, mustard oil, man mustard oil, bạru oil, Mahua oil, castor oil, bherṇḍa oil, rae rui mustard oil, this oil, reading, what will appear, a witch may appear, an imp may appear, a female demon may appear, poison may appear, who reads, the guru reads, the guru's knowledge, mae (the mother) reads, do read by Kạhri's knowledge, by Kamru's grace, grace he reads[5].

Having done this he puts it down on the ground for a little while. Thereupon taking off one leaf he looks at it, and they ask him: Do make an offering first; what have you found? Only when you tell us, we shall understand. Now the ojha has, before making

[3] Cf. the writer's Santal Medicine and Connected Folklore, Asiatic Society of Bengal's Memoirs, Vol. X. [4] See Dictionary s. v. Kạmbru. [5] This formula has been dealt with in Santal Medicine.

the divination, selected what the different spots are to stand for, viz., here is a witch, here is the house bonga, here is a bonga of the outskirts, here is a disease, and here is poison. In what place on the leaf it comes up, in small bubbles, he tells them; if a witch then a witch, if a bonga then a bonga, if disease then disease, and if poison then poison. If witches are shown, the village headman and his deputy together with the village council will in the evening call out at every house: Beware you so and so, so and so is ill, may he get well; we have caught you; if he does not get well, we shall certainly not call you good. If the patient gets well by this, well and good; otherwise the village headman sends men in pairs to the neighbourhood to have divination in oil made. In the evening they come together, and they ask the men who went to get divination in oil made, each one separately. If they have brought the answer from three persons, that it is a witch, they fix branches in the ground to single out the person, and if their reports do not agree, they have again fresh divinations made.

If the house bonga is shown up, they say to the patient: Do appease your bonga. He then libates water to him and makes a vow, saying: When I get well, I shall fill thee. If a bonga of the outskirts is shown up, the ojha scatters rice out for the bonga, making this invocation: Here then, thou so and so bonga, my own blood, pricked-out blood I am giving thee, handing to thee; may he get well, may he recover; whoever hired thee, invited thee, her (his) principal son mayest thou provide with food, with provisions for the journey; from to-day mayest thou forswear, for ever leave this house; where thy place, thy residence may be, go there, get up with thee. Scattering out rice also to Maraṅ buru and Pargana he makes invocations to them: Beware then, as is seen here, in such and such headman's house an eating bonga, an eating mountain spirit had applied himself, had struck against (a person); I caught him, I grasped him, his broken grain, his rice grain I gave; please be witness to it, be favourably present at it; from to-day may the ill person get well, may he recover. In this way the ojha makes invocations separately to Maraṅ buru and Pargana. Finally he makes invocations to the bongas of roots and stumps and those near the boundary, scattering out rice to them: Beware then, ye also, of the roots, of the stumps, of the recesses, of the holes, of the boundary, of the side, splendid ones, spirited ones, carrying the water-bottles, carrying on your backs the sandals, ascetics, friends, managing ones, come near, and ye that cannot come, be witnesses, be eye-witnesses from far away.

If disease is shown up, they will crush medicines for the patient and let him drink these; and if it is poison, they will bite the patient or rub him with a cotton ball. First, pronouncing an incantation, they exorcize and bring it together in one place; thereupon they bite it out and spit it out into a leaf-cup, that is to say, the ojha does this. Or where the disease is situated, there they rub with a ball of flour, pronouncing an incantation. When the patient gets well, they give the ojha fowls for offering to his bonga. When he has sacrificed them, he eats them, and he gives a share to a couple of the village people.

c. Planting branches.

Branch planting is done as follows: If witches or bongas or disease is shown by the divination, they plant branches at the water's edge to prove this. To stand as a witness they first plant a branch in the middle; thereafter one in the name of the house-bonga; thereupon one in the name of the bonga of the house-wife's old home, thereupon one in the name of the man's brother and male relatives; thereupon one in the name of the daughters and the sisters; thereupon one in the name of an epidemic, and after this they plant one branch in the name of each separate house in the village. They apply sindur to every branch as it is planted. Thereupon they scatter out rice and make invocation: Be greeted then, Siṅ bonga in heaven! Thou art spread out like a mat, the four corners, the four worlds thou hast covered; here then we are trying to find, to trace by ordeal; what is guilty thou wilt show guilty, may that dry up, may it wither — thou wilt call witnesses, — and if it is not so, mayest thou sprout like a sedge sprouts; thou wilt remain unchanged (that is the witness branch).

Again they speak: Have a care then, if thou art a bonga, may this dry up, may it wither; if it is not thou, may it remain unchanged. Thou wilt call witnesses. In the same way they make invocations in the name of all at each branch. When they have acted in this way, they go home. Some five hours afterwards they return to have a look at the branches. Which branch, standing in anybody's name, has died, they find out for certain. If it has been proved to stand for witches, then in so many houses as the branches have whithered there there are witches. Afterwards they seek fresh proofs in other villages in the same way, in two or three places. Thereupon they say to the suffering person: We have ascertained these things for you; are you taking us to the guru, or is it well as it is? He will say in reply: I am not getting well; we must bring a clear decision from the guru. They fix a day and go to the witchfinder.

d. The witchfinders.

The witchfinders are our High-court in connexion with witchcraft. Whom they pronounce to be witches, these we call true witches. Whether they really find them, or it is false, so far as we are concerned, we believe that they really find them; they have namely received initiation from Maraṅ buru. And we also test them, whether they speak inspired by the bongas, or they deceitfully act as witchfinders.

If a person does not become well by medicine, we first let divination be made by an ojha; thereupon we plant branches in the villages; then only we go to the witchfinder. If the whole village is ill, the village headman invites all men and takes us along; and if only one person is ill, he cries to the village headman; then a couple of men on the side of the patient, and the husband or the brothers of the person who has been found by the divination to be responsible, and five or six men from the village as witnesses go to the witchfinder. They stay together, in order that none of them shall be able secretly to tell the witchfinder anything. They do not go straight to the witchfinder; they camp somewhere outside. From where they are, what their names are, in whose name they have come, and what kind of illness the patient suffers from, about these matters they do not tell anybody anything. They say to the headman of the witchfinder's village: Please, Father, let us get divination in oil made at the guru's. He then asks them: How many are you, who will have offerings made? They say to him: We are so and so many men. The headman takes them to the witchfinder. The headman makes them bring forward the necessaries for offering, viz., one betel nut, one leaf-cup, sun-dried rice, oil, sindur, resin of the Sal-tree, and Bael[6] leaves.

Now the witchfinder says to them: Please come presently at this or that time. They return to their lodgings. When people of the village or anybody come there and ask them anything, they do not speak, or, even if they speak, they do not tell them their country and their village; they mention another country and another village. At the appointed time they go to the witchfinder. Sometimes the witchfinder will prophesy for them in his own house, and sometimes in the sacred grove or in the open field. They sit there quietly, and he himself puts down small quantities of sun-dried rice in many places in the name of the bongas, and puts Bael-leaves down at each place; thereupon he makes marks of sindur at each small heap of sun-dried rice, after having mixed it in oil. And the Sal-resin he throws into the fire in the earthenware lid of a vessel. He blows a conch and rings a bonga bell, and he invokes his bongas; then he becomes filled with the spirit of inspiration, and in this state he makes his utterances. First he names their country, thereupon their village, thereupon how their village street is situated, these things he mentions; thereupon their village headman, thereupon the complainant, thereupon the younger and elder brothers of his father, his brothers, his sisters, his sons, his daughters, and how many all these are, — all these he mentions by name.

Thereupon he asks them: How is it, Sirs, have I spoken these matters right or not? They then say: Absolutely right; we are convinced; please let us hear the oracle. The witchfinder answers them: Give me, pay down the fee; then naturally I shall tell you. Then they give him one rupee. And if they have come after having made an agreement, he also asks them to give as many rupees as they have agreed on; only when they give this, will he tell them whether it is a witch or a bonga, and who they are. Thereupon the witchfinder says to them: In so and so many places you have planted branches, did you do this properly or not? They answer: Yes, Father, we have done these things. Then the witchfinder says to them: If you are not satisfied, go and consult seven men of insight. If it

[6] Aegle Marmelos, Correa.

turns out to be otherwise at seven such people, I shall return you your fee money. Now they go home. If it has been shown to be a bonga, the patient will promise him a sacrifice; and if it has been shown to be witches, they harrass and fine these, and they drive them ignominiously away from the village. If the people who have been pronounced to be witches at one witchfinder's are not satisfied, they take them to another witchfinder, to get fresh proof. But this is futile, because if they have been pronounced to be witches in one place, even if they go to a thousand witchfinders, they will all say the same. Only a very few witches are able by magic to muddle up a witchfinder's prophecy. If the wife of a village headman is caught as a witch, they will not be able to drive her away; she will on the contrary herself say to the person who has been eaten: Do look out for yourself, if you are not feeling comfortable somewhere; I have got a village, where shall I go?

Nowadays the witchfinders act very deceivingly; there is no trustworthiness in them as it was formerly, as with the honest witchfinders. Formerly the witchfinders did not learn to become witchfinders, it would come to them of its own accord. They were not filled by the spirit of divination; they got it at night through dreams, or they had visions in day-time. The bongas appeared and told them, viz.: Such and such people are coming for this or that purpose, you tell them in this way. Nowadays there are no such witchfinders; mostly they hypocritically blacken people and take their money. For this reason they keep secret informers, to remove hindrances. And witchfinders, who have no secret informers, make their prophecies, feeling their way. They try mentioning half a name, and keep their eyes on the persons who want to be informed, to see whether it is right or not, and if it is incorrect, they again try some other name. Therefore the words of the witchfinders do not agree nowadays. The witchfinders who keep secret informers are easily able to find all out; if such a witchfinder is unable to name it correctly, he says to them: Sirs, there is an occult hindrance; get this removed first. They then go to the secret informer. What different things have to be given to remove the occult hindrance, this the witchfinder has told them. The secret informer offers this, a fowl, or a grasshopper, or a frog, or some fungus, or a white cat. Before he performs the sacrifice, he asks them: In whose name am I to get the occult hindrance removed? Then they tell him the names of the village headman and of his deputy; they tell him the name of the complainant; and as they tell him a few other matters, he performs the sacrifice. Thereupon he says to them: If you have any doubt, watch me; I shall not go to the witchfinder. But to his own house he goes, and his wife can talk with the wife of the witchfinder; thereby much deceit may happen. Let the witchfinders at once openly tell all as in former times, in that case there is nothing to be said. But where do the present day witchfinders act in this way? The secret informers get one four-anna bit to remove the occult hindrance.

e. To be possessed.

About being possessed I have already spoken: at the time when they make the bongas come up in the sacred grove, they cause men to be possessed, and at the Flower festival they become possessed of their own accord; but also at times of fever and illness they cause men to be possessed, in order to ask them and to be informed. When a bonga has inspired a man, he gets into a trance and is possessed, and the bonga speaks through his mouth. We ask the bongas at such time: Do please, my Lord, here filling the bed, overfilling the mat, we are lying, we are curled up, feeble, scantily clad, where it ran into seed and ripened, in what way it was half-done, was indifferently done, this one thing tell us, show us; where it started, had its origin, carefully using a split bamboo, a stretched out thread, make a way, make a road in connexion with this, Lord Father my Ṭhạkur[7]. Then the possessed men tell that they are possessing bongas, saying: We have one day, half-a-day desired, have coveted, we have frightened, have alarmed, where should we lay the blame, the fault. Then they quickly make a sound that it is allright. The men then answer: Well then, now we have got to know, we have understood, we have had warning, have become conscious, please, at the Flower festival or at the Sohrae we shall give ye this portion; well then, this fever, this illness ye at once carry along, carry along in a sling, and medicine leaf-cups, large leaf-cups with medicine we shall apply, shall put on; may he get well, may he recover, that he may say from to-day: please give me rice, please give me food; may he eat, may he take food; have a care then, don't deceive us, let us see your trustworthiness. Then at this moment the bongas answer: Look then, so long a time, so long an age our (word) has not been false, not been falsified; for what purpose should we let it loose, set it free? like a stone, like a rock we have pressed it, we have pressed it down. Then when they have got confidence, the people say: Well, my Lords, it has become late and a long time, the horses, the umbrellas have become tired, please let it come to an end. Thereupon the possessed ones come to.

The ancestors have said that when those to be possessed are inspired, they become unconscious; they do not remember anything. But nowadays the possessed ones remember everything. Perhaps these also are like the deceitful witchfinders of the present day, probably they are. Also due to greediness they become possessed in the present age, that they may get excellent beer under false pretences. One man[8] has told the following: When I get possessed, I remember everything, and I hear and follow clearly all their talk, and I have got for myself a good deal of excellent beer by false pretences. This man lives in Benagaria; all people know his name. He has told: If I do not get excellent beer at some festival, then I meditate in my mind how I shall get tasty beer. And I say: O, I shall

---

[7] No Santal has been able to tell the writer what the real meaning of the rigmarole is. [8] The man referred to was Biram, who later on became Skrefsrud's principal assistant in Santali.

be possessed as Mạṅjhi haṛam. Thereupon I quickly become possessed, and they ask me: Who are you, Lord? Then I tell: Mạṅjhi haṛam. Then they take me to their house; at the door they wash my feet on a brass plate. Thereupon they take me inside and make me sit down on a stool. Then they bring me some very tasty poured out beer in a brass-cup. When I have drunk about two brass-cups, I come to. In many villages I have fraudulently obtained beer by becoming possessed in this way.

When they tie the bullocks to the posts in the street at the Sohrae and forget any customary act, I look intently at it, in order that when they ask me, after my having become possessed, I may be able to tell exactly why I, the Mạṅjhi haṛam, have come. Having become possessed I say to them: I have come because you have done wrong in connexion with this or that. Then they say to me: Well, my Lord, don't be offended; we did something wrong; please put up with it, endure it. Then they again give me one additional brass-cup full of beer.

f. Application of the (evil) eye.

Application of the eye is also a trouble that we have. The eye of women is applied because of envy. When they see that someone has earned well, they say: Nothing happens to so and so; they are earning exceedingly; they will surely have no trouble. This speech of theirs takes effect. Then these people become ill; their cattle die, and they get much suffering. When they let divination be made in connexion with this the ojhas say: Envy and malevolence have been applied to you. Consequently they give fowls to the ojha, that he may make them well by sacrificing them. Therefore, however wise we Santals may be, or however much we may be able to work, we do not exert ourselves too much; we rather suffer hunger.

g. Of being bewitched.

We are also afraid of being bewitched. People say, it is told, if people whose tongue is spotted look at you when you are eating, you will vomit a good deal, afterwards you will get diarrhoea, and in case it is a child, they will also cry much. On such occasions we let persons who know how to do it, feel the pulse. They will then say: This one has been bewitched, get me some marking nut, one half of the pod of the fruit of jo̤m lạr[9], some charcoal and a straw of a worn broom. They bring him this, and keeping his breath he three times makes exorcizing passes over the bewitched person, and when he is performing this, he takes these things below and under his legs; thereupon he throws it all away on to the homestead field of some other person.

---

9 Bauhinia Vahlii, W. & A.

h. About digging out bongas.

To dig out bongas is also a work we have. We make the ojhas dig, if it has been proved that a bonga has been buried. Witches deposit (bury) bongas in the house or cowshed of some person, in order that these people may die. On such occasions we fetch an ojha, that is to say one who knows how to dig out bongas. Not all ojhas know this. The ojhas first make divination, to find out where the buried bongas are. When they have ascertained this, they dig out the bongas. We have seen bongas that have been dug out. Deposited bongas are of two kinds. One kind of bonga is a white stone to which sindur has been applied, covered by hair wrapped round it, and another kind of bonga is all kinds of agricultural seeds and a white stone with sindur applied to it, put into an empty cocoon. When the bonga has been dug out, the diseased persons sometimes get well, sometimes they also get worse thereby. When they dig out bongas, sacrifices have to be given, one ram, one pig, one goat, five fowls and one pair of pigeons. The ojha gets for the offering of his blood five four-anna bits in money, and when the diseased person gets quite well, the ojha at the same time next year gets five rupees and a loin-cloth.

i. The bonga of the old home of a wife.

If the bonga of the old home of a wife follows her, they will get well only when he is taken back there; otherwise they are taken ill and they die. If they sacrifice every year to a bonga of the wife's old home, who has followed to the son-in-law's home, he will not eat them; if they do not sacrifice to him, they will have to give various things to make him go back. As much as they have brought from the house of the bride's father, only when they send all this back, will the bonga of the wife's old home leave them, and they will also have to take along to the home of the bride's father two animals to be sacrificed. They call the bonga of a wife's old home acraeḷe boṅga. If the bongas of the wife's old home become angry, they eat awfully; therefore people make sacrifices to them from fear; or they send them quickly back.

j. About exorcizing bongas.

When bongas are exorcized, a good many requisites in connexion therewith have to be given, otherwise they do not go out. They exorcize the wealth-bongas. The wealth-bongas make them who have taken them in, very wealthy; but if they become obstinately angry, they eat people in large numbers. Therefore people are saved only when they exorcize them; otherwise they will eradicate the whole family.

If they get proofs through ojhas or witchfinders, that the wealth-bongas are eating, they procure the requisites: one silk cloth, one small box with sindur, a hair-knot tassel, a plait of cow-tail hair, a hair-pin, a small box with eye-paint, a winnowing-fan, a small flat basket, an iron stick, five chains, five nails, a pair of sandals, a wooden slab to sit on, a small cart, a bundle with grains of all crops, five rupees, two cows, one pig, one goat, a ram and five fowls. On the ram they put a small bell. When they have gathered all this, they bring the ojha.

The ojha then calls on the bonga to come. He makes the bonga take possession of a man. The ojha puts a worn-out winnowing-fan in front of the person to be possessed; in this winnowing-fan he puts about one handful of sun-dried rice; then he says: Come here, Lord, come to such and such a house, thou so and so bonga, I am calling on thee, crying to thee, in hurry and haste come running, come quickly, as a disciple, as a medium he is sitting, he is seated (the one to be possessed). Now the man quickly becomes possessed. Then they ask him: Please then, Lord, thy owner has come to an end worshipping thee, adoring thee; listen, he will not keep thee any more; what do you say? Then the bonga quickly mutters that it is right; and he says: If he will not keep me, I shall go; let him deliver up to me all that is mine.

Thereupon they bring out to him all the collected requisites. They say to him: Look, here is all that is yours; well then, are you satisfied or not? He says: Satisfied. Now he enters the cowshed to select cows for himself. He slaps two and comes away. He comes out, and they ask him: How is it, have you got everything? He says to them: Yes, I have. Thereupon they open the gate, and the two cows that he has chosen, come out of their own accord. They bind them with ropes. Thereupon they take all the collected requisites and say to him: Come along, where you have your place and abode, guide us there. Then he comes to.

Now the two cows of their own accord go in front, and these two guide the people along. The winnowing-fan the ojha takes along, carrying it in his armpit. Where the two cows stop and lie down, there they behead the sacrificial animals. Through the head of the ram they put a chain, and they hammer this fast to a tree. The flesh of the sacrificed animals they all of them cook into a hash with rice, and they all eat it there, before they go away. And the things they leave there; none will touch these; if they touch them, the wealth-bonga will follow after these. And the man from whom the bonga was exorcized, will, before a year is passed, become utterly poor; his cows and buffaloes will also all die; his paddy and rice will also be blown away, who knows where; the inhabitants of this house become utter paupers. This is what we have seen with our eyes. Unrighteous wealth will not stay.

k. Spiriting away by bongas.

We are very much afraid of bongas spiriting away; they spirit away people, and things also they cause to disappear. The bongas, who spirit away, are female bongas. They spirit away young Santal men. Some live in water, and some in mountain caves. It is told they like young Santal men very much; therefore they spirit them away to themselves, that they may be married to them. In the shape of Santal girls they beguile them and take them in. Down in the water, it is told, they have what is like kingly palaces, and in the mountain caves also the same. They give them excellent rice and curry, it is told; if young men spirited away bring these things out in the world, it at once becomes earth. Formerly, people tell, young Santal men had got children with bonga girls. One bonga girl once ran in to a young Santal man. They lived together for a long time and got children. When she had run in, the bonga girl said to the young man: When we may become angry for some cause and quarrel or scold each other, you may beat me with anything, but do not kick me with your foot. When she had become the mother of two or three children, the young man was one day milking a cow; at that time the bonga girl was in the door leading into the cowshed, giving breast to her child. Somehow or other she was making the child cry; getting angry at this the young man suddenly kicked her. Then the bonga girl became deadly hurt. She cried awfully. That very day she went out and away. The young man tried again and again to bring her back, but was unable to make her come back. When bonga girls, it is told, have been married to Santal men, they do all kinds of work, only they do not throw cow-dung away, and they do not eat rice and curry with salt; if they eat salt, they will disappear. Many young men who were spirited away by bonga girls, have come back, both from the water and from the mountain caves. At the present day also some such ones are living. The bonga girls, it is told, have the heels turned forwards and the instep backwards.

l. About bongas appearing.

We have also seen bongas revealing themselves. They look like real; but as you continue looking at them, they disappear to sight these bongas. Formerly the bongas appeared in visions to the righteous witchfinders and told them what they had to say. The bongas who reveal themselves cannot be caught like other bongas. They speak, that is so. If the people of the country or the people of any village have done anything wrong, the bongas reveal themselves and tell them, as they leave: You have done this or that wrong; now observe religious abstinence and do so and so; otherwise it will go bad with you.

m. About goblins and ghosts.

There are also goblins and ghosts. Women who die during pregnancy become goblins (cuṛin), and children who die in the womb, become ghosts (bhut), people tell. Children who die without having been ceremoniously cleansed also become ghosts. The head of the goblins, it is told, looks like a spinning wheel, standing out, and the ghosts are very small, indistinctly seen. The goblins suck people, when they find them alone, and the ghosts frighten people in a thousand shapes.

We have further belief in various matters. People say: If husband and wife name each other's name, the children become deaf; therefore they do not name each other's name. And if a man and the wife of his younger brother, or a woman and the husband of her younger sister, or the wife of her younger brother name each other's name, they will not, it is told, burn when they are cremated after death; therefore they do not among us name each other's name. Husband and wife call on each other saying, father or mother of so and so child, and when they have not as yet got any children, they call on each other using some general expression [10].

---

10 For a number of details in connexion with the customs here mentioned the reader is referred to the writer's paper 'On Taboo and Customs connected therewith among the Santals' in the Journal of the Asiatic Society of Bengal, Vol. LXVII, Part III, 1898.

XI. DEATH AND FINAL FUNERAL CEREMONIES

a. Death.

When people among us die, our women cry awfully; they cry alas, alas; they wail, they beat their breast, they knock their forehead against the ground; they sing mourning songs, mentioning various matters. When a mother is dead, they cry:

Alas, alas, my milk tree,
My milk tree, O mother, fell down.
Going in which direction
Might I catch sight of the form of the milk tree?

Alas, alas, up to now
Like a hen-mother she covered us with her wings.
To-day, O mother, like chickens,
To-day, O mother, you shook us off and left us.

Alas, alas, up to now
When we came from anywhere,
Our mother sitting in the door
Was meeting us with caresses like maena chickens.

When a father has died, they cry in the same way:

Alas, alas, the author of my life,
The author of my life left us to-day.
Going in which direction
Might I catch sight of the form of the author of my life?

When the husband dies, the mistress of the house will cry:

Alas, alas, my shading umbrella,
My shading umbrella, O mother, is blown away.
Going in which direction
Might I catch sight of the form of my shading umbrella?

Alas, alas, my pigeon-mate,
My pigeon-mate and I, our pair is broken.
Going in which direction
Might I catch sight of the form of my pigeon-mate?

When children die, their mother cries:

Alas, alas, my parakeet,
My parakeet, O mother, flew away.
Going in which direction
Might I catch sight of the form of my parakeet?

They mention again and again various griefs of their heart, not what they have heard from others: just what at the moment comes up in their heart, this they mention in their lamentation.

b. The cremation.

We cremate people on the day they die. We inform the village headman and his deputy, and these two give the Goḍet an order: Do call the people together, we shall go to carry firewood in such and such a house. And they assemble in the house of death, taking axes with them. The women of that house grind turmeric and roast cotton seed and paddy. The men catch a fowl, apply fire to a straw-rope and pull out some thatching-grass from the eaves; the roasted cotton-seed and paddy and the thatching-grass from the eaves and the fowl they place in a worn-out winnowing-fan. And what the people of the house send with the dead one, all this they place on the bedstead, viz., clothes, a brass-cup, rupees, pice, a battle-axe, bow and arrows, a stick, a flute and all his implements. When they have finished arranging all this, four men come in, and taking hold of the four bedstead-legs they carry the dead one out; when they have brought him out into the courtyard, they carry him on the bedstead on their shoulders to the junction of roads at the end of the village street; here they put him down for a short while. Here all the women of the house and of the village anoint him with oil and turmeric, and they put a sindur mark on his forehead, and the roasted cotton seeds and paddy they drop down in small heaps at the four bedstead-legs.

Thereupon an ojha exorcizes the dead one with the fowl mentioned, waving it three times round over him. Now the women return home, and the men carry the dead one on their shoulders to the place where he is to be cremated. If the man has a low rice-field with running water, they will cremate him there, and if he has not, then at a river. There they build the funeral pyre running North and South, after having cut wood. At the four corners they fix four posts to prevent it from falling down. These they call pyre-corner-posts. Thereupon they wash the hands and feet of the heir of the dead one; they rinse his eyes and pour a little water on his mouth. Thereupon the carriers lift him (the dead one) up and carry him three times round the pyre; when they have done this, they lift him up on the pyre; they put him down with his head towards the South.

The clothes of his body, necklaces, and loin-string they loose, rings, ear-rings, all of his they take off, the things sent with him they remove from him, and they cover his private parts with a branch, and they put down on him four pieces of wood, one on his breast, one on his stomach, one on his waist, and one on his feet; this they call covering wood.

The village men stand round the pyre. Any one whose wife is enceinte, stands some distance away. Now the ojha exorcizes them, waving the fowl mentioned three times round them; thereupon he nails the fowl to the pyre corner-post, and he cuts the bedstead and comes away from it. Thereupon the heir breaks off a sedge-culm and, uncoiling some threads of the fringes of the cloth of the dead one, he twists this round the sedge. Having kindled this he sets fire to the mouth of the dead one, while looking away to another side. This they call ag mukh[1].

Thereupon all the brothers and cousins first throw each one branch of firewood on the dead one; after them all the village men. Then they recite: Here then, we have all of us given thee one branch of firewood; do not keep us long, go like the wind. Thereupon they set fire to it round about. Thereupon they sit down together at a distance. Here one man shaves them. They are all shaved, and at the same time the dead one is cremated and finished. Now they quench the fire by pouring water on. When this is done, the heir rinses the bones with water and pours turmeric water and milk on them, and he puts them into an earthenware vessel. As we nowadays live very far away from the Damuda river they put only the skull and collar bones, three pieces, into a small earthenware vessel On this small vessel they place a potsherd, and in the middle of this there is a hole for the dead one to breathe; and into this hole they insert a crab-straw; on this the dead one wanders out and in. Round it they close it up by smearing on turmeric. The other bones the ashes, and the charcoal they push out into the water of the river and immerse it there When they pick up the bones, they sing[2]:

Above the funeral pyre
The vulture is sweeping round;
My father's bones
Pick out for me.

Here, take it, vulture,
The gold in the ear.
My father's bones
Pick out for me.

---

1 Ag means fire, mukh means mouth, both Hindi words.

2 In a corrupt form of Bihari.

Thereupon they put a winnowing-fan over the middle of the place where he was burnt; treading on this the men who carried him dig round it, and the one who was the last one to dig hacks the winnowing-fan and leaves it. Then one man mixes cowdung water in a brass-cup and sprinkles it on the places there up to where they had put him. Thereupon they scatter the remaining roasted cotton-seed and paddy over the place where he was cremated. And they say to it: Have a care then, so long a while the earth was closed up, now we are purifying thee. Thereupon some three men bury the small earthenware vessel containing the flower-bones in a copse at the end of the village street. In this place they cover with earth the earthenware vessel, over which they have put bark pressed down with a stone. Thereupon they all go to bathe. When they have bathed, they come to the end of the village street and stand there. They have some Sal-resin that they have taken off (some tree) when they came. One man asks for fire and brings it out from the village. Into this fire they throw the resin, and all of them are fumigated by this resin. Thereupon they go to their respective houses. All that was sent with the dead person they sell and buy a castrated goat (or pig), and the village people eat this the same day. But the people of the house where the death occurred, do not eat of it.

When it becomes evening, elderly men go to the house of death to console the inhabitants of this house. They say to them: Do not be constantly grieving; he is gone, he is happy; we shall also one day in the future have to go. If we should be continually crying, our body would suffer, our work would also be neglected; the landlords are there, the usurers and money-lenders are there, the relatives are there, our own stomach and soul are there; so long as we are alive, we shall surely not give up eating and drinking; therefore work, do what is to be done. Then from to-day keep your soul down with a stone-rock. People tell, they say: If you cry all day long, they will rap him who is gone on the head, like a buffalo-calf. In the other world they will say to him: Please you, dance, they are singing for you. Therefore do not wail and lament all over the country, or they will give him much hardship.

c. The ceremony of purification after death.

On the fifth day they have the purification ceremony[3]. They assemble in the house of the dead person and are shaved. The people of the house pound flattened rice, and they make three cakes, boiling them in oil. Now the people of the village go to bathe. They take a little soapy earth for washing the hair, oil-cake, oil, three tooth-brush twigs, and three or four leaves with them to the place where they are to bathe. The women go to a separate place. The men divide the earth and the oil-cake that they have brought to the bathing place on three leaves, and the tooth-brush twigs they also put down along

---

[3] The Santal words tel nahan literally mean "oil bathing" and are taken from Hindi.

with these. Thereupon they offer this earth with the left hand to the bongas. They make an invocation: Here then, thou who hast died, hast fallen, to-day we are bathing, we are washing our hair for the sake of purification, mayest thou also bathe, wash thy hair. After this they make offering to the first human pair; they make this invocation: Here then, Pilcu haṛam, for the sake of purification we are bathing, are washing our hair, may you two also bathe and wash your hair; now then this one who has died, has fallen here, him also you two bring in and keep, lead in and keep with you; under the eaves of a stranger, at the back of a stranger's house do not put him, you two. At last they offer to Maraṅ buru; they make an invocation: Here then, Maraṅ buru, for the sake of purification we are bathing, washing our hair; mayest thou also bathe, wash thy hair; have a care then, also this one who has been extinguished, has fallen down, bring him in and keep him, lead him in and keep him with thee.

When they have bathed, they return home. The women also come. The widow of the dead man comes in wet clothes, and she wrings the water out of her cloth at the place where her husband died. When the village people have had food, they again assemble in the house of the dead one. Then they call on the dead one to come. Three persons become possessed, one by the dead one, one by Porodhol[4] and one by Maraṅ buru. When the possessed ones have been inspired, the village people ask them: Please, Lords, who are you who have stretched yourselves out like a straw-rope? Only when you tell, when you show your kind, your birth, then only we shall know, shall recognize, that you are this bonga, this mountain-spirit; then only we shall worship him, pay homage to him. Two of them say it is right, and they tell who they are, viz., I am Porodhol, and I am Maraṅ buru. One of them does not speak. They then sprinkle water on him, and washing his face they slap him on his back. Then he says it is right. Then they ask him: Please, Lord, who art thou who hast come, hast arrived; tell thy kind, thy birth. He then says: I the extinguished one, the fallen-down one have come, have arrived. They then give rice to the three bongas and say to them: Here please, Lords, broken grains, rice grains, understand ye, explain ye first; it has no eyes, no ears. Then they seek to understand among themselves. When they have understood, they put the rice back into the winnowing-fan. They then ask them: Please, Lords, how did ye understand, did ye explain, tell us, show us, how did we die, did we fall? They then say: One day, half-a-day what was ill, what was diseased was accepted, was pricked. Now they ask the dead one: Please, Lord, thou the extinguished one, the fallen down one, how didst thou go, didst thou get up? He then says: I got finished of my own accord; or, if witches have eaten him, he will say: There was no room for me in the eyes of people, therefore I went.

Now they say to him: Wilt thou not ask for water? He answers: I shall ask for it. He then asks every one of the village people for water, commencing with the people of

---

[4] Porodhol, lit. the whitehaired one, is used here about the spirit of the first man.

his own family. All give him water. After this they give him beer, a couple of brass-cups, until he is satisfied. Marañ buru and Porodhol they also give each one leaf-cup with water and beer. Thereupon they ask the dead one: Please, as thou knowest, we are going to take thee to the Damuda river, may nowhere on the road, in the forest stomach-ache, headache be created, be formed. He then says: Do it, youngsters, nothing will happen, like the wind you will go, like the wind you will come back. When they have had this talk, they make them come to.

Thereupon they wrap up one seer of flattened rice, three cakes, and one seer rice. They stitch together a purse of the cloth of the dead one; taking this with them they go to the end of the village street. Women bring water along in brass-cups, besides turmeric. When they have reached the end of the village street, they stand together at the cross road. Now three men go to fetch the flower-bones[5]. They take fire with them. When they have dug it up, they set fire to the burial place and come away. Then they say: The old woman's hut is burning, hey! Now they come straight along, they do not look back. This they call the burning of the old woman's hut. They cut and bring along three ebony sticks, short ones. These three they tie into a bundle, and on top of this they put the small earthenware vessel. They take out the flower-bones and call on the women to come near. With a leaf-cup these (women) pour water on the flower-bones, after this turmeric water, after this milk. The heir of the dead one puts the flower-bones into the purse. Thereupon the people move away some distance. One man among the three who brought the flower-bones takes an ebony stick and goes three times round the small earthenware vessel; then he at once strikes the vessel into pieces with his left hand; thereupon the three men go with the flower-bones half-way, that is, up to past one village boundary. The other people go back to the house of death after having bathed. They drink a couple leaf-cups of beer.

It becomes evening. They catch and bring a few fish. When they have brought these, they cook them and a fowl into curry and rice without salt. When they cut up the fowl, they cut off and keep one leg and one wing. This leg and wing they tie to a small piece of wood, and when it has become dark, three men go to the cross-road at the end of the village street; they take with them two or three other small pieces of wood, a little thatching-grass from the eaves, and fire, and one man among them drags the leg and wing that is tied to the piece of wood along the ground. When they have reached the cross-road, they build a semblance of a house, thatch it with the thatching-grass, and when they have thrown the fowl's leg and the wing into this house, they set fire to the hut and come away. They say: The old woman's hut is burning, hey! Thereupon they come straight back to

---

[5] Lit. jañ baha, bone flower, the three bits of bone that are to be taken to the Damuda river. No Santal has been able to explain why these bones are called "flower", some think, that it may possibly be due to the bones being white.

the house. When they reach the entrance to the courtyard of the dead person, they see that they have in the meantime placed water in a wooden mortar. Into this they dip their left foot and go inside to the courtyard. When the last one of them has dipped his foot into the wooden mortar, he kicks and upsets it.

Now all the people who have come to take food sit down. Two persons of the family take food from karam leaves, and the village people from half-finished Sal-leaf-plates. One leaf-cup with rice, one leaf-cup with curry, and one leaf-cup with water placed in a small basket they hang up in a carrying-sling at the place where the death took place. The people of the family make a pretence of eating with their left hand; at this time the village people sprinkle water on them with roots of the khus khus[6] plant, to remove their uncleanness. The food they have eaten they call food after cremation.

The three men who have gone half-way to take the flower-bones away eat the flattened rice and the cakes that they have brought with them inside the boundary of another village; thereupon they return to the house with the flower-bones. In the house they put bedsteads and wooden slabs to sit on before them; they pour out water to them; they salute them. Thereupon they go inside the house; they put the flower-bones into a new vessel and hang this up and keep it in a safe place. Thereupon they give them food. After this the village people go to their respective homes. When day dawns, they take down the carrying sling in which they had put the leaf-cup with rice, and look at it, whether he has eaten it, or it is there. If he has eaten it, they find a crumb in the leaf-cup with water, and if he has not eaten, there is nothing. Now they put these things and the leaf-plates on which they took food in the evening, into a broken basket and throw it away at the cross-road at the end of the village street, the basket included.

d. Going to the Damuda river.

There is no fixed time for going to the Damuda river. Santals who live near the Damuda river set the flower-bones afloat the same day they cremate a person. Some take flower-bones to the Damuda one month afterwards, and others five months afterwards, and people who live in a distant country only after two or three years. They go there mostly in the month of Aghăṛ (middle of November to middle of December). They provide the necessary food for the journey; they also collect the necessary things: A cloth three cubits long, five cowries, one wristlet, a little sindur, one seer flattened rice, three cakes, and one seer rice. As they fear the dangers of the forests and thieves, people of only one village do not go to take the flower-bones away. People of two or three villages, where people have died, invite each other to go in company, and then they go, each taking their separate

---

[6] Andropogon muricatus, Retz.

flower-bones along. The ears of the sacrificial animal that they are to give to the dead one at the final funeral ceremonies, they cut off and let the blood drip down on the rice, and this rice they put in with the flower-bones.

Our first place of descent at the Damuda is Gạı ghaṭ (cow descent place), next Tirio ghaṭ (flute descent place), after this Telkupi bạrni ghaṭ; after this still further down they have arranged a place of descent, this they call Hatkundạ banda ghaṭ; the last places of descent are Haḍa bhaṅga and Dạmạliạ. Some people take the flower-bones to Guạ river[7], viz., members of the Hembrom sept.

When the men who go to the Damuda river reach there, they first buy right to descent with the cowries, that is to say, they put them down at the place of descent, and they make three marks of sindur at the place of descent; the wristlet they also put down there. Thereupon they go down to the river. First they make a small pool in the sand. When they have done this, they put on a loin-strip of new cloth, and the heir of the dead one takes the flower-bones in his hand; when he has done this, he goes down into the water of a deep pool, and turning towards the sun-rise he dives and at once lets the bones float away together with the bloody rice. When he has been bathed, he comes back to the small pool. Now he puts on other clothes. The stripped-off clothes the Doms of the place there take, and also the cowries and the wristlet.

Thereupon the heir offers earth. First he puts portions of earth on three leaves, and three tooth-brush twigs, that he has broken off on the road and brought along, these also he offers on the leaves. Thereupon he makes an invocation: Be greeted then, thou who hast been extinguished, hast fallen down, here I am performing the last rites for thee, I have bathed and washed my hair, mayest thou also bathe and wash thy hair. After this he offers earth to Pilcu haṛam and Pilcu buḍhi; he makes invocation: Here then, Pilcu haṛam, Pilcu buḍhi, I have bathed and washed my hair; may you two also bathe and wash your hair. For the extinguished one, the fallen-down one I have performed the last rites; now you two bring him in and keep him, lead him in and keep him with you from to-day. After this he offers to Porodhol and makes invocation: Here then, Porodhol, I have bathed and washed my hair, mayest thou also bathe and wash thy hair; now as is seen here, I have performed the last rites for the extinguished one, the fallen-down one, bring him in and keep him, lead him in an keep him with you.

After this he puts small heaps of flattened rice on three leaves, and on every leaf he puts one cake. Thereupon he worships, making the same kind of invocation. Then he himself and those of his own village who have come with him, eat this flattened rice and the cakes. The other people also act in the same way. The wrapped-up flattened rice and the rice left over from what has been offered to the bongas, the Doms at this descent to

[7] The Guạ river is said to be to the South of the Santal Parganas district. The different ghats mentioned will not be found on any map; they are known to the Santals as places where their ancestors have been.

the river take. When they start to return home, they call out horibol three times in the Damuda river and come away. When they come home, the people of their home call the village headman and his deputy and give beer to these two and the men returned from the Damuda river. And they ask each other about the state of matters. Thereupon they separate.

e. The final funeral ceremonies.

The bhaṇḍan is our final act in connexion with death. By the final funeral ceremonies we make propitiation in connexion with the dead person. We brew beer, we provide all that is necessary for a feast. On the day appointed the relatives and the village people come together; we are shaved; we bathe and come back; in the evening we call on the dead person, the ancestors, and Maraṅ buru to come; when they have taken possession of some, we ask them: Please, Lords, as ye see here we are to-day giving the extinguished one, the fallen-down one his share and portion; you two, Maraṅ buru and Porodhol, look after what is his (hers), pay attention to what is his (hers). They both say: Well and good. Thereupon we say to the dead one: Have a care then, we are giving thee, handing thee thy share, thy portion to-day; receive it, accept it with pleasure, with delight. He says: Well and good. Thereupon they give them water and beer. They drink; thereupon they make them come to.

In the courtyard they plant a branch of the Sal tree; there they plaster with cow-dung, and put a leaf-plate with rice; thereupon they first fell the sacrificial animal whose ears they cut off when they went to the Damuda river. At this time they make an invocation: Here then, thou so and so (the dead one), thy share, thy portion we are giving thee, handing thee; thou wilt receive it, accept it with pleasure, with delight; mayest thou fondle this, consider this great, Father my Ṭhạkur. (He has become a bonga, is it not so?) Thereupon all the relatives and the village people, making the same kind of invocation, fell the sacrificial animals that they have brought along (they have also brought beer), in the name of the dead one. They do not give sacrificial animals to other bongas. And they pour out beer as a libation to him. They make an invocation: Have a care then, after that done we are pouring out, baling out shield-water, fight-water to thee; mayest thou be pleased with, agree to this Lord, Father my Ṭhạkur. Also to Maraṅ buru and to Porodhol they libate beer, making invocation in the same way.

When they singe and cut up the sacrificed animals, they take off and keep aside one forequarter of the animal they first felled, and the head and the liver and lungs they bring into the house to the owners for sacrificing purposes, and the neck-portion they cut off and keep aside. Now the village people bring out from the house of the owner one earthenware vessel with beer, three half-seers of rice, three joints turmeric, salt, tobacco, one bundle of leaves, bits of straw, one bundle firewood, one iron ladle, and one narrow-mouthed earthenware vessel. Thereupon they make the owner of the house where the death has occurred standing take in his hand the forequarter meat mentioned; the elderly men sit round with him in the middle; then how many countries we have from the beginning "grazed" on our wanderings, and what our ancestors of old have from time to time introduced of customs and rules, all these matters they recite, as at the chaṭiar. When they have finished reciting this, they continue reciting: One so and so headman discovered a rising ground with partridges; he said: Come along, I have discovered virgin ground, virgin forest, you will burn and clear jungle for yourselves, you will support yourselves, you will obtain a living. Hearing this we came together like decoy quails, like decoy doves, under the feet of so and so village headman, to support ourselves, to obtain a living. We saw the bait, the snare we did not see, to die here and to fall down there, this we did not know, honourable fathers. So as you see here, we have died, we have fallen down, honourable fathers. Then so and so village headman, honourable fathers, under his feet we have died, we have fallen down, honourable fathers. Then, as you see here, we called on you to come, we invited you, honourable fathers. As is seen here, you came, you arrived, crying with us, standing with us, honourable fathers. By this also we are satisfied, honourable fathers. Eye-water, tears, by this we are also satisfied, honourable fathers. Carrying out on the shoulders, leading out, by this also we are satisfied, honourable fathers. One branch of firewood, by this also we are satisfied, honourable fathers. Assisting to dig, assisting to hoe, by this also we are satisfied, honourable fathers. Then, as is seen here, our so and so village headman, honourable fathers, we called, we invited, you came, you arrived, you did not let us wait and become stale, honourable fathers. Then, honourable fathers, so and so village headman, as is seen here, to-day we have shaved them, have had their clothes washed, we have bathed, have washed our hair. As is seen here, our so and so village headman, honourable fathers, as is seen here, we had our head full of ashes, our mouth full of blood, honourable fathers, our shoulders were full of firewood, to-day, our so and so village headman, honourable fathers, you have made us white like the paddy-birds, we were like crows. You came walking on your legs, in connexion with courteous behaviour, in all we were deficient, high wooden slabs to sit on, a high verandah, in this respect we are also deficient, honourable fathers; one cup of water and one bowl of tobacco, in respect of this also we were deficient, honourable fathers, — in respect of all we were deficient; in respect of this you village people be especially grieved for us, viz., these friends where can they be settled, be kept, just now we wanted these things and those things, all they have brought into desuetude for us.

The village people then answer: The grieving ones have presumably gone in advance to Somae's narrow valley to prop up the hut, the booth on the fine sand. You rather say: These friends, where can they be settled, be kept; what is not sanctioned by custom they have sanctioned; what is not usage they have made so, a great many things they scraped me clean of, fined me; these things ought not to be given; over this matter be especially grieved. Then he says in reply: The grieving ones, Father, have gone in advance to Somae's narrow valley to be crocodile-herds.

Now they bring the forequarter, the rice, the beer, the water, all out into the village street. This the village council men eat and drink. This they call kand kạṭhi daka[8]. The owner's people cook the liver and lungs and the head into a hash with rice. In the courtyard where they felled the animals, they sacrifice to the dead one. They make an invocation: Be greeted then, thou so and so, rotten food, rotten cooked rice is being given to thee, being handed to thee; with pleasure, with delight thou wilt receive it, accept it; mayest thou be pleased with, mayest thou agree to this. We also shall eat, put into our mouth; may stomach-ache, headache not be created, be formed, Lord, Father my Ṭhạkur. In the same way they make invocations to all dead forefathers, so far as they are known, and sacrifice to them.

Thereupon they cut up the sacrificed animals to prepare curry. The sacrificed animals brought by relatives they cut into two equal parts; one part they cut off for the village people, and one part they put aside. When the rice and curry is ready, they all, small and big, eat. When they have had food, they lie down. The young men and girls do not dance at the final funeral ceremonies. When day dawns, they give the relatives a couple leaf-cups of beer and also food. When they have eaten this, they say goodbye to them. They take their forequarter with them. If co-parents-in-law have come to the final funeral ceremonies, they have besides the sacrificial animals brought with them two pots of beer, two suli[9] rice, two suli parched and flattened rice, salt and oil. When they say goodbye to these, the owners of the house at once kill a goat for them; only the forequarter and the head they keep. One suli rice, one suli flattened and parched rice, one pot beer, salt, and oil they also send with them. They see them off.

When the relatives have departed, they bring the village headman and his deputy and a couple of the village people together and give them the presented beer. The neck-part that they have kept, the barber gets; one seer rice, one seer parched and flattened rice, three branches of the root of turmeric, salt, tobacco, and one small earthenware vessel with beer they also present him with. Thereupon they speak to him: Look here, Father, you are the barber, for twelve years we had uncleanness, we were like consecrated he-goats with hair kept growing; this uncleanness thou hast taken down and made away with for us; in case you had been somewhere else, who knows how much thou might have got by working for wages, by gleaning; as is seen here, we have caused thee to lose time, we have not made thee satisfied with anything; for this mayest thou be especially grieved. He answers: The grieving ones are presumably gone in advance, Father, to Somae's narrow

---

[8] See Dictionary s. v. [9] The suli is a measure of 20 half-seers.

valley. He then takes what he has got with him to his home, and the village headman and his deputy and those with them also go.

When a person dies, the people of this house do not perform any sacrifice, until the final funeral ceremonies for the dead have been gone through; neither do they use sindur on themselves; they do not libate beer, nor do they have any marriage.

People say, it is reported: At the final funeral ceremonies they give the dead ones all, cows, goats, pigs, fowls, all these they make wander along, and in the other world they look after what is theirs.

XII. ABOUT THE OTHER WORLD

Our ancestors of old have said: Ṭhąkur has sent us to the world; he has himself measured out to us our seer, and when this seer is finished for us, he takes us away to the other world. There he judges about our good and bad deeds and gives us a place in accordance with them. They who were good get a good place there, and they who were bad in this world, they get a bad place. The bongas or mountain-spirits have no authority over good people; but to the persons who were bad they give an awful amount of suffering. When I lived in the village Asonlea in the Paṇḍra country, I was dead for three days, after having been ill. Old Buḍhạn and old Jugiạ, now of Citragaria, lived at that time in that village. They both know this. When I died, I went to the other world, to a bad place. There was a very large door into that prison-house. When I had gone inside, they at once shut the door. I saw a very large house, big like a country. I saw places for inflicting different kinds of suffering. I saw a cavity like an immense trench for cooking. There was fire in this, and in this fire-cavity a countless number of persons were thrown down. Climbing with hands and feet they were trying to get up and out of it; but Marań buru was stabbing them, meeting them with an iron fish-spear; thereby they were getting still more suffering.

Seeing this I became awfully afraid and was fidgeting to get out; I was unable to get out, because the door was shut, and soldiers were standing at the door. Just then they opened the door to bring a new person in. O mother, I saw that from my body and outside a thin thread was stretched out! Catching hold of this thread I at once crossed under their feet and came out. I escaped, I ran all I could; I came back to the world; I got well.

People say, it is reported, that what different kinds of sins they have committed in this world, they have in the other world an awful wish to commit the same sins; but they do not get an opportunity of sinning, so that they feel great distress there. They who in this world covet meat much, these persons, it is told, in the other world all day long carry meat on their head, smelling offensively; it is a strong smell; they are unable to eat. They who have not in this world paid their debts before they leave, of them they demand payment in the other world, and as they have nothing to pay with, they flay their back and sow salt there, and when it heals, they do the same to them over again.

The words of the ancestors are ended. I learnt from Buku guru in the village Pabea in the Paṇḍra country, and I have made you two, Kerap Saheb[1] and old Jugiạ my disciples. As you two have become gurus, make disciples in the country, in order that the words may not be lost; may they remain generation after generation.

We Kerap Saheb and Jugiạ haṛam of Citragaria in Nankar have written down the words of the ancestors that our guru old Kolean finished telling us on the 15th February 1871, in accordance with the original paper.

The old guru is no more; therefore we here below write a couple of matters that were not written at that time: The twelve septs of the Santals were in Campa again divided, every sept into twelve subsepts. Santals cannot marry one of their own sept, and not their mother or aunt or wife of mother's brother or father's sister, nor the children of these. As in Campa people of the Kisku sept and of the Marṇḍi sept became at enmity with each other, they do not intermarry even now, and because people of the Ṭuḍu sept and of the Besra sept became at enmity there, they do not contract marriages up to this day. Even if they join them together by force, they do not get on together.

Benagaria, the 5th August 1887.

L. O. Skrefsrud.

Jugiạ haṛam.

---

[1] The Santali corruption of Skrefsrud Sahib.

XIII. ADDITIONAL ACCOUNT BY OLD JUGIẠ

Because of the harassing of the Dekos and the distress through lack of food after we had crossed the Ajae river, we were, as time passed, spread about towards the North and the East, on the hills in the North East right up to the Ganges river. At that time there was only forest, and here and there Bhũyas[1] and on the hill tops Maṛ Muṇḍas[2]. The Muṇḍas they also call Sãurias. The Bhũyas and the Maṛ Muṇḍas were the landowners at that time. They allowed us to take up land in peace, and they took a very small amount of rent from us. Under them we had no distress at all. But as time passed, the Dekos entered trading, and finally they settled down as money-lenders. They also became the money-lenders of the landlords. The landlords borrowed money and clothes from them and gave the country to them as security. In this way the Deko money-lenders got the country from them by fraud, they themselves became the landlords, and the real landlords became paupers and became like us. The Deko landlords living at the foot of the hill country also took possession of what belonged to the Maṛ.

We cleared the hill country and the forest country at our expense for the new landlords, after they had become money-lenders, and they gradually increased the land-rent for us. The money-lenders give us very small amounts, and they take very much. The crops of the year they take away from us, all of it, and we get through life by again incurring debts with them. However much we pay back, still it is not cleared off. If they are not satisfied with the crops of the year, they drive our cattle away; and if they are not content even by this, they make us, wife and children, serve with them as slaves for a couple of half-seers (of rice). At that time there were no magistrates; to whom could we complain? Afterwards Deko police came in; but these dismiss our cases, taking the white pice of their own race. We had very great distress. With the whole country we became bewildered.

Then different rumours arose. First this: The two Lag Lạgin[3] snakes are coming; they will swallow people. To remove the adverse influence men of five villages gathered and walked about to five other villages, during one night, being religiously very abstinent. To our village those of five villages came, one man to every separate house. In the village

---

[1] A semi-hinduized caste, living here and there near the Santals. [2] A Dravidian tribe living on the hills in the northern parts of the Santal Parganas. [3] Lag Lạgin, a Bengalized form of Nag Nạgin, a pair of fabulous snakes.

street outside the house of the village headman they danced round, drumming the kettle-drum. At their waist they had tied wooden bells and small metal bells. As they were swaying, these made an awful noise. Two young unmarried men had taken on the sacred thread of the twice-born, and they were carrying about two very small ploughs, on to which sindur had been smeared, these were of Nim and Bael and put into a small flat basket. When they had finished wandering to their five villages, they gathered us of our five villages in the open plain outside the last village. There they offered Bael leaves, sun-dried rice, and oil and sindur in the name of Lag Lạgin. After this they that were coming along taught us songs, before they left; then having put the sacred thread of the twice-born on two unmarried young men of ours and having handed the two ploughs to them, they went to their respective homes. Thereupon we also in the same way wandered round to five villages. When we had finished wandering we gave the two ploughs over to the people of the five villages that we had wandered round to; we turned the sacred thread of the twice-born to two unmarried young men of theirs; we offered in the name of Lag Lạgin, and having taught them the songs we came home. When we had reached home, we men plastered the courtyards with cow-dung, and we brought one large vessel with water. Our women, that is to say, mothers of children, did not put their feet down on the ground during the whole night that we were away; they had put cow-dung down near the bedsteads, and putting their feet on this they sucked their children.

After this they again started a rumour, viz., that women who had got the same number of children should exchange vows, two and two; the pair should give each other clothes, and all should eat and drink. Who knows for what reason. Perhaps in order that all should become related and then be of one mind, so that if an insurrection or the like arose, they should not tell tales about each other, and if anything happened, it might remain hidden.

Those two rumours went round. Again one other matter was rumoured, viz., a buffalo-cow is coming. Where she may find grass in the village street outside somebody's house, there she will graze and lie down. She will not get up until the people of this house have all died. Hearing this the people of the whole country dug their village streets clean.

Then a rumour about the Doms was started, viz.: In the Ganges river a Dom touched a golden boat, thereby the boat sank, therefore they will kill all Doms. Fearing this the Doms were running about like forest deer; they put on clothes and ornaments like Santals, and stayed in Santal houses.

Then it was rumoured, viz.: In the Layo fort a Subạ[4] has been born by an unmarried girl; let all people go there to hunt. The Layo fort[5] is to the west of Hazaribagh. Some men went; they saw the Subạ and together with him they also hunted through the Kanchon forest. They brought the deer they had killed together to the same place and cut them

---

[4] Subạ (or Subạ Ṭhạkur) is used about an inspired leader. [5] The Layo gaṛ was far to the West from the places where most of the insurrection occurred.

up. And the people brought with them one leaf each to receive their portion. They counted these leaves; they saw how many thousands country people had come together. The Subạ paid all the expenses. When we were about to disperse, the Subạ said to us: We shall hunt over the Ṭir mountain, that is near to Deoghar; assemble there. But for some reason or other they did not hunt there.

After this it was rumoured, viz.: Some people, who knows who, are coming to kill the Dekos. As for you, at the end of the village street hang up the hide of a bullock and a pair of flutes, that they may know that you are Santals; otherwise they will kill you with the others. Fearing this we hung these things up in every village.

Then it was heard, viz.: In Bhognaḍi in the Pạṛ country[6] a Subạ Ṭhạkur has appeared. Hearing this the people of the country commenced to go, each taking with them one half-seer of sun-dried rice and the milk of one cow. There they saw that they had built an altar, and that they had put up a fence round it. In the middle Ṭhạkur was sitting in the shape of Sido of that village. Throwing themselves down on their face before him the people of the country worshipped him, and they brought rice and milk together in his name at the same place. Then a police head-constable from the courts came. He said to them: What order have you? out with it, I wish to see your authority. Then Sido said: Look here is my authority, and with a clasp-knife he killed him. Then the insurrection commenced. When they heard that they had killed the head-constable, the soldiers came. At the Kõcpaṛa market place they fought against Sido and his brother Canhu and the country people. The soldiers were vanquished; therefore the courage of Sido and Kanhu and their party greatly increased. Then Sido and Kanhu gave an order: The landlords and usurers we shall kill every one of them, and the other Dekos we shall drive away to the other side of the Ganges; the reign will be ours. Then the people of the country became raving mad; many Subạ Ṭhạkurs appeared.

Now there happened fighting at Pakaur and Mohespur; here also the soldiers were vanquished. After this Mạni Pargana from Jamolpani and Ram Mańjhi from Baromasia in Nankar became Subạ. With a host of the country people these two plundered Naranpur and Moluti. Binud Mańjhi from Tilabani in Belparta became a Subạ, and with a host of country people he plundered Deocha and Gunpura. At Gunpura the Santals were vanquished. Thereupon they had a fight at the Nangolia police station. There a great number of Santals were killed. From there they fought at Laubaṛia on the other side of the Mor river. Here a great many soldiers fell, and a European also was killed. And Santals were shot dead in heaps. The Santals could not prevail; the Santals ran away into the Saptola forest and the Satbehoṛ hill. Here they remained for about two months, in the months of Asin and Kartik (from the middle of September to the middle of November). Here the

---

6 Most of the places mentioned by Juglạ may be found on the large maps of the Santal Parganas. The Pạṛ country is in the north-eastern part of this district.

Santals plundered each other, because of the distress through lack of food. Thereupon the Europeans surrounded us; they drove us out, and to the villages Sikarpur and Ramkhuṛi.

Us men they caught and took every one of us to Dhasnia, the village of the landlord, that is to say, so many as they caught. Having kept us here for something like one month they brought us to Kumṛabad near the Mor river. At that time the Europeans cozened us, they said to us: Why will you suffer? Tell who the Subạ are; then we shall set you free now this moment. Then the country people told who they were. The Europeans caught the Subạ; some of them they hanged there, and some they transported to an island[7]. A few they also set free. Sido had in the meantime died in the fighting, and Kanhu and his followers they caught afterwards. They hanged Kanhu and a couple others, and some, who knows how many, they transported to an island. Ram Mańjhi and Binud escaped. The Lieutenant Governor came and pacified us the people of the country; we returned to our respective villages.

During the insurrection we suffered severely. From Asaṛ (middle of June to middle of July) for fully three months we lived in the hills at the foot of trees; rain was continually pouring down on us, and we were nearly dying from hunger, because of the guiles of the Subạ Ṭhạkurs. During the insurrection many of us lost our cattle; therefore when we returned to our villages, we suffered much distress. There were no plough-cattle, there was nothing to eat, and the Dekos mocked us very irritatingly. We had again to fall into the hands of the same money-lenders. Some people unrighteously became rich during the insurrection by unlawfully taking possession of other people's cows and buffaloes.

From after the insurrection the Europeans have appeared in the Santal country. First Telbor Saheb was our magistrate. At that time he judged our cases without charging money; but nowadays much money has to be paid in court-cases: the writers take a couple of rupees, the muktiạr (pleader-babus) take earnest-money in advance, stamps have to be put on, and if the orderlies are not given a little, they push you straight away when you come, and if you do not go and have trouble three-four times, the case is not settled. This we feel a distress; otherwise the Europeans judge well.

---

7 i. e. the Andamans.

XIV. WHAT HAS BEEN ADDED BELOW IS BY SIDO DESMAŃJHI SARDAR OF AMBAJOṚA[1]

a. About adoption.

When a man marries a second wife[2], and this second wife has a son of her first husband brought with her, then if he wishes to give him full adoption, the man tells the village headman of this, that is, he informs him what they have both decided. The village headman then invites those who can claim this child, and they come to talk the matter over. In the presence of the village headman they consult together, whether they shall set the child free or not. If they set the child free, they say: Well, Father headman, we the claimants have before you and before the village people renounced all claims on this child. So from to-day he belongs to this stepfather of his. Consequently he has no right to his natural father's lands or cattle, money and so on; he will not get anything.

When this is said, they ask the stepfather for five four-anna bits, the provision of the sitting village council. Thereupon they salute each other and separate.

Now the stepfather fixes a day for adopting the child. Then on the day fixed he calls out for being shaved, as at the name-giving festival. They are shaved in the same way, and in the same way they drink Nim-gruel. And then the "midwife" informs the gathered men and women of the stepfather's sept. Thereupon they separate.

Now they give the child the Baha Sǫhrae, i. e., the real original bonga's sacrificial meat and rice. From this time the child has become his own child. And this child will get an equal share with his stepfather's own sons of his agricultural lands, money, and cattle. But while the real sons have a right to the property of cousins when they die out, he has in the same way no right to their property; only to the property of his stepfather he has a full right.

b. About adopted children.

Now and then they adopt orphan children and support them. And when they grow into maturity, these also get an equal share to those of the proper children in the agricultural lands, money, and cattle. If such a boy dies and falls away, and there is any property of

---

1 What here follows was added at the request of many Santals. Sido was the man best qualified to do this. He had for many years as dẹs mạṅjhi had to do with these matters; he had also been an honorary magistrate.

2 Naturally a widow.

his, then the sons of the adopting man get this property or that of his wife. But the cousins of the adopted man get nothing. That is to say, the sons of the adopting man will have the responsibility for the expenses with the final funeral ceremonies and so on. And if he has children, it naturally belongs to them. And when any married people have no children, they may take children of both sides, i. e., children of the wife's brothers, or children of her younger sister, children of the husband's younger or elder brothers, take them to themselves as adopted ones, to be supported by them until death. These adopted ones also, in the same way, get their share of the agricultural lands, if children of the adopting pair have been born. And if they have got no children, all property will naturally belong to the adopted son. Mostly such childless people take in sons as adopted ones.

Now and then they have taken in real adopted ones. When formerly — it is now some three scores of years ago — there was an insurrection, then they adopted many. At the present time they also now and then adopt. Nowadays, since the European missionaries have come, these show mercy to orphans. Rather, these European teachers are like claimants following up and finding their rice-lands and other lands. This is a righteous act much greater than everything else they do. They are teaching them knowledge at their own expense. They do not seek to be supported until death like us; they are rather themselves supporting others.

c. Wife's children taken in.

When a man takes a second wife, and she brings with her children, viz., of her former husband, we call such children saṅgha lọṭọm (taken in by wife's second marriage). If they are boys, these children have no right to get the stepfather's agricultural lands and so on. But the stepfather will with pleasure procure land and a homestead field for such a one from the village headman, giving money of his own household as salami. And when the remarried woman has any earnings of her own, these belong to the children she has brought with her. But for keeping it in safe custody, she will give the uterine brothers a portion; otherwise they have no right to it.

d. Taking possession on settling.

If any one after having done some planting of trees runs away, and the headman of that village settles a man who has come running there, in the run-away man's agricultural land and homestead field, then if there are Mahua trees or water-reservoirs, etc., in that homestead field or in the village street outside the house or in the unit of land, the new settler gets all, including these. Even if there are heirs of the run-away man in this village, they cannot lay claim to the things mentioned, because the new man has taken possession on settling. And even if the run-away man should sometime return to this village, he will not get these trees or water-reservoirs, etc., even if he lays claim to them at the landlord's door, because that man has taken possession on settling.

e. Becoming unfitted for use.

Becoming unfitted for use happens in two ways. One way is this: When somebody sets castrated animals aside for the Jǫm sim, and before they sacrifice them some venerable old man of their sept dies, then these castrated animals become unfit for being sacrificed; these castrated animals are not sacrificed, they only slaughter them.

The other is in connexion with the rights of daughters or sisters. When a man separates his own sons, or brothers set up separate households, sisters get one cow each, when their father is living; when the father dies without having given a cow to his daughters or sisters, and these girls afterwards ask for this right of theirs from their brothers, then the council people say: Why did you not ask for it while your father was living? Now your right has been cancelled; but the women who follow up their right say: Don't, Fathers, cancel my right; the man is dead; quite so, judgement has not died; this really is, that judgement has been overthrown.

And concerning any rights in connexion with marriage they say: Don't, Fathers, cancel my right; this is my right.

f. The sum total of the law of the rights of women.

When a man makes separate establishments for his sons, then he also gives to each of his daughters one cow or calf, or a sheep or a goat. When he gives this to married ones or to spinsters, he gives the same to all. And in this right of theirs, or, if their goats or sheep multiply, in this increase the brothers of a husband of theirs have no right, because the father of the girls has given them this of his own accord. When he made separate establishments for his sons, at that time the girl received them in the presence of her brothers, from her own father. At this very time the matter of father and brothers has been finally settled. But if sons or daughters of her brother herd them, they get wages. And if they multiply in the house of her husband, then the nephews or nieces of the girl will herd them. These she will also in the same way give wages, and if the two wish so, they may give a heifer or a bull calf to the children on both sides. But on both sides they have no right to get this.

If there are no cattle, then they will give to each one brass-cup. When selling this brass-cup they buy a calf or a goat for the money they get thereby, and when these multiply, in the same way the heirs on both sides have no right to get any of these either. A pig, or a goat, a sheep, a cow the woman herself may sell, and she will keep the money, and she may also use the money for her clothes and apparel. Such people have now and then, by giving a bullock or a cow with calf as salami, acquired rice and other land in a separate place, and somewhere they have even founded a village after having given salami. Formerly when the Paharias were landlords in this country, they very much appreciated pigs or castrated goats. They were great drunkards; they were eating anything along with liquor. They were easily and quickly beguiled by pigs and castrated goats.

g. To neutralize the effect of an eclipse.

To neutralize the effect of an eclipse is done as follows. In a year when an eclipse of the sun or the moon is taking place, a mother of children will say: Do, my sons or daughters, go for us to the family of your maternal uncle to neutralize the effect of the eclipse. If they live in the same village, they go that very day to the family of their maternal uncle. When they have reached there, they say: We have come, uncle, to neutralize the effects of the eclipse. They say to them: All right, my boy (or my girl). Now the mother of these children has brewed beer and takes this to her father's house; and they drink this, pouring some out as a libation. If her father is living, he says to her: What is it, my girl, that you have in mind and have brought? If her father is not living, her brothers will also ask her in the same way. She then says: You remember, your nephews or grandchildren came to neutralize the effets of the eclipse; it is in connexion with this that we have come. Now if the old man is alive, he calls all the boys together. If he is not alive, the brothers come together and consult each other. And they give them a fowl or a goat or a sheep or a pig. If these multiply, then only these children have a right to this property because the wives of all the sons fetch this eclipse-neutralizing from their father or brothers. Therefore the heirs on both sides have no right to get anything of the possible increase of these. Only of their own accord the brothers of both sides may give the children a bull- or a heifer calf. They say that formerly, when the cows or the sheep or goats multiplied in the home of a wife's father, and the girl was bringing this live stock from there to her husband's home, then the bonga of her father's home would also come along. Then if this bonga did not return, her husband would have to worship the bonga of the old home of his wife.

h. About harvest perquisites.

The harvest perquisites are as follows: When a man's daughter, while unmarried, gets harvest perquisites, her father and brothers will lend her perquisites to somebody at 50 pct. And when these perquisites increase, and from this also cattle multiply, then at the time when her husband brings to his home what has multiplied in the old home of his wife, the bonga of some people will also, it is told, follow together with this property. Therefore some people do not let what they have remain there for a long time, fearing that the bongas will come along. And when anyone marries them, also the brothers of the husband have a right to the harvest perquisites property. But then the father and the brothers of the girl will call out to get a higher brideprice; because they say: We are sending with this our daughter or sister, or: what she owns, half our houshold. Therefore we shall take a higher brideprice, and of this you will not get anything in return. And when she acquires harvest perquisites after having become a widow or been divorced and this increases, then, in case friends apply for her and she is remarried, this woman alone has authoritative right to the increase mentioned, because this is her property, that of her husband or her children. The brothers or heirs of her new husband have no right to this. But if both of them have no descendants when they die, then the heirs are the true claimants to the goods of these two.

i. About cuman.

The cuman is as follows: When a man procures a wife for his son, then the elder sister of this young man, or his younger sister, or his paternal uncles, or his mother's brother's wife, or elder or younger female cousins will put a rupee in the bridegroom's brass-plate at the waving ceremony at the marriage. This they call the cuman rupee. And for this they point out a calf to the girl. If there is any increase from this calf, or it is turned into money, paddy, or rice, this the children of this woman only will get. The heirs of her husband will not get anything. And if she dies without having had children, it will naturally belong to the heirs.

XV. A NEW AGREEMENT

On the 15th February 1916 the Parganas, Desmańjhis, Sardars, and different other people of the Dumka district gathered in Dumka and talked about their daughters and widows. Having talked the matter over, they came to the conclusion: It would be very good, if what is printed here below became law:

Daughters.

1. If a man has only daughters, these will be his heirs when married, that is to say, their husbands will get the rice- and other land.

The brothers of the father will get half the cattle. The man who sets fire to the mouth of the dead will get a calf. If a girl, for whom they have brought a house-son-in-law dies without having children, the house-son-in-law gets nothing; he goes out and away with his calf.

2. When a man has sons and daughters, and the sons die without having children, the girls become the heirs, that is to say, the father or the brothers may bring house-sons-in-law for the girls, or they may bring the husband to the girl's father's home to live there.

3. If a girl is married without a house-son-in-law being brought for her she will not become heir.

4. If a house-son-in-law does not stay, his rights end.

5. If a girl for whom they have brought a house-son-in-law dies after having borne children, her children will get the rights of their mother; and the house-son-in-law will stay there until he remarries, and his children will support him. If he remarries, he will go out and away.

Widows.

When a woman becomes a widow, she has the right to be supported from her husband's home, so long as she lives.

If she is married again, her right in the house of her first husband ceases.

Until she is married again, a widow may manage the house of her husband; but when the woman dies or is married again, all rice- and other land will belong to the brothers of her husband or their heirs.